Mastering vRealize Manager
Second Edition

Analyze and optimize your IT environment by gaining a
practical understanding of vRealize Operations 6.6

Spas Kaloferov
Scott Norris
Christopher Slater

BIRMINGHAM - MUMBAI

Mastering vRealize Operations Manager
Second Edition

Commissioning Editor: Vijin Boricha
Acquisition Editor: Heramb Bhavsar
Content Development Editor: Sharon Raj
Technical Editor: Prashant Chaudhari
Copy Editor: Safis Editing
Project Coordinator: Virginia Dias
Proofreader: Safis Editing
Indexer: Priyanka Dhadke
Graphics: Tom Scaria
Production Coordinator: Nilesh Mohite

First published: May 2015
Second edition: March 2018

Production reference: 1070318

Published by Packt Publishing Ltd.
Livery Place
35 Livery Street
Birmingham
B3 2PB, UK.

ISBN 978-1-78847-487-0

www.packtpub.com

`mapt.io`

Mapt is an online digital library that gives you full access to over 5,000 books and videos, as well as industry leading tools to help you plan your personal development and advance your career. For more information, please visit our website.

Why subscribe?

- Spend less time learning and more time coding with practical eBooks and Videos from over 4,000 industry professionals

- Improve your learning with Skill Plans built especially for you

- Get a free eBook or video every month

- Mapt is fully searchable

- Copy and paste, print, and bookmark content

PacktPub.com

Did you know that Packt offers eBook versions of every book published, with PDF and ePub files available? You can upgrade to the eBook version at `www.PacktPub.com` and as a print book customer, you are entitled to a discount on the eBook copy. Get in touch with us at `service@packtpub.com` for more details.

At `www.PacktPub.com`, you can also read a collection of free technical articles, sign up for a range of free newsletters, and receive exclusive discounts and offers on Packt books and eBooks.

Contributors

About the authors

Spas Kaloferov has been a technology professional since 2004 and holds over 30 industry certifications. His experience is focused around the Microsoft and VMware portfolios. He studied in Germany and now lives in Sofia, Bulgaria. Spas joined the VMware family in 2014, and he is currently part of a team delivering high-level training across the VMware **Software-Defined Data Center** (**SDDC**) product stack.

> *First, I express my gratitude to my family and friends for supporting me while writing this book. I thank the editors and publishing staff at Packt, especially Sharon Raj, Content Development Editor, who worked with me patiently.*
> *I also thank VMware Technical Support University team, Alex Wulf from the VMware Global Support Services team and Peter Oberacher for their valuable contributions to the content.*

Scott Norris has 12 years of professional IT experience. Currently, he works for VMware as a Consulting Architect. Scott specializes in multiple VMware technologies, such as ESXi, vCenter, vRA 6 and 7, vCD, vCOps (vROps), vRO, SRM, and Application Services. He is a VMware Certified Design Expert (VCDX-DCA and VCDX-CMA #201).

For the past 10 years, Scott has worked on VMware products and technologies, supporting small environments from a single server to large federal government environments with hundreds of hosts.

Christopher Slater is a VMware Principal Solutions Architect and a member of the Office of the CTO - Global Field. He specializes in designing and implementing VMware technologies for the Software-Defined Data Center. His technical experience includes design, development and implementation of virtual infrastructure, Infrastructure as a Service, Platform as a Service, and DevOps solutions.

Chris also holds a double VCDX in Virtualization and Cloud Management and Automation. He is also the co-author of *Mastering vRealize Operations Manager 6* by Packt Publishing.

About the reviewer

Mathias Meyenburg is an accomplished business unit manager, solution architect, and senior consultant with more than 15 years of experience in the IT industry.

From a system administrator to large-scale data center operations and administration, his career has evolved through constantly updating and expanding his know-how as well as acquiring advancing certifications, CCNA, MCP, and VCP to name a few.

In 2016, he was recruited by vleet GmbH as a solution architect and senior consultant for server and desktop virtualization specializing in vSphere, vROPS, NSX, and vSAN.

> *I would like to express my gratitude to my wife, Andrea, who had to carry the burden while I was occupied with this book and my career, and who lovingly looked after our kids while studying herself.*

Packt is searching for authors like you

If you're interested in becoming an author for Packt, please visit `authors.packtpub.com` and apply today. We have worked with thousands of developers and tech professionals, just like you, to help them share their insight with the global tech community. You can make a general application, apply for a specific hot topic that we are recruiting an author for, or submit your own idea.

Table of Contents

Preface

When I was initially approached to write this book, the first and most obvious question was *why should I do this?* However, upon reflection, I thought of my personal experiences with the product and considered the real-world difference it made during times where we needed to troubleshoot performance problems or report on capacity trends. We also considered those customers with whom we had either demonstrated or run knowledge transfer sessions of vRealize Operations, and how only after a few hours, the energy in the room changed as people begin to grasp the power and concept of how vRealize Operations can benefit them on a daily basis.

The second reason is based on the observation that in some environments that had the product deployed, many of the concepts, terminology, and settings were not well-understood. As a result, customers were not getting the maximum value from their investment simply because they weren't familiar enough with the product. The product has extensive and great documentation; however, most product documentation is generally very thin on the why; such as, why should I enable some containers for capacity management and not others? Through this book, I attempt to fill this gap and hopefully show the positive impact this product can bring to an environment.

Who this book is for

Mastering vRealize Operations aims to help readers gain a deep understanding of VMware vRealize Operations and learn how to apply the product to everyday operations management use cases in the best way. This book aims to move beyond the standard product documentation and explain both why and how vRealize Operations should be deployed, configured, and used in your own environment.

Although this book is aimed at mastering vRealize Operations, expert knowledge of vRealize Operations is not a required. The various chapters vary in the requirement of skill level and expertise, as well as in the useful theory versus practical step-by-step content. We expect this book to be useful for the following people:

- Systems administrators responsible for the day-to-day smooth running of a virtualized enterprise IT environment
- Infrastructure architects and engineers responsible for designing and building solutions that improve the reliability and maintainability of virtualized environments

- Current-day customers who want to know how to get the most out of vRealize Operations, such as what the badges actually mean and how capacity management policies should be configured for a typical production environment
- Anyone who is keen to know more about vRealize Operations for specific reference look-ups, from badges to capacity planning and the new API

What this book covers

Chapter 1, *Going Ahead with vRealize Operations*, begins by taking you through the key vRealize Operations 6.6 components architecture. We will cover some of the main services and databases and their purposes. We will then discuss the different vRealize Operations node types. We will also discuss what High Availability is and how it works in vRealize Operations 6.6.

Chapter 2, *Which vRealize Operations Deployment Model Fits Your Needs*, discusses how things such as High Availability, Remote Collectors and Remote Collector Groups, number of users, and deployment size can affect how we design a vRealize Operations deployment. Finally, we will take a look at the most popular deployment examples.

Chapter 3, *Initial Setup and Configuration*, takes you through all the steps of installing, expanding, and upgrading an existing installation of vRealize Operations.

Chapter 4, *Extending vRealize Operations with Management Packs and Plugins*, discusses what a vRealize Operations solution is. We will also take a look at some of the most popular solutions and how to install them. Finally, we will talk about how we can import data into vRealize Operations using a REST API.

Chapter 5, *Badges*, describes what vRealize Operations badges are, what they represent, and how they are calculated.

Chapter 6, *Getting a Handle on Alerting and Notifications*, talks about vRealize Operations Symptoms, Recommendations, and Actions, and how to create them. We will also discuss what Alert notifications are and how we can push Alerts to external systems.

Chapter 7, *Capacity Management Made Easy*, explains the different resource capacity models that we can use in vRealize Operations. We will also discuss what capacity management policies are and how to correctly define them.

Chapter 8, *Aligning vRealize Operations with Business Outcomes*, discusses what Business-Oriented Reporting is. We will also look at how this can be achieved in vRealize Operations using Tags, Application Groups, and Custom Object Groups.

Chapter 9, *Super Metrics Made Super Easy*, describes what vRealize Operations Super Metrics are. We will look at different metric types, terminology, and definitions. Finally, we will build our own Super Metrics and compare them to Views.

Chapter 10, *Creating Custom Views*, explains what vRealize Operations Views and Reports are and how to create and use them.

Chapter 11, *Creating Custom Dashboards*, discusses what vRealize Operations Dashboards and Widgets are and how to use them together to display information. We will create our own custom dashboards using some of the most popular widgets.

Chapter 12, *Using vRealize Operations to Monitor Applications*, shows what Endpoint Operations Management is, what the Endpoint Operations Management Agent is used for, and how to install and reinstall it. Finally, we will take a look at some of the monitoring functionalities the Agent provides.

Chapter 13, *Leveraging vRealize Operations for vSphere and vRealize Automation Workload Placement*, discusses what vRealize Operations Intelligent Workload Placement is and how we can use vRealize Operations to rebalance workloads in our environment. We will also look at how Intelligent Workload Placement can be used to optimize vRealize Automation workload placement.

Chapter 14, *Using vRealize Operations for Infrastructure Compliance*, explains how we can use vRealize Operations to monitor configuration compliance in our environment to comply with industry-standard compliance standards such as PCI and HIPAA.

Chapter 15, *Troubleshooting vRealize Operations*, discusses how we can use vRealize Operations for troubleshooting. In particular, we will take a look at the Self-Monitoring Dashboards, which come out of the box. We will then discuss some of the key vRealize Operations components and how to troubleshoot them.

To get the most out of this book

To get the most out of *Mastering vRealize Operations Manager*, you should have a basic understanding of X86 virtualization, network, storage, VMware vSphere, and of course, vRealize Operations (or its previous version, vCenter Operations Manager). Although vRealize Operations 6.6 is no longer as vSphere-centric as its previous versions, most of the examples and the step-by-step guides in this book are based on vSphere objects and concepts.

A useful way to reinforce the content in this book is to follow some of the step-by-step guides and theory in your own vRealize Operations environment, be it either at work or in your own lab. For those without access to either, or wanting access to a structured practical lab component, we highly recommend that they check out the VMware Hands-on Labs (HOL) at `labs.hol.vmware.com`. The catalogs are updated often and always contain at least a few comprehensive labs on vRealize Operations with step-by-step online instructions.

Download the color images

We also provide a PDF file that has color images of the screenshots/diagrams used in this book. You can download it from `https://www.packtpub.com/sites/default/files/downloads/MasteringvRealizeOperationsManagerSecondEdition_ColorImages.pdf`.

Conventions used

There are a number of text conventions used throughout this book.

`CodeInText`: Indicates code words in text, database table names, folder names, filenames, file extensions, pathnames, dummy URLs, user input, and Twitter handles. Here is an example: "Remote collector nodes only communicate over GemFire using ports `10000-10010`"

A block of code is set as follows:

```
{
  "description" : " My REST imported recommendation (USR)",
  "others" : [ ],
  "otherAttributes" : {
  }
}
```

Any command-line input or output is written as follows:

```
${this, metric=sys|osUptime_latest}<=300)
```

Bold: Indicates a new term, an important word, or words that you see onscreen. For example, words in menus or dialog boxes appear in the text like this. Here is an example: "Once all the correct information is entered, click on **Finish**, and the OVA Template will now deploy the first vRealize Operations node."

 Warnings or important notes appear like this.

 Tips and tricks appear like this.

Get in touch

Feedback from our readers is always welcome.

General feedback: Email `feedback@packtpub.com` and mention the book title in the subject of your message. If you have questions about any aspect of this book, please email us at `questions@packtpub.com`.

Errata: Although we have taken every care to ensure the accuracy of our content, mistakes do happen. If you have found a mistake in this book, we would be grateful if you would report this to us. Please visit `www.packtpub.com/submit-errata`, selecting your book, clicking on the Errata Submission Form link, and entering the details.

Piracy: If you come across any illegal copies of our works in any form on the Internet, we would be grateful if you would provide us with the location address or website name. Please contact us at `copyright@packtpub.com` with a link to the material.

If you are interested in becoming an author: If there is a topic that you have expertise in and you are interested in either writing or contributing to a book, please visit `authors.packtpub.com`.

Reviews

Please leave a review. Once you have read and used this book, why not leave a review on the site that you purchased it from? Potential readers can then see and use your unbiased opinion to make purchase decisions, we at Packt can understand what you think about our products, and our authors can see your feedback on their book. Thank you!

For more information about Packt, please visit `packtpub.com`.

1
Going Ahead with vRealize Operations

vRealize Operations Manager 6.6 is a solution from VMware to help customers monitor, troubleshoot, and manage the health, capacity, and compliance of their virtual environment.

Throughout this book, I may occasionally refer to vRealize Operations as vROps. vROps is not an official VMware acronym or name for the vRealize Operations product.

The vRealize Operations 6.6 release offers a combined experience with VMware vRealize Business for Cloud and VMware vRealize Log Insight, delivering a complete intelligent operations solution that is designed to help customers plan, manage, and scale their **Software-Defined Data Center (SDDC)**and multi-cloud environments to meet business needs.

As we said, vRealize Operations is, first of all, a monitoring solution. But what does monitoring mean? In a traditional sense, monitoring can be defined as observing the current, real-time behavior of any system to make sure that it runs as expected, or well within the defined boundaries. It helps answer questions that are faced by IT on a day-to-day basis. Be it the IT or cloud administrators who manage the IT systems and infrastructure, the application owners monitoring their critical application stacks, or the executives who are responsible for making strategic decisions around capacity and growth, the latest release of vRealize Operations caters to all the personas with multiple use cases out of the box. For future reference, in this book, we will combine all of these personas, or anybody else using vRealize Operations, under the name **virtual infrastructure admins**, or **vAdmins**.

By that definition, vRealize Operations is not a monitoring solution. It does not monitor and gather data in real time as, for example, a typical performance monitoring tool would gather real-time resource (CPU, memory, disk I/O, and so on) utilization information from a system. Although we may refer to it as a monitoring solution throughout the book, make sure to differentiate it from a typical real-time monitoring solution. vRealize Operations is more of a historical analytics and forensics tool that uses predictive analytics and dynamic thresholding to show vAdmins not only what is currently (again, not actual real time, as we will see later in the book) wrong in their environment, but what will go wrong in the future.

Moreover, the predictive analysis engine feature also allows vAdmins to run capacity plans on their environments, ensuring that there are always enough resources to run mission-critical workloads without stress. VMware provides out-of-the-box dashboards and reports to quickly view key predictive analysis features, as well as health and performance metrics.

vRealize Operations is a great tool for vAdmins to gather historical analytics and forensics data from their VMware environments, and do predictive analytics based on that data. But its greatness doesn't stop there. The need for vAdmins to be able to gain visibility into other environments and applications gave birth to the vRealize Operations adapters and management packs to enable communication to those monitored endpoints.

Some of these management packs further extend the monitoring capabilities of vRealize Operations into the VMware product ecosystem.

For example, the Management Pack™ for vRealize Automation™ extends the operational management capabilities of the vRealize Operations platform to provide tenant-aware operational visibility of the infrastructure supporting private clouds to cloud provider administrators.

With the vRealize Operations Management Pack for vSAN™ installed, you can make vSAN operational in a production environment. You use dashboards provided with the solution to evaluate, manage, and optimize the performance of vSAN objects and vSAN-enabled objects in your vCenter Server system.

Other management packs extend into third-party products and hardware vendors.

The Oracle Enterprise Manager Management Pack for vRealize Operations allows the VMware admin to see Oracle metrics side by side with the VMware metrics, allowing for quick diagnosis of the root problem.

There are a number of management packs available to the vAdmin to help gain this visibility, and ensure there are no hardware failures of the underlying hardware infrastructure. These management packs range from EMC and Trend Micro to Dell, NetApp (from Blue Medora), and Hewlett-Packard.

A compatibility guide and a list of recent updates in the management packs can be found at `https://www.vmware.com/resources/compatibility/pdf/vi_vrops_guide.pdf`.

In this chapter, we will cover the following topics:

- **Return on investment (ROI)** with vRealize Operations
- What vRealize Operations can do
- Key component architecture
- Node types and their purpose
- **High availability (HA)** and scalability

ROI with vRealize Operations

There is a lot of promise in the **Internet of Things (IoT)** as a means to create business value, but there is also a lot of hype. In fact, an unclear business benefit is one of the top barriers to IoT efforts overall.

Why do we make business investments?

The short answer is, we make business investments because, after all, this is the cost of doing business. This is the cost you have to pay to be able to stay in business.

How do we stay in business?

By making smart decisions guided by intelligent and reliable information. The main drivers that affect the ability to stay in business are the following:

- Reducing costs
- Improving price-to-performance ratios
- Lowering risk, or in other words, increasing the change to avoid failures that can lead to catastrophic costs for the business

As IT leaders continue to struggle with translating value into business terms, they need a simple language with relevant and reliable metrics to not only be able to stay in business, but also to grow the business by increasing business revenue growth and enhancing products, services, and experiences for customers. And for those who are looking for new market and product horizons, this will help you transform your business and stay competitive, or even become a market leader.

What tools do we need to stay in business?

In the IT world, it really helps to achieve those business goals by helping out your IT by giving the infrastructure and application teams the tools that will enable them to perform:

- **Application-aware monitoring**: Accelerate time to value, and troubleshoot smarter with native integrations, unified visibility from applications to infrastructure health, and actionable insights combining metrics and logs.
- **Automated and proactive workload management**: Simplify and streamline operations with the fully automated management of infrastructure and applications performance, while retaining full control. Automatically balance workloads, avoid contention and enable proactive detection and automatic remediation of issues and anomalies before end users are impacted.
- **Capacity planning and optimization**: Optimize cost and resource usage through capacity management, reclamation, and right-sizing, improve planning and forecasting, and enforce IT and configuration standards.

The VMware vRealize Operations product portfolio provides the necessary functionality to satisfy the above use cases. It delivers a complete intelligent operations solution that is designed to help customers plan, manage, and scale their SDDC and multi-cloud environments to meet business needs.

VMware commissioned Forrester Consulting to conduct a **Total Economic Impact** (**TEI**) study, and examine the potential ROI enterprises may realize when deploying intelligent operations solution. Working with four VMware customers, Forrester identified and quantified the key benefits of investing in this intelligent operations solution, including the following:

- A 20% improvement in operational efficiency
- Over 10% savings in hardware costs
- A 75% reduction in unplanned downtime

The TEI study demonstrates quantifiable ROI of 119%, a payback period of 3 months, and $1.4M NPV over 3 years.

If you would like to estimate the potential 3-year cost savings and benefits of deploying and using the tools included in this intelligent operations solution, use the vRealize Intelligent Operations Estimator Tool at `https://tools.totaleconomicimpact.com/go/vmware/vrops/`.

What can vRealize Operations do?

vRealize Operations collects data from objects in your environment. Each piece of data collected is called a **metric observation**, or **value**. Metrics can be grouped together in a vRealize Operations view.

Views are resource-type-specific, self-contained, reusable displays of information.

You have to define the resource type (or types) that you want to use as the "subjects" for the view. This is necessary so that you can select metrics that are specific to a resource type.

A view configuration is entirely independent of other views or settings. A view will display exactly the same everywhere it is used.

Due to their self-contained nature, and thanks to extensive integration points provided throughout vRealize Operations, views can be reused extensively. You can create valuable vRealize Operations views, and reuse them for every table or chart.

You can configure views to show transformation, trend, and forecast calculations:

- The transformation type determines how the values are aggregated.
- The trend option shows how the values tend to change, based on the historical raw data. The trend calculations depend on the transformation type and roll-up interval.
- The forecast option shows what the future values can be, based on the trend calculations of the historical data.

vRealize Operations provides several types of views. Each type of view helps you to interpret metrics, properties, policies of various monitored objects including alerts, symptoms, and so on, from a different perspective.

Views can be added to dashboards via the view widget. Dashboards present a visual overview of the performance and state of objects in your virtual infrastructure. You use dashboards to determine the nature and time frame of existing and potential issues with your environment.

Views are also the building blocks for reports. A report captures details related to current or predicted resource needs.

Used separately, or in reports, or dashboards, views can increase ROI in multiple ways.

Standalone views let you package up multiple key performance metrics into one view, removing the repetitive task of digging through metric menus. They are available for both parent and children resources, enabling you to quickly get key information for resources up and down the stack.

When used in reports, views increase your vRealize Operations ROI by combining vital configuration and performance information across your stack in a simple and reusable package. Report execution and delivery can also be automated, saving you even more time!

When used in dashboards, views allow you to define your resource KPIs in one place (the view), then reuse it elsewhere (reports and dashboards).

vRealize Operations has come a long way in recent years, but the more interesting and exciting features have come in the latest releases of the product. Here is a short overview of the new and enhanced features in the latest release of vRealize Operations, 6.6.

vRealize Operations offers simplified usability and faster time-to-value capabilities, as follows:

- A new HTML5 user interface provides an easier and consistent experience. The new UI is clarity-based, which is a standard used by all the products of VMware. This allows you to seamlessly go from one area of the solution to another, whether it is metrics, logs, or cost, without learning the menus or impacting your user experience.
- Consolidation and simpler grouping of menus, leading to the enhanced user experience.
- The **Getting Started** dashboard allows for quick navigation.
- Persona-based dashboards provide answers in one place. Dashboards are separated into categories such as **Operations**, **Capacity and Utilization**, **Performance Troubleshooting**, **Workload Balance**, and **Configuration and Compliance**.
- Out-of-the-box integration with vSAN, vRealize Log Insight, vRealize Business for Cloud, and vRealize Automation provides quick time to value:

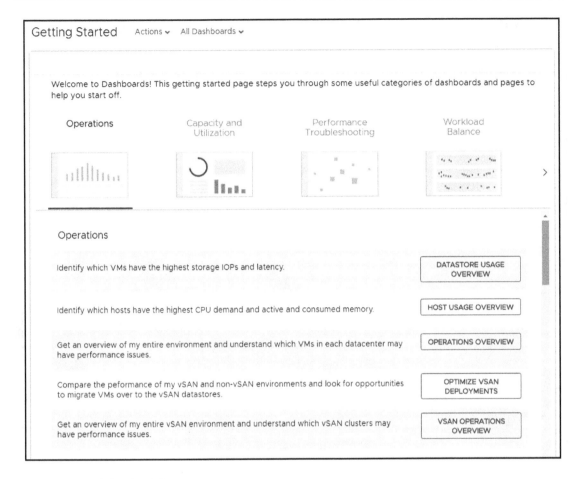

It is optimized for SDDC management:

- Native vSAN management capabilities allow for centralized management across vSAN stretched clusters
- Ability for complete vSAN management, which includes administering performance, capacity, logs, and configuration and health
- Deploy vSAN with confidence with complete visibility down to disk level

- Operationalize vSAN with performance and capacity monitoring, including deduplication and compression benefits:

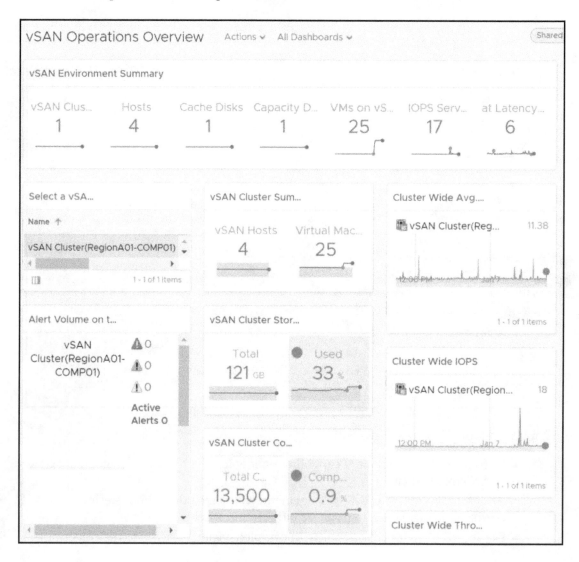

The Service Discovery Management Pack discovers all the services running in each VM and then builds a relationship or dependencies between services from different VMs, based on the network communication. The management pack can create dynamic applications based on the network communication between the services:

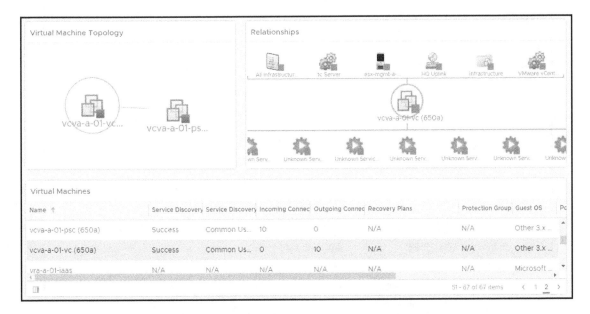

It has intelligent workload placement featuring fully automated workload balancing:

- Ensures performance across data centers with fully automated workload balancing, across clusters and across data stores (with storage vMotion)
- Ensures DRS configurations, and provides the option to set DRS automation level for individual objects
- Predictive DRS takes action to pre-empt resource contention

- Utilizes operations analytics to optimize initial placement of workloads through vRealize Automation:

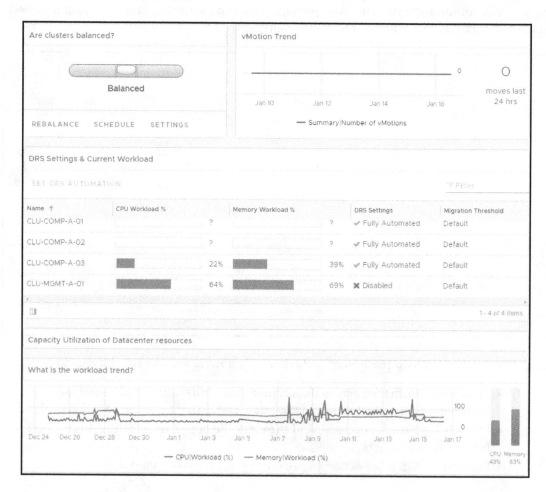

It has log integration:

- Full integration in-context within vRealize Operations for faster troubleshooting:
    - Direct launch of the **Log Insight** dashboard
    - Direct launch into **Log Insight Interactive Analytics** mode
    - Object auto-initiated log management
    - vRealize Operations alerts auto-initiated log management:

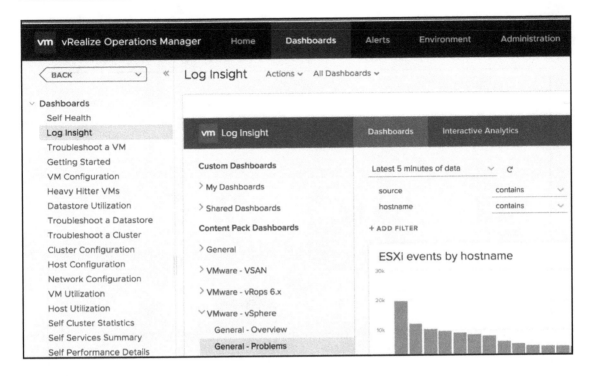

It enables cost management:

- Optimize public cloud spending with more visibility:
    - **Cost visibility**: Costing analysis for all services on AWS and Azure
    - **Usage visibility**: VM level usage visibility into public clouds
- Enhanced planning by correlating capacity and costs:
    - Fine-grained cost analysis for private cloud
    - Makes capacity optimization quantifiable
    - Procurement planning

It has the following additional out-of-the-box compliance and hardening capabilities:

- Ability to tackle compliance problems through the new vSphere hardening dashboard
- Extends compliance through PCI and HIPAA compliance for vSphere

- Ensures business configurations through new cluster, host, and VM configuration dashboards:

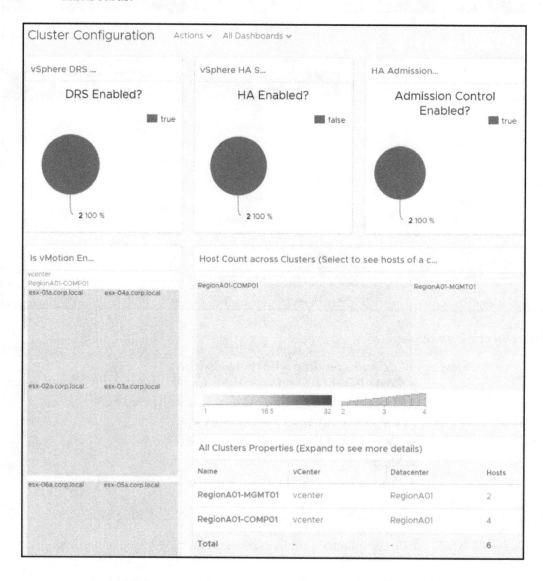

It has sizing and scalability enhancements:

- You can now scale to six extra large nodes in a cluster, which can support up to 180,000 objects, and 45 million metrics
- You can now monitor up to 60 vCenter servers with a single instance of vRealize Operations
- A large remote Collector can support up to 15,000 objects

vRealize Operations key component architecture

In vRealize Operations 6.0, a new platform design was introduced to meet some of the required goals that VMware envisaged for the product. These included the following:

- The ability to treat all solutions equally, and to be able to offer management of performance, capacity, configuration, and compliance to both VMware and third-party solutions
- Provide a single platform that can scale to tens of thousands of objects and millions of metrics by scaling out with little reconfiguration or redesign required
- Support a monitoring solution that can be highly available, and support the loss of a node without impacting the ability to store or query information

With that new common platform, the design came a completely new architecture.

The following diagram shows the major components of the vRealize Operations 6.6 architecture:

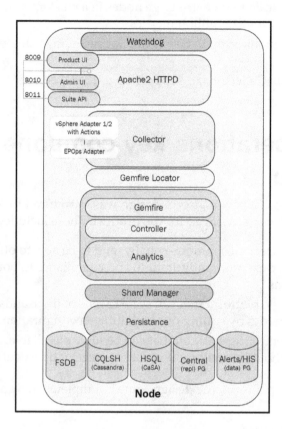

The components of the vRealize Operations 6.6 architecture are as follows:

- **Watchdog**
- **The user interface**
- **Collector**
- **GemFire**
- **GemFire Locator**
- **Controller**
- **Analytics**
- **Persistence**

The Watchdog service

Watchdog is a vRealize Operations service that maintains the necessary daemons/services and attempts to restart them as necessary should there be a failure. The `vcops-watchdog` is a Python script that runs every five minutes by means of the `cops-watchdog-daemon` with the purpose of monitoring the various vRealize Operations services, including the **Cluster and Slice Administrator (CaSA)**.

The Watchdog service performs the following checks:

- PID file of the service
- Service status

The user interface

In vRealize Operations 6.6, the UI is broken into two components the Product UI, and the Admin UI. The Product UI is present on all nodes, with the exception of nodes that are deployed as remote collectors.

The Admin UI is a web application hosted by Pivotal tc Server (Java application Apache web server), and is responsible for making HTTP REST calls to the admin API for node administration tasks. The CaSA is responsible for cluster administrative actions, such as the following:

- Enabling/disabling the vRealize Operations cluster
- Enabling/disabling cluster nodes
- Performing software updates
- Browsing log files

The Admin UI is purposely designed to be separate from the Product UI and to always be available for administration and troubleshooting-type tasks. A small database caches data from the Product UI that provides the last known state information to the Admin UI in the event that the Product UI and analytics are unavailable.

The Admin UI is available on each node at `https://<NodeIP>/admin`.

The Product UI is the main vRealize Operations graphical user interface. Like the Admin UI, the Product UI is based on Pivotal tc Server, and can make HTTP REST calls to the CaSA for administrative tasks; however, the primary purpose of the Product UI is to make GemFire calls to the Controller API to access data and create views, such as dashboards and reports.

The Apache2 HTTPD also provides the backend platform for another Tomcat instances. The Suite API is a public-facing API that can be used for automating/scripting common tasks. It is also used internally by vRealize Operations for carrying out numerous administrative tasks. The End Point Operations Management Adapter, HTTP Post Adapter, and Telemetry are also run by this Tomcat instance.

As shown in the following diagram, the **Product UI** is simply accessed via HTTPS on TCP 443. Apache then provides a reverse proxy back to the Product UI running in tc Server using the Apache APJ protocol:

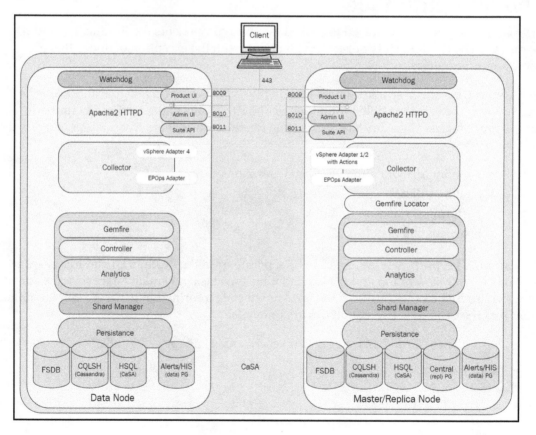

The Collector

The **Collector** process is responsible for pulling in inventory and metric data from the configured sources. As shown in the following diagram, the **Collector** uses adapters to collect data from various sources, and then contacts the **GemFire** locator for connection information to one or more **Controller** cache servers. The **Collector** service then connects to one or more **Controller** API GemFire cache servers, and sends the collected data.

It is important to note that although an instance of an adapter can only be running on one node at a time, it does not imply that the collected data is being sent to the **Controller** on that node.

The **Collector** will send a heartbeat to the **Controller** every 30 seconds. This is sent via the HeartbeatThread thread process running on the **Collector**. It has a maximum of 25 data collection threads. Vice versa, the **Controller** node, vice versa, runs a HeartbeatServer thread process which processes heartbeats from Collectors. The CollectorStatusChecker thread process is a DistributedTask which uses data from HeartbeatServers to decides whether the **Collector** is up or down.

By default, the **Collector** will wait for 30 minutes for adapters to synchronize.

 The **Collector** properties, including enabling or disabling the self-protection, can be configured from the collector.properties properties file located in /usr/lib/vmware-vcops/user/conf/collector.

The vSphere adapter provides the **Collector** process with the configuration information needed to pull in vCenter inventory and metric data. It consists of configuration files and a JAR file. A separate adapter instance is configured for each vCenter Server.

The Python adapter provides the **Collector** process with the configuration information needed to send remediation commands back to a vCenter Server (power on/off VM, vMotion VM, reconfigure VM, and so on).

The **End Point Operations Management** adapter is installed and listening by default on each vRealize Operations node. To receive data from operating systems, the agent must be installed and configured on each guest OS to be monitored.

The Horizon adapter provides the Collector process with the configuration information needed to pull in the Horizon View inventory and metric data. A separate adapter instance is configured for each Horizon View pod, and only one adapter instance is supported per vRealize Operations node with a limit of 10,000 Horizon objects:

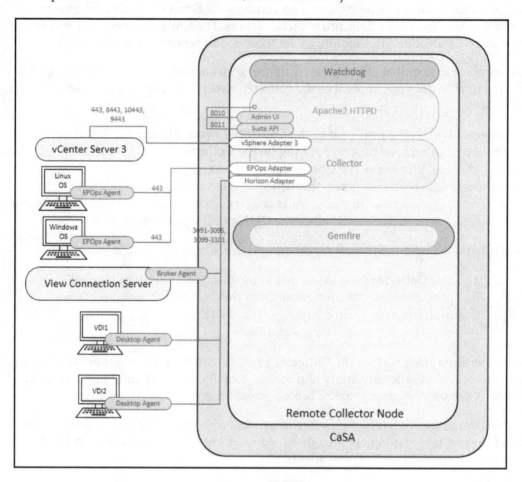

The GemFire

VMware vFabric® GemFire® is an in-memory, low-latency data grid, running in the same JVM as the Controller and Analytics, that scales as needed when nodes are added to the cluster. It allows the caching, processing, and retrieval of metrics, and is functionally dependent on the GemFire Locator.

Remote collector nodes only communicate over GemFire using ports `10000-10010`.

The GemFire locator

The vFabric GemFire locator runs on the master and master replica nodes. The data nodes and remote Collectors run GemFire as a client process.

The Controller

The Controller is a sub-process of the Analytics process, and is responsible for coordinating activity between the cluster members. It manages the storage and retrieval of the inventory of objects within the system. The queries are performed leveraging the GemFire MapReduce function that allows for selective querying. This allows for efficient data querying, as data queries are only performed on select nodes rather than all nodes.

The Controller will monitor the Collector status every minute. It also monitors how long a deleted resource is available in the inventory, and how long a non-existing resource is stored in the database.

 The Collector properties can be configured from the `controller.properties` properties file located in `/usr/lib/vmware-vcops/user/conf/controller`.

Analytics

Analytics is the heart of vRealize Operations, as it is essentially the runtime layer for data analysis. The role of the Analytics process is to track the individual states of every metric, and then use various forms of correlation to determine if there are problems.

At a high level, the Analytics layer is responsible for the following tasks:

- Metric calculations
- Dynamic thresholds
- Alerts and alarms
- Metric storage and retrieval from the Persistence layer

- Root cause analysis
- **Historic Inventory Server** (**HIS**) version metadata calculations and relationship data

Analytics components work with the new GemFire-based cache, Controller, and Persistence layers. The Analytics process is also responsible for generating SMTP and SNMP alerts on the master and master-replica nodes.

Persistence

The Persistence (the database) layer, as its name implies, is the layer where the data is persisted to disk. The layer primarily consists of a series of databases performing different functions, and having different roles.

vRealize Operations uses two data storage solutions:

- **Postgres**: This is a relational database that stores the configuration and state of the data
- **FSDB**: This is a proprietary high-performance filesystem-based repository that stores all the time series data

Understanding the Persistence layer is an important aspect of vRealize Operations, as this layer has a strong relationship with the data and service availability of the solution.

vRealize Operations has five primary database services, as follows:

Common name	Role	DB type	Sharded	**Location**
Cassandra DB	User preferences and configuration, alerts definition, customizations, dashboards, policies, view, reports, licensing, shard maps, activities	Apache Cassandra	No	`/storage/db/vcops/cassandra`

Central (Repl) DB	Resource inventory	PostgreSQL	Yes	`/storage/db/vcops/vpostgres/data/`
Alerts /HIS (Data) DB	Alerts and alarm history, history of resource property data, history of resource relationship	PostgreSQL	Yes	`/storage/db/vcops/vpostgres/data/`
FSDB	Filesystem database containing the following: •RAW metrics •Super metrics data	FSDB	Yes	`/storage/db/vcops/data` `/storage/db/vcops/rollup`
CaSA DB	Cluster and Slice Administrator data	HSQL (Hyper SQL Database)	No	`/storage/db/casa/webapp/ hsqlbd`

 Prior to 6.3, a common administrator task was to re-index the database. The 6.3 release, and later releases, contain a scheduled task to re-index the database. The script itself is available at the following location: `/usr/lib/vmware-vcops/user/conf/persistence/vpostgres/vpostgres_sharded_d b_index_rebuild.sh`.

Sharding is the term that GemFire uses to describe the process of distributing data across multiple systems to ensure that compute, storage, and network load is evenly distributed across the cluster.

Cassandra DB

The Cassandra database was introduced in 6.1 to replace the Global xDB database. Apache Cassandra is a highly scalable, high-performance, distributed database. It is designed to handle large amounts of structured data across many nodes. It provides HA with no single point of failure. Cassandra is highly scalable, as it allows us to add more vRealize Operations nodes in the future to the existing cluster.

Currently, the database stores the following:

- User preferences and configuration
- Alerts definition
- Customizations
- Dashboards, policies, views
- Reports, licensing
- Shard maps
- Activities

Cassandra stores all the info that we see in the CONTENT folder; basically any settings that are applied globally.

Central (repl) DB

The Postgres database was introduced in 6.1. It has two instances in version 6.6. The Central Postgres DB, also called repl and the Alerts/HIS Postgres DB, also called **data**, are two separate database instances under the database called vcopsdb.

The Central DB exists only on the master and the master-replica node when HA is enabled. It is accessible via port 5433 and it is located in /storage/db/vcops/vpostgres/repl.

Currently, the database stores only resource inventory information.

Alerts /HIS (Data) DB

The Alerts DB is called **data** on all the data nodes including Master and Master-replica node. It was again introduced in 6.1. Starting from 6.2, the Historical Inventory Service xDB was merged with the Alerts DB. It is accessible via port 5432, and it is located in /storage/db/vcops/vpostgres/data.

Currently, the database stores the following:

- Alerts and alarm history
- History of resource property data
- History of resource relationship

HSQL DB

The HSQL (or CaSA) database is a small, flat, JSON-based, in-memory DB that is used by CaSA for cluster administration.

FSDB

The FSDB contains all raw time series metrics and super metrics data for the discovered resources. It stores the data collected by adapters, and data that is calculated/generated (such as a system, badge, and metrics) based on the analysis of that data.

FSDB is a GemFire server, and runs inside the analytics JVM. It uses Sharding Manager to distribute data between nodes (new objects). We will discuss what vRealize Operations cluster nodes are later in this chapter. The FSDB is available in all the nodes of a vRealize Operations cluster deployment.

vRealize Operations node types

vRealize Operations contains a common node architecture. Every vRealize Operations cluster consists of a master node, an optional replica node for HA, optional data nodes, and optional remote collector nodes.

When you install vRealize Operations , you use a vRealize Operations vApp deployment to create roleless nodes. After the nodes are created, you can configure them according to their role. You can create roleless nodes all at once or as needed. A common as-needed practice might be to add nodes to scale out vRealize Operations to monitor an environment as the environment grows larger.

Here is a low-level overview of the different node types, the component roles they can have, and the communication ports they use:

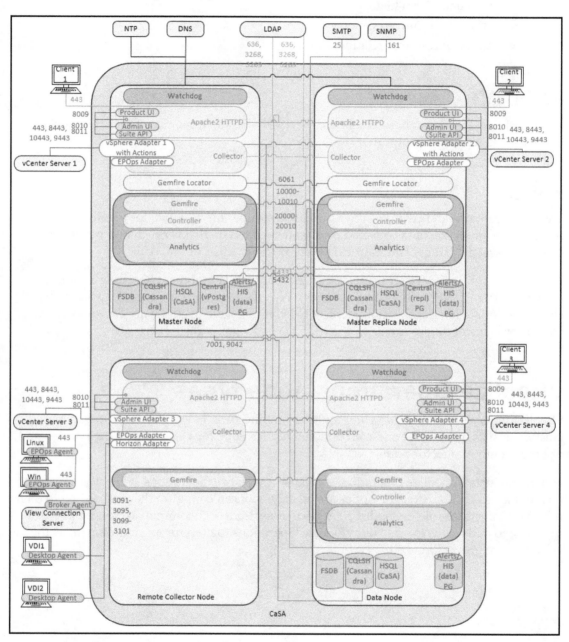

Although deployment will be discussed in detail in later chapters, from a design perspective it is important to understand the different roles, and what deployment model best fits your own environment.

The master and master replica nodes

The master or master replica node is critical to the availability of the vRealize Operations cluster. It contains all vRealize Operations services, including UI, Controller, Analytics, Collector, and Persistence, as well as critical services that cannot be replicated across all cluster nodes. These include the following:

- NTP server
- GemFire locator

During a failure event of the master node, the master replica DB is promoted to a full read/write master. Although the process of replica DB promotion can be done online, the migration of the master role during a failover does require an automated restart of the cluster. As a result, even though it is an automated process, the failure of the master node will result in a temporary outage of the vRealize Operations cluster until all nodes have been restarted against the new master.

The master also has the responsibility for running both an NTP server and client. On initial configuration of the first vRealize Operations node, you are prompted to add an external NTP source for time synchronization. The master node then keeps time with this source, and runs its own NTP server for all data and collector nodes to sync from. This ensures all nodes have the correct time, and only the master/master replica requires access to an external time source.

The final component that is unique to the master role is the GemFire locator. The GemFire locator is a process that tells starting or connecting data nodes where running cluster members are located; this process also provides load balancing of queries that are passed to data nodes that then become data coordinators for that particular query:

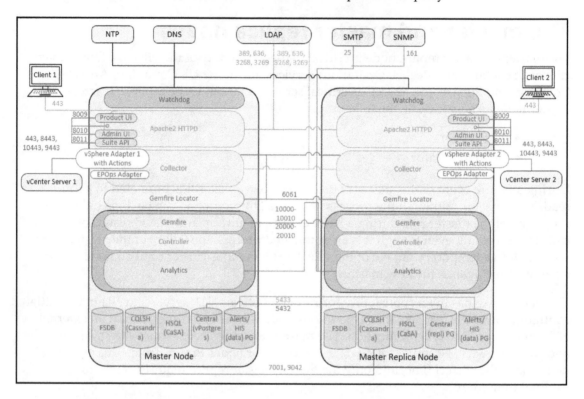

The data node

The data node is the standard vRealize Operations role, and is the default when adding a new node into an existing cluster. It provides the core functionality of collecting and processing data and data queries, as well as extending the vRealize Operations cluster by being a member of the GemFire Federation that, in turn, provides the horizontal scaling of the platform.

As shown in the following diagram, a data node is almost identical to a master/master replica node, with the exception of the Central vPostgres database, NTP server, and GemFire locator:

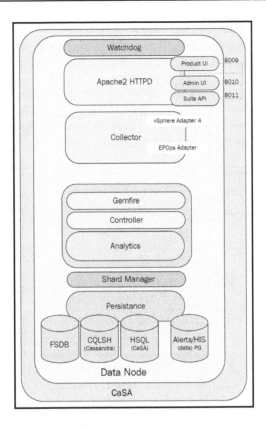

The remote collector node

The remote collector node is a continuation of the vCenter Operations Manager 5.x installable concept around having a standalone collector for remote sites or secure enclaves. Remote collectors do not process data themselves; instead, they simply forward on metric data to data nodes for analytics processing.

Remote collector nodes do not run several of the core vRealize Operations components, including the following:

- Product UI
- Controller
- GemFire locator
- Analytics
- Persistence

As a result of not running these components, remote collectors are not members of the GemFire federation, and although they do not add resources to the cluster, they themselves require far fewer resources to run, which is ideal in smaller remote office locations:

 An important point to note is that adapter instances will fail over to other data nodes when the hosting node fails, even if HA is not enabled. An exception to this is remote collectors, as adapter instances registered to remote collectors will not automatically fail over.

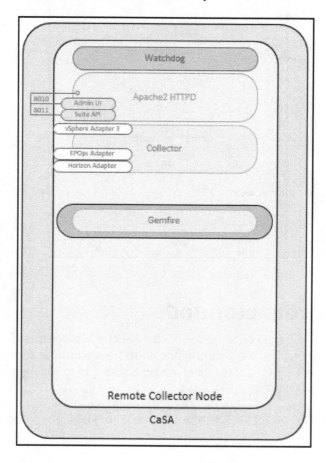

Multi-node deployment, HA, and scalability

So far, we have focused on the new architecture and components of vRealize Operations 6.6, as well as starting to mention the major architectural changes that the GemFire-based Controller, Analytics, and Persistence layers have introduced. Now, before we close this chapter, we will dive down a little deeper into how data is handled in multi-node deployment, and, finally, how HA works in vRealize Operations 6.6, and what design decisions revolve around a successful deployment.

We are also going to mention what scalability considerations you should make to configure your initial deployment of vRealize Operations based on anticipated usage.

GemFire clustering

At the core of vRealize Operations, 6.6 architecture is the powerful GemFire in-memory clustering and distributed cache. GemFire provides the internal transport bus, as well as the ability to balance CPU and memory consumption across all nodes through compute pooling, memory sharing, and data partitioning. With this change, it is better to then think of the Controller, Analytics, and Persistence layers as components that span nodes, rather than individual components on individual nodes:

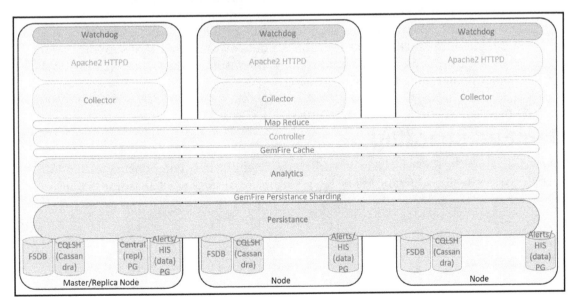

During deployment, ensure all your vRealize Operations 6.6 nodes are configured with the same amount of vCPUs and memory. This is because, from a load balancing point of view, vRealize Operations expects all nodes to have the same amount of resources as part of the controller's round-robin load balancing.

The migration to GemFire is probably the single largest underlying architectural change from vCenter Operations Manager 5.x, and the result of moving to a distributed in-memory database has made many of the new vRealize Operations 6.x features possible, including the following:

- **Elasticity and scale**: Nodes can be added on demand, allowing vRealize Operations to scale as required. This allows a single Operations Manager instance to scale to 6 extra large nodes in a cluster, which can support up to 180,000 objects and 45,000,000 metrics.
- **Reliability**: When GemFire HA is enabled, a backup copy of all data is stored in both the Analytics GemFire cache and the Persistence layer.
- **Availability**: Even with the GemFire HA mode disabled, in the event of a failure, other nodes take over the failed services and the load of the failed node (assuming the failure was not the master node).
- **Data partitioning**: vRealize Operations leverages GemFire data partitioning to distribute data across nodes in units called **buckets**. A partition region will contain multiple buckets that are configured during a startup, or migrated during a rebalance operation. Data partitioning allows the use of the GemFire MapReduce function. This function is a data-aware query, that supports parallel data querying on a subset of the nodes. The result of this is then returned to the coordinator node for final processing.

GemFire sharding

When describing the Persistence layer earlier, we listed the new components related to Persistence in vRealize Operations 6.6, Now it's time to discuss what sharding actually is.

GemFire sharding is the process of splitting data across multiple GemFire nodes for placement in various partitioned buckets. It is this concept in conjunction with the controller and locator services that balance the incoming resources and metrics across multiple nodes in the vRealize Operations Cluster. It is important to note that data is sharded per resource, and not per adapter instance. For example, this allows the load balancing of incoming and outgoing data, even if only one adapter instance is configured. From a design perspective, a single vRealize Operations cluster could then manage a maximum configuration vCenter by distributing the incoming metrics across multiple data nodes.

 In vRealize Operations 6.6, the maximum number of VMware vCenter adapter instances certified is 60, and the maximum number of VMware vCenter adapter instances that were tested on a single collector is 40.

vRealize Operations data is sharded in both the Analytics and Persistence layers, which is referred to as GemFire cache sharding and GemFire Persistence sharding respectively.

Just because data is held in the GemFire cache on one node, this does not necessarily result in the data shard persisting on the same node. In fact, as both layers are balanced independently, the chance of both the cache shard and Persistence shard existing on the same node is $1/N$, where N is the number of nodes.

 In an HA environment, the databases that use GemFire sharding are Central, Alert/HIS, and FSDB. The Cassandra DB uses its own clustering mechanism.

Adding, removing, and balancing nodes

One of the biggest advantages of a GemFire-based cluster is the elasticity of adding nodes to the cluster as the number of resources and metrics grows in your environment. This allows administrators to add or remove nodes if the size of their environment changes unexpectedly; for example, a merger with another IT department, or catering for seasonal workloads that only exist for a small period of the year.

From a deployment perspective, we want to hide the complexities of scaling out from the user, so we deploy the whole stack at a time. When one instance/slice of the stack runs out of capacity (CPU/disk/memory), we can spin up another, and add more capacity. We can keep doing this as necessary to handle the scale.

Although adding nodes to an existing cluster is something that can be done at any time, there is a slight cost when doing so. As just mentioned, it is important when adding new nodes that they are sized the same as the existing cluster nodes; this will ensure during a rebalance operation that the load is distributed equally between the cluster nodes:

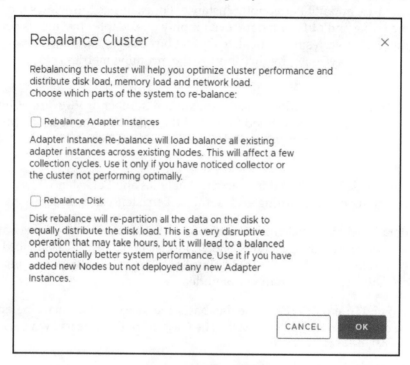

When adding new nodes to the cluster sometime after initial deployment, it is recommended that the **Rebalance Disk** option be selected under **Cluster Management**. As seen in the preceding figure, the warning advises that this is a very disruptive operation that may take hours and, as such, it is recommended that this be a planned maintenance activity. The amount of time this operation will take will vary depending on the size of the existing cluster and the amount of data in the FSDB. As you can probably imagine, if you are adding the eighth node to an existing seven-node cluster with tens of thousands of resources, there could potentially be several TBs of data that need to be re-sharded over the entire cluster. It is also strongly recommended that when adding new nodes the disk capacity and performance match that of existing nodes, as the Rebalance Disk operation assumes this is the case.

This activity is not required to start receiving the compute and network load balancing benefits of the new node. This can be achieved by selecting the **Rebalance GemFire** option, which is a far less disruptive process. As per the description, this process re-partitions the JVM buckets, balancing the memory across all active nodes in the GemFire federation. With the GemFire cache balanced across all nodes, the compute and network demand should be roughly equal across all the nodes in the cluster.

Although this allows early benefit from adding a new node into an existing cluster, unless a large number of new resources is discovered by the system shortly afterward, the majority of disk I/O for persisted, sharded data will occur on other nodes.

Apart from adding nodes, vRealize Operations also allows the removal of a node at any time, as long as it has been taken offline first. This can be valuable if a cluster was originally oversized for a requirement, and is considered a waste of physical compute resource; however, this task should not be taken lightly, as the removal of a data node without HA enabled will result in the loss of all metrics on that node. As such, it is recommended that removing nodes from the cluster is generally avoided.

If the permanent removal of a data node is necessary, ensure HA is first enabled to prevent data loss.

High Availability in vRealize Operations 6.6

One of the features that came in vRealize Operations 6.0 was the ability to configure the cluster in an HA mode to prevent data loss. This still remains an impressive feature, used even today in vRealize Operations 6.6. Enabling HA makes two major changes to the Operations Manager cluster:

- The primary effect of HA is that all sharded data is duplicated by the Controller layer to a primary and backup copy in both the GemFire cache and GemFire Persistence layers.
- The secondary effect is that the master replica is created on a chosen data node for replication of the database. This node then takes over the role of the master node in the event that the original master fails.

How does HA and data duplication work?

As we just said, HA duplicates all incoming resource data so that two copies exist instead of one in both the GemFire cache and Persistence layers. This is done by creating a secondary copy of each piece of data that is used in queries, if the node hosting a primary copy is unavailable.

It is important to note that as HA is simply creating a secondary copy of each piece of data, as such only one node failure can be sustained at a time (*N*-1) without data loss, regardless of the cluster size. If a node is down, a new secondary shard of the data is not created unless the original node is removed from the cluster permanently.

When a failed node becomes available again, a node is placed into recovery mode. During this time, data is synchronized with the other cluster members and when the synchronization is complete, the node is returned to active status:

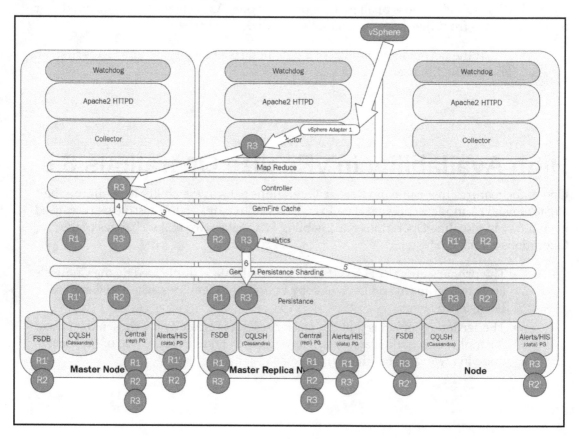

Let's run through this process using the diagram above for an example, about how incoming data or the creation of a new object is handled in an HA configuration. In the above diagram, R3 represents our new resource, and R3' represents the secondary copy:

1. A running adapter instance receives data from vCenter, as it is required to create a new resource for the new object, and a discovery task is created.
2. The discovery task is passed to the cluster. This task could be passed to any one node in the cluster, and once assigned, that node is responsible for completing the task.
3. A new analytics item is created for the new object in the GemFire cache on any node in the cluster.
4. A secondary copy of the data is created on a different node to protect against failure.
5. The system then saves the data to the Persistence layer. The object is created in the inventory (HIS), and its statistics are stored in the FSDB.
6. A secondary copy of the saved (GemFire Persistence sharding) HIS and FSDB data is stored on a different node to protect against data loss.

The following diagram shows the same duplication process, but this time for a non-HA setup:

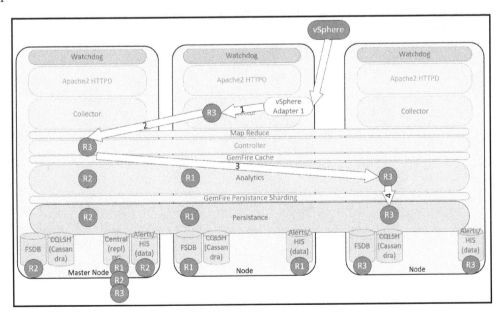

In a non-HA scenario, the following happens when a new object is discovered:

1. A new object is discovered by the adapter, which is located in the Collector.
2. The Collector receives the object's metric and property information from the adapter.
3. The Collector sends the object information to the Controller.
4. The global database is updated with the new object type information. The object is created in the central database.
5. The object is also cached by the analytics component.
6. The Alerts database is updated with object information.

Summary

In this chapter, we discussed the new common platform architecture design, and how vRealize Operations 6.6 differs from previous versions. We also covered the major components that make up the vRealize Operations 6.6 platform, and the functions that each of the component layers provides. This then moved into the various roles of each node type, and finally how multi-node, HA deployment functions.

In the next chapter, we will cover some design considerations and requirements around vRealize Operations 6.6.

2
Which vRealize Operations Deployment Model Fits Your Needs

In this chapter, we will guide you through the design considerations you have to be aware of as part of architecting your solution. This will include the following topics:

- Design considerations around vRealize Operations High Availability
- Remote collectors and collector groups, and how they can affect the design
- Importance of proper vRealize Operations sizing
- Deployment examples

Design considerations

Let's take a look at some high availability and scalability considerations we must be aware of when designing for vRealize Operations architecture. We will also take a look at what role vRealize Operations remote collector nodes and collector groups can play in a design.

To HA or not to HA?

You have to have a good grasp of the geographical layout of the infrastructure, including remote offices and data centers that you want to monitor.

'You should also consider the number and type of objects for which you want to collect data, which includes the type and number of adapters installed. Determine whether you want to enable high availability.

Based on that information you can determine what type of nodes need to be deployed in your vRealize Operations cluster to meet those requirements.

As you may remember from the previous chapter, you can deploy vRealize Operations on a single node, or on multiple nodes, to create a multi-node cluster for either scalability, availability, or both.

Every node in the cluster is assigned a role:

- Master
- Master replica
- Data
- Remote collector

vRealize Operations supports high availability by enabling a master replica node for the vRealize Operations master node.

Although enabling HA is simple enough, it should not be done without proper consideration.

As mentioned earlier, both cache and persistence data is sharded per resource, not per metric or adapter. As such, when a data node is unavailable, not only can metrics not be viewed or used for analytics, but also new metrics for resources that are on affected nodes are discarded, assuming the adapter collector is operational, or failed over. This fact alone would attract administrators to simply enabling HA by default, considering how easy it is to do so.

Each time you enable high availability for the vRealize Operations cluster, a re-balance process takes place in the background, which may sometimes take a long time. This is a necessary action if you lose the master or master replica nodes. You can take advantage of all the benefits vSphere has to offer, such as DRS anti-affinity rules, to make sure nodes are not residing on the same vSphere cluster nodes. vRealize Operations HA ensures you can recover your data when a single node is lost. If more than one node is lost, the loss of data is irreversible.

Do not stretch your vRealize Operations cluster nodes across different geographical zones or logical data centers, even if they are on the same LAN or subnet. It is not supported.

Although HA is very easy to enable, you must ensure that your cluster is sized appropriately to handle the increased load. As HA duplicates all data stored in both the GemFire cache and Persistence layers, it essentially doubles the load on the system. We will be discussing the sizing considerations in detail later in this chapter.

It is also important to consider that vRealize Operations should not be deployed in a vSphere Cluster where the number of vRealize Operations nodes is greater than the underlying vSphere Cluster hosts. This is because there is little point enabling HA in vRealize Operations if more than one node is residing on the same vSphere host at the same time.

After deploying all your vRealize Operations nodes and enabling HA, ensure a DRS affinity rule is created to keep all nodes on separate vSphere hosts under normal operation. This can be achieved with a DRS separate virtual machine, or a virtual machine to host an affinity rule.

Last, but not least, enabling HA ensures that vRealize Operations can tolerate the loss of only a single cluster node without loss of data. Adding more additional cluster nodes does not increase the number of lost nodes vRealize Operations can tolerate.

Do I need remote collectors and collector groups?

As we mentioned in the previous chapter, a vRealize Operations remote collector node is an additional cluster node that enables vRealize Operations to increase the number of objects that it can store into its inventory for monitoring. Unlike all other nodes, remote collector nodes only include the collector role of vRealize Operations. Collector nodes are not responsible for processing any analytics functions or storing any data.

Formatting of data is handled by the adapter on the Collector. Remote collector nodes always start communication with the vRealize Operations cluster. The cluster does not poll the remote collector for data.

Tactically, you deploy a remote collector node for any of the following reasons:

- So that you can navigate between firewall-protected networks
- Reduce network-related bandwidth between data centers or geographical locations where vRealize Operations components are being deployed
- To connect over **wide area networks** (**WANs**) to remote data sources
- Reduce the operational load on the vRealize Operations analytics cluster

What about collector groups?

If your environment has remote collectors, you can create a collector group, and add remote collectors to the group.

Use collector groups to achieve the following benefits:

- **Adapter resiliency**: If a collector in a collector group becomes unavailable, the total workload is redistributed within the collector group
- **Load balancing**: Automatically instantiates adapter instances based on the collector load of all adapter instances running in the remote collector group

 If an adapter is assigned to a single node, in the event of adapter failure, it will not be moved to a remaining cluster node. To overcome this, make sure to assign it to a collector group instead. Exceptions are made for hybrid adapters. Refer to the official documentation for specific adapters for more information.

Does size matter?

Doing proper scaling before you go and deploying vRealize Operations is very important.

Scaling in vRealize Operations can be achieved by two methods:

- Scaling vertically by either adding resources or storage
- Scaling horizontally by adding nodes

The resources needed for vRealize Operations depends, on the following factors:

- Size of the environment that you expect to monitor and analyze
- Number of objects that you plan to monitor
- Number of metrics that you plan to collect

As you can see from the following table, VMware offers various sizes during installation, each of which consume a certain amount of CPUs and memory to be able to handle a given amount of objects and collected metrics:

Node size	Maximum number of nodes in a cluster	Single-node maximum objects	Single-node maximum collected Metrics	vCPUs	Initial memory (GB)	Maximum memory (GB)
Extra-small	1	250	70,000	2	8	N/A
Small	2	2,400	800,000	4	16	32
Medium	16	8,500	2,000,000	8	32	64
Large	16	15,000	4,000,000	16	48	96
Extra-large	6	35,000	10,000,000	24	128	N/A

If you have first deployed extra-small, small, medium, or large nodes you can reconfigure the node's vCPU and memory. The storage can be increased independently.

The best approach to addressing sizing is through self-monitoring. Allocate as many objects as possible, but create an alert for a situation where the capacity falls below a particular threshold. The alert must allow enough time to add nodes or disks to the cluster.

You can always initially size vRealize Operations according to the existing environmental monitoring needs. After the vRealize Operations instance is no longer capable to handle the environment/object grown, you must expand the cluster to add nodes of the same size.

To maintain a VMware supported-configuration, the size of the data and analytics nodes must match across the respective clusters.

For complete sizing guidelines, you can refer to the vRealize Operations 6.6 Sizing Guidelines (KB2150421) article.

When designing your vRealize Operations cluster, as a general rule, you will need to double the number of nodes if you are planning to enable HA.

Now let's talk about cluster disk space.

You can calculate the amount of disk space needed for your vRealize Operations installation by using the sizing guidelines spreadsheet. This spreadsheet is available in the VMware knowledge base (KB2150421) article.

In this spreadsheet, you enter the number of VMware vSphere objects of each type: virtual machines, host systems, datastores, and so on.

For objects other than vSphere, VMware suggests that you install the adapter and collect the data for at least an hour. You can then look up the number of objects and metrics that the adapter instance collects and enter them into the spreadsheet.

You can find the number of objects and metrics the cluster collects by navigating to the Cluster Management page in the user interface, as explained before.

 You add to the data disk of vRealize Operations vApp nodes when space for storing the collected data runs low.

What about the number of users?

Let's talk briefly about concurrent user access to the vRealize Operations UI.

There is no hard guidance on the maximum concurrent users per node. It is considered that four users is the recommended maximum per node, irrespective of node size, but depending on the use case, that number may be a lot higher.

Let's give an example:

Let's say you have 100 dashboards that your vRealize Operations users, constantly monitor. This means the vRealize Operations UI needs to load, build up, and populate those dashboards with information from the databases and the GemFire caching layer for each user viewing them. Four users are considered to be the maximum number of concurrent users before degradation in user performance may start to take place. Let's say a fifth or sixth user logs in. They will still be able to log in, but they may notice performance degradation, such as slow UI responsiveness.

On the other hand, you may have 20 or 30 concurrent vRealize Operations users where each of them only has permissions and views on only a limited subset of dashboards. In this case, you may not see performance degradation at all.

As we said, these are just example numbers, there is no hard guidance on this. So, make sure to plan user access accordingly. Try to stick to a tight group of vRealize Operations users and give them permissions only to dashboards that are relevant to their business unit or role.

Deployment examples

Let's take a look at a few common deployment scenarios:

Example 1:
In this scenario, you have multiple vCenter Server instances in a single data center.

Deploy at least one node, and scale out as needed:

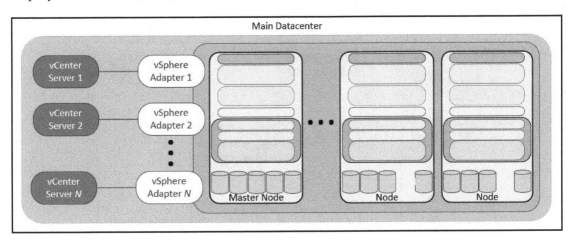

In this scenario, you deploy a vRealize Operations cluster in the main data center. You configure a vCenter adapter for each VMware vCenter Server instance. You monitor all vCenter Server instances from a single product user interface.

Example 2:

In this scenario, you have multiple vCenter Server instances in one data center, like you did in the previous example, but in addition, you have a vCenter Server instance in each remote data center location:

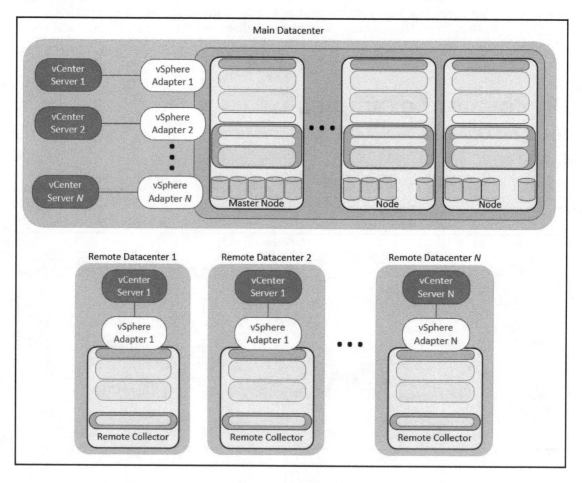

In this scenario, you deploy a vRealize Operations cluster in the main data center. You configure a vCenter adapter for each VMware vCenter Server instance in the main data center. You monitor all vCenter Server instances from a single product user interface.

In addition, you deploy a remote collector node in each remote data center location. Each remote collector node has a vCenter adapter installed that monitors the vCenter Server instance at that location.

Users at the remote locations log into the product user interface at the main data center:

Example 3:

In this scenario, you have multiple vCenter Server instances in two main data centers. This is the same design as in Example 1, but it has been replicated for each data center.

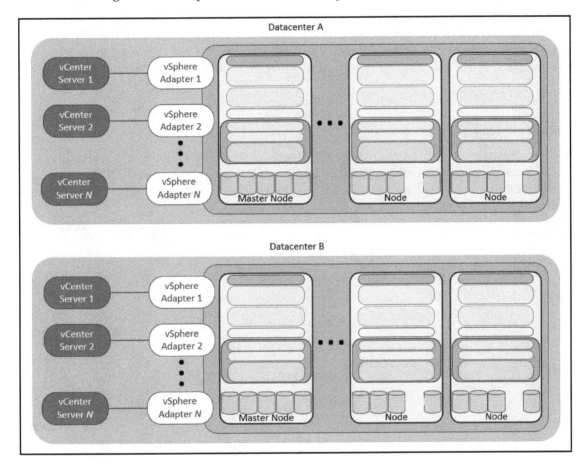

In this scenario, you deploy separate vRealize Operations clusters in each data center. You configure a vCenter adapter for each VMware vCenter Server instance in each of the data centers. You monitor the vCenter Server instances in a data center from a single product user interface. Users log in locally to their cluster.

Seems too complex? Need help?

As you have seen from these first chapters, and as you will see in the next one when we discuss the prerequisite requirements and perform our first vRealize Operations deployment, planning for a proper deployment and architecting a solution that can accommodate the load and complicity of your environment may be a complex task.

The good news is that you can always engage VMware's professional services for some guidance and help to design, implement, upgrade, or migrate your vRealize Operations environment. Make sure to contact your local VMware representative for more info.

Summary

In this chapter, we discussed some vRealize Operations high availability and scalability design considerations. Then we moved on to discuss remote collectors and collector groups, and what they can be used for. At the end, we looked at a few common vRealize Operations deployment examples and use cases.

In the next chapter, we will discuss the deployment prerequisite requirements vRealize Operations has, and perform our first install.

3
Initial Setup and Configuration

Now that we have a good general understanding of the components that make up vRealize Operations, it's time to move on to how to install and upgrade vRealize Operations.

In this chapter, we will guide you through the process of architecting and deploying vRealize Operations 6.6. This will include the following topics:

- Understanding the installation requirements
- Understanding the different installation steps, formats, and types
- Performing a fresh installation
- Performing an upgrade

Meeting the requirements

Before moving on to the actual installation and configuration of vRealize Operations, let's first go through the sizing and networking installation requirements the product has.

Sizing requirements

We discussed the sizing requirements in detail in the previous chapter when we discussed the different deployment models. If necessary, go back and revise them before you continue.

Networking requirements

Before you deploy nodes and build up clusters, it is important to get familiar with all the networking requirements that vRealize Operations has. These requirements must be met to ensure not only successful deployment, but also successful operational continuity of the nodes and full VMware support in case of issues.

Most of the requirements are pretty standard industry requirements for any piece of software, such as having IP and FQDN forward and reverse DNS lookup resolution for all nodes. Others are more specific to the product, such as using one IP subnet and layer 2 network, or having 5 ms or less latency between all analytic cluster nodes.

It is worth mentioning that, although introduced a while ago, **Internet Protocol version 6 (IPv6)** is still not widely used in the public space. If you are one of those enthusiasts that have implemented IPv6 in your environment and are using it, vRealize Operations supports the protocol. Although the product supports IPv6 implementation, with certain limitations, my recommendation to you is to stick to IPv4 until a necessity comes that requires you to move to IPv6.

 Although IPv6 addresses are supported, you cannot mix IPv6 and IPv4.

vRealize Operations uses several network ports to communicate with VMware vCenter Server®, VMware Horizon View, and vRealize Operations components between node instances. You must ensure the following ports are opened across firewalls, between the corresponding servers, or vRealize Operations components:

Source server	Destination server	Port	Protocol	Description
End user workstation	All cluster nodes	22	TCP	Enables SSH access to the vRealize Operations vApp
End user web browser	All cluster nodes	80	TCP	Redirects to port 443

Source server	Destination server	Port	Protocol	Description
End user web browser	All cluster nodes	`443`	TCP	Used to access the vRealize Operations admin portal and the vRealize Operations product user interface
End user web browser	Remote collector	`443`	TCP	Remote collector admin user interface
vCenter Server	All cluster nodes	`443, 22`	TCP	Used for the collection of metric data
Remote collector	All cluster nodes	`443`	TCP	Cluster nodes CASA
Remote collector	All cluster nodes	`6061, 10000-10010, 20000-20010`	TCP	GemFire locator and data
Remote collector	vCenter Servers	`443, 10443, 8443, 9443`	TCP	Data collection and access to vCenter inventory service
Remote collector	DNS servers	`53`	TCP/UDP	Name resolution
Remote collector	NTP servers	`123`	UDP	Time synchronization
All cluster nodes	Remote collector	`443`	TCP	Remote collector CASA and admin user interface
All cluster nodes	SMTP	`25`	TCP	Alert notifications
All cluster nodes	LDAP	`389`	TCP	**Lightweight Directory Access Protocol (LDAP)**
All cluster nodes	All cluster nodes	`25, 161, 5432, 10000-10010`	TCP	All cluster nodes should be on the same LAN with no firewall or NAT between them

Source server	Destination server	Port	Protocol	Description
Master	Master replica	5432, 5433, 7001, 9042	TCP	Replication of vital cluster information
All cluster nodes and remote collectors	LDAP servers	389,686,3368,3369	TCP	Required for LDAP authentication
Endpoint operations manager agent	All cluster nodes and remote collectors	443	TCP	Collection of endpoint operations data from agents
All nodes containing the central DB	All nodes containing the central DB	1235	TCP	Used by all nodes to transmit resource data and key-value data for the Central database instance
All nodes collecting data from Horizon View	View connections servers	3091-3095, 3099-3101	TCP	Used to access data from VMware Horizon View

 vRealize Operations does not support customizing the server ports it uses.

For a full list of vRealize Operations, 6.6 networking requirements and limitations, make sure to check the VMware official product documentation.

It is also very important to be aware of the following latency requirements:

- Network latency between Analytics nodes should be <5 ms
- Network latency between remote collectors and Analytics nodes should be <200 ms
- Network bandwidth should be >= 1 GBps between analytics nodes
- Storage latency should be <10-15 ms per virtual disk of vRealize Operations nodes

Installation steps, formats, and types

Before we start with the actual installation, let's take a quick look at the general setup steps, the installation formats, and installation types vRealize Operations 6.6 supports.

Installation steps

When you perform a fresh installation and configuration of vRealize Operations, you will go through the following general steps:

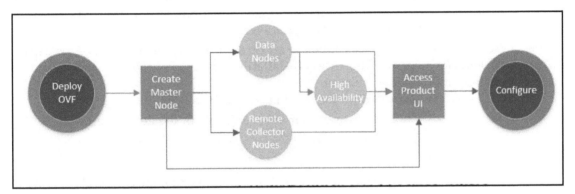

1. Deploy the OVF to create a master node
2. Run initial setup to create a master node
3. (Optional) Set up data nodes
    1. (Optional) Enable High Availability
4. (Optional) Set up remote collector nodes
5. Log in for the first time in the product user interface
6. Configure the new installation

Installation formats

As you may have noticed, when we previously went through the general installation steps, we only mentioned OVF as a deployment format. This is because, as of vRealize Operations 6.6, this is the only installation format that is supported.

vRealize Operations 6.4 was the final one to support installing on Microsoft Windows operating systems. Similarly, version 6.5 was the final one to support installing on RHEL operating systems.

Installation types

When the vRealize Operations initial setup program begins, as we will see later in this chapter, you can select one of the following installation options (or types):

- **Express Installation**: This option is the quickest and easiest option. Use this option to set up the first node in a vRealize Operations cluster. This option uses the default values for all the configuration options.
- **New Installation**: Use this option to set up the first node in a vRealize Operations cluster. However, unlike **Express Installation**, you can configure advanced configuration options, such as:
  - Password for the admin user account
  - Choose between your own certificate or the default certificate
  - The name of the node
  - The name of your NTP server
- **Expand an Existing Installation**: Use this option to add nodes to the cluster, after the first node has already been configured.

Installation and upgrade

Now that we have a good understanding of the prerequisites, let's go through the steps required to install and configure a fresh installation of vRealize Operations and to upgrade an existing one.

Installing a new vRealize Operations instance

First, we will go through the process of deploying a fresh vRealize Operations instance, and perform some initial configurations to make it ready for use.

Deploying the vRealize Operations virtual appliance

Deploying the vRealize Operations 6.6 virtual appliance is very similar to any standard OVF/OVA deployment on vSphere. First, download the latest OVA appliance from VMware. Then deploy into the environment using the Deploy OVF Template wizard.

This can be done through the vSphere Web Client. The vSphere Web Client will be used as it is the only available client since vSphere 6.5. The thick C# client is deprecated and no longer available.

Browse to `https://<vCenter FQDN>:9443/` or just `https://<vCenter FQDN>:vsphere-client/`.

1. If you have deployed any OVF or OVA package before, this process is no different. Select Deploy OVA Template on the cluster as shown in the following screenshot.
2. Select the vRealize Operations 6.6 OVA Template and follow the bouncing ball through the different selections. In here, configure:
    - **Name and folder**: Name of the virtual machine and the folder it will reside in.
    - **Configuration**: This is where you can select the size of the deployment. In this deployment, we will be doing extra small, which is 2 vCPU and 8 GB RAM. Note that extra small and small nodes are primarily intended for test and proof of concept environments.
    - **Storage**: This is the datastore where the virtual machine will be placed and in what disk format it will be placed (Thick or Thin). It is recommended to select the thick provisioned eager-zero option when possible.
    - **Networks**: Which port group the virtual machine network card will be assigned to.
    - **Customization**: This is where we configure the time zone and networking details.

3. Once all the correct information is entered, click **Finish** and the OVA Template will now deploy the first vRealize Operations node.
4. When the node has been deployed, ensure that is has been powered on. Once the virtual machine has booted up the following splash screen indicates that you are ready to begin configuring the vRealize Operations cluster.

As per the previous example, browse to the URL of `https://<ip or fqdn>` and you should be presented with a screen similar to the following screenshot:

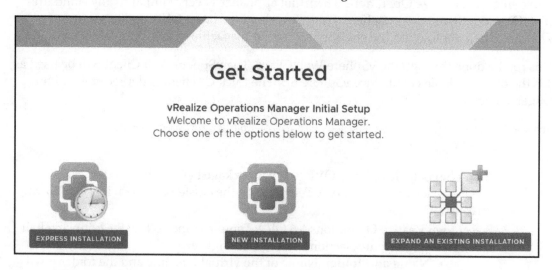

Configuring a new vRealize Operations instance

The next step is straightforward as it contains three installation type options:

- **Express Installation**
- **New Installation—Standard Installation** (the example we will cover now)
- Expand an **Existing Installation**

We discussed the difference between the installation types previously in this chapter. Since this is the first node in our vRealize Operations cluster instance, we will select the New Installation method.

If you remember your installation workflow, you are at the state where we are creating our master node:

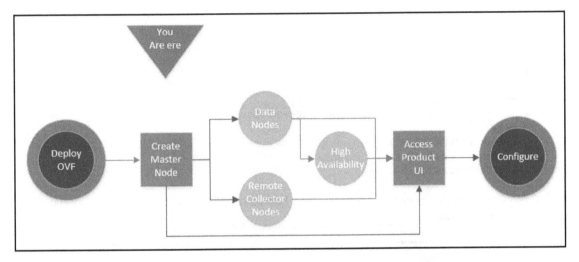

Click on the **New Installation** button, and the initial setup wizard will be presented:

1. The first wizard page is the getting started page; this will show a workflow diagram of the process of setting up vRealize Operations. Click **Next** to move on.
2. Next is to **Set Administrator Password**. Enter a password that fits with the minimum requirements listed on the page. Once entered, click **Next** to move on.
3. The third step on the list is to **Choose Certificate**. Once an option is selected, perform any necessary additional steps and click **Next** to move on.

You can either choose to use a self-signed certificate or one issued by a trusted **Certificate Authority (CA)**.

A valid vRealize Operations certificate signed by a trusted private or public CA is vital during installation, especially if this vRealize Operations instance will go into production. You have to configure a vRealize Operations certificate signed by a CA before you configure End Point Operations Management agents.

In this demonstration, I will use a certificate from a trusted certificate authority.

The certificate applied must be in PEM format, and requires the entire chain, as in the following example:

```
-----BEGIN RSA PRIVATE KEY-----
(Your Primary SSL certificate: PrivateKey.key)
--END RSA PRIVATE KEY-----
-----BEGIN CERTIFICATE-----
(Your Primary SSL certificate: Server.crt)
-----END CERTIFICATE-----
-----BEGIN CERTIFICATE-----
(Your Intermediate certificate: Intermidate.crt)
-----END CERTIFICATE-----
-----BEGIN CERTIFICATE-----
(Your Root certificate: TrustedRoot.crt)
-----END CERTIFICATE-----
```

It also requires that the **Server Authentication Enhanced Key Usage** attribute be present as in the following example:

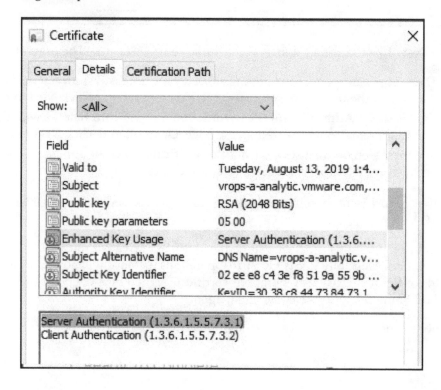

The certificate must contain a private key and not be secured/encrypted with a password. When using a custom certificate, the certificate is only added to the first node of the cluster. When the cluster is expanded by adding a node, the additional nodes take on the same certificate. This means the certificate should be planned out with additional SAN names to include future nodes.

 If self-signed certificates are used the first node becomes the CA for the vRealize Operations cluster and will issue certificates to any future nodes.

You must include the names of all the vRealize Operations analytics and remote collector nodes in the **Subject Alternative Names** field of the certificate. In addition, you must also include the load balancer DNS names.

Here's an example of the subject alternative names I've included in the certificate for this demonstration:

- DNS Name=vrops-a-analytic.vmware.com
- DNS Name=vrops-a-analytic
- DNS Name=vrops-a-epops.vmware.com
- DNS Name=vrops-a-epops
- DNS Name=vrops-a-analytic-01.vmware.com
- DNS Name=vrops-a-analytic-01
- DNS Name=vrops-a-analytic-02.vmware.com
- DNS Name=vrops-a-analytic-02
- DNS Name=vrops-a-analytic-03.vmware.com
- DNS Name=vrops-a-analytic-03
- DNS Name=vrops-a-remote-01.vmware.com
- DNS Name=vrops-a-remote-01
- DNS Name=vrops-a-remote-02.vmware.com
- DNS Name=vrops-a-remote-02

- DNS Name=vrops-a-remote-03.vmware.com
- DNS Name=vrops-a-remote-03
- DNS Name=vrops-a-epops-01.vmware.com
- DNS Name=vrops-a-epops-01
- DNS Name=vrops-a-epops-02.vmware.com
- DNS Name=vrops-a-epops-02
- DNS Name=vrops-a-epops-03.vmware.com
- DNS Name=vrops-a-epops-03

 As you can see, personally I prefer to add both the FQDN name and the short DNS name to the subject alternative name field for every entry. Usually, just the FQDN should suffice.

Deployment Settings is the fourth section. In this section, enter the master node name and enter an NTP server. Even though the first node of a vRealize Operations cluster is always the master node initially, there is no guarantee it will remain so. This would be the case if a vRealize Operations cluster was deployed and **High Availability (HA)** was enabled, then at a later time the first node were to fail. As the master is a role that can move between two servers (the master and master replica), it is recommended to use a name that is relatively generic, such as vrops-analytic-01, vrops-analytic-01, or vrops-node-01, vrops-node-03, and so on. The NTP server will only be added if the vRealize Operations server is able to connect to the service. The master node will become an NTP server itself for other data nodes in the cluster.

Once you've done all the configuration, click **Next** to move on.

The next step is the last step, but here we don't actually do anything. We just list the next steps involved in the configuration of the new vRealize Operations installation. Click the **Finish** button.

When the **Finish** button is clicked, the web page will be redirected to the admin interface of vRealize Operations. To get to this interface manually, enter https://<IP or FQDN>/admin.

If you remember your installation workflow, you are at the state where the shutdown of vRealize Operations nodes or addition of nodes to the cluster is done. This is also where you can apply patches, updates, and collect logs if required:

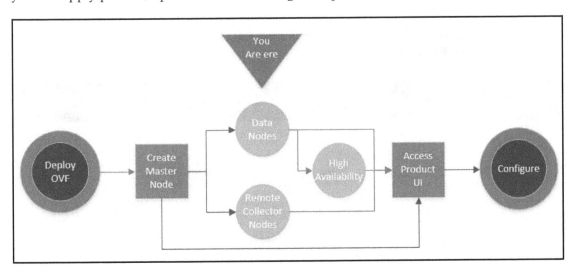

As seen in the previous image the node that was just installed is visible and currently offline. At this point, you would deploy as many nodes as would be required to meet your desired scale for the target environment. Although you can add additional nodes at any time (as discussed in the previous chapter), when doing so, certain actions, such as rebalancing of the GemFire cluster are required. As such, it is highly recommended to aim to size your cluster correctly initially to avoid these tasks in the future.

If you're completely unsure on the eventual end state of the environment regarding how many objects vRealize Operations will be collecting metrics from, it is recommended to start off with a smaller number of nodes. This is because, like many things in life, it is easier to add than take away.

1. Start vRealize Operations by pressing the **START vREALIZE OPERATIONS MANAGER** button:

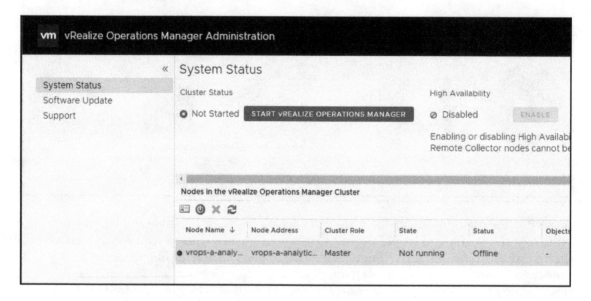

Then a pop-up window will be presented, asking if we are sure and whether we have all the nodes we need.

2. Click **Yes** to move on.

 vRealize Operations will take some time to start.

When vRealize Operations has started up, the web page is redirected to the new vRealize Operations login page. The first login is where the final configuration is done, but we can go back at any time to configure any of the parts configured next.

3. Log into vRealize Operations with the username `admin` and the password entered during the first part of the configuration phase, making sure the authentication source is set to **local users**.

4. Once successfully logged in, we are presented with a new window. Click **Next,** and you will then be presented with the normal EULA. Check the accept box and move on to the licensing section. Enter the vRealize Operations 6.6 license key. If you are licensed for vCloud Suite or vRealize Suite, that license is what would be used. Another option is to use the trial, and enter a permanent license later.

5. On the VMware's **Customer Experience Improvement Program** (**CEIP**) page, we select if we want to join the CEIP program. Joining CEIP is something you may consider doing if you are deploying a production instance for vRealize Operations. Click **Next** to move on. On the last wizard page, click **Finish** to complete the configuration.

6. Once the configuration has finished, the web page is redirected to the **Solutions** section on the **Administration** tab within the vRealize Operations user interface. Here we configure the vCenter servers vRealize Operations is to monitor. Select the VMware vSphere, and click on the configure icon as shown in the following screenshot:

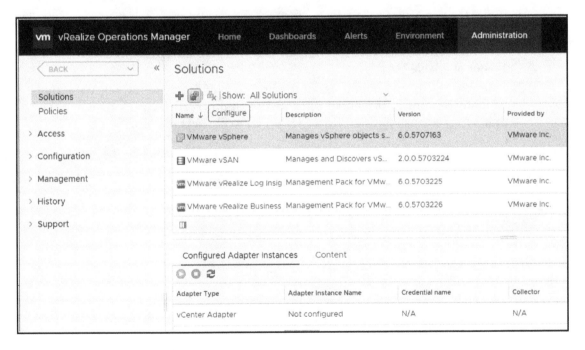

We will be performing the configuration of the vCenter servers later in this chapter.

Expanding the existing installation

At this point, we have installed a single node in our vRealize Operations cluster. Next, we will add one additional node to expand the existing vRealize Operations cluster.

Adding a node to the vRealize Operations cluster

It is recommended that all nodes be added before the cluster is originally started. In this instance though, we will be adding a node to an existing running instance, as this is also supported and works well.

1. Deploy another vRealize Operations node with the same OVA file used previously. When at the **Getting Started** screen, choose the **Expand an Existing Installation** option this time. When this option is selected we will be presented with the expanding existing installation wizard pop-up window.

2. In the **Node Settings and Cluster Info** section, give the new node a name and select the node type. Here we only have two options, **Data** and **Remote Collector**. Select **Data** from the **Note** type menu. This will give the option to expand the cluster or enable HA.

3. Enter the FQDN and IP address of the first node of the cluster. Click **Validate** to validate the node information. Click to **Accept this certificate**, as shown in the following screenshot. Click **Next** to proceed to the next section:

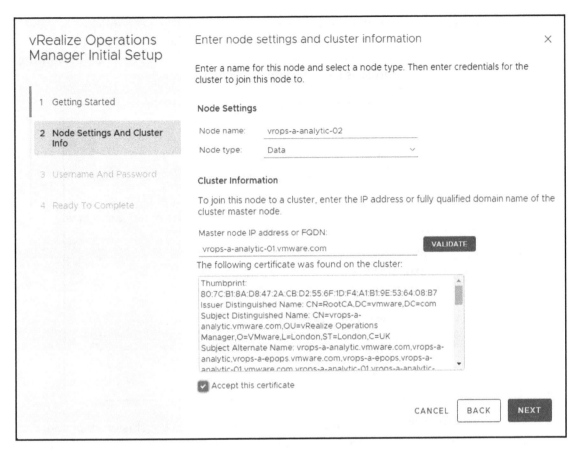

4. The **Username and Password** section is where we enter the password of the admin account of the first node deployed, or we use the shared passphrase if one was generated. A passphrase is a temporary password that you can set by using the administration user interface. Use a passphrase when you want non-administrative users to add a node to the cluster, but you do not want them to access the administration user interface. In this instance, we will just use the password of the admin account. Click **Next** to proceed to the next section.

5. On the **Ready to Complete** section, click **Finish**. Once the setup finishes, we will be redirected to the admin interface. Here we can see the original vRealize Operations node and the newly-added data node, which will be in a **Not running** state and **Offline** status, as shown in the following screenshot:

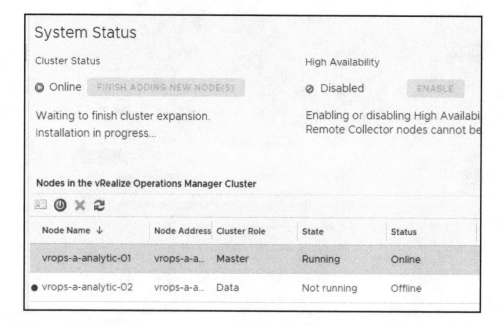

System Status

Cluster Status

○ Online   FINISH ADDING NEW NODE(S)

Waiting to finish cluster expansion.
Installation in progress...

High Availability

⊘ Disabled   ENABLE

Enabling or disabling High Availabi
Remote Collector nodes cannot be

Nodes in the vRealize Operations Manager Cluster

Node Name ↓	Node Address	Cluster Role	State	Status
vrops-a-analytic-01	vrops-a-a...	Master	Running	Online
● vrops-a-analytic-02	vrops-a-a...	Data	Not running	Offline

If you used the admin credentials to add the node to the cluster, then you remain logged into the administration interface. If you used a passphrase to add the node to the cluster, then you are logged out of the web browser session immediately after the node has been added to the cluster. So, someone with admin credentials is required to verify that the node has been added successfully.

6. As you can see from the preceding screenshot, under **Cluster Status**, the **Finish Adding New Node(s)** button is grayed out. It will remain grayed out until the addition of the node completes. Wait for the operation to complete and click the **Finish Adding New Node(s)** button. A confirmation dialog will appear. Click **OK** to confirm the addition of the nodes to the cluster. Once the addition of the node to the cluster has completed, you will see both nodes shown with **Running** state and **Online** status, as shown in the following screenshot:

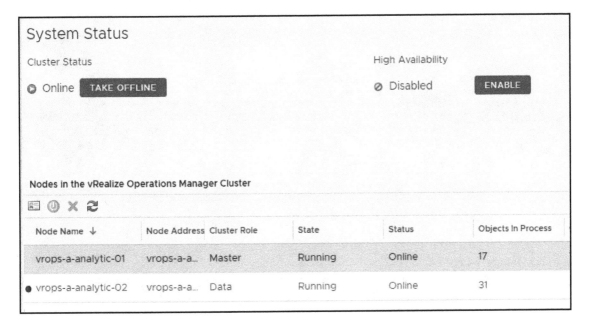

You can enable high availability now, or you can bring your vRealize Operations online instead. You can enable high availability later. In this example, the `vrops-a-analytic-01` data node is selected to be the master node.

Regardless of how many nodes you add to a HA configuration, vRealize Operations can tolerate only the loss of a single node without data loss.

Enabling High Availability

At this point, we have installed two nodes in our vRealize Operations cluster. If you remember your installation workflow, you are at the state where the configuration of HA is done:

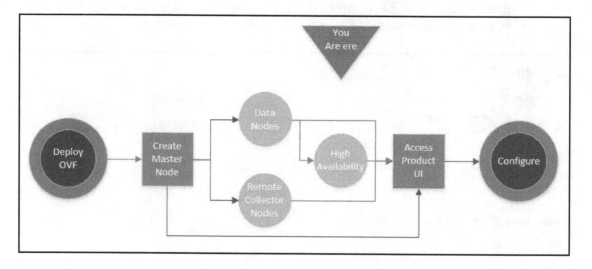

Enabling HA

Perform the following steps to enable HA, on the vRealize Operations cluster:

1. Open the vRealize Operations Admin UI by navigating to `https://<vRealizeOperationsIP or FQDN>/admin`. Once you've logged in, navigate to **System Status**. Navigate to **Cluster Status** and click **Bring Offline** to bring the cluster offline. Wait until the status of the cluster changes to **Offline** and all nodes are in an **Offline** status.

2. Under **High Availability**, click the **Enable** button to enable high availability for this.

3. In the **Enable High Availability** window, select the **Enable High Availability** checkbox and click **OK**. Wait until the status changes to **Enabled** under **High Availability**, as shown in the following screenshot. Once it is enabled, under **Cluster Status** click **Bring Online** to bring the vRealize Operations cluster online. The cluster should now be online and enabled for HA as shown in the following screenshot:

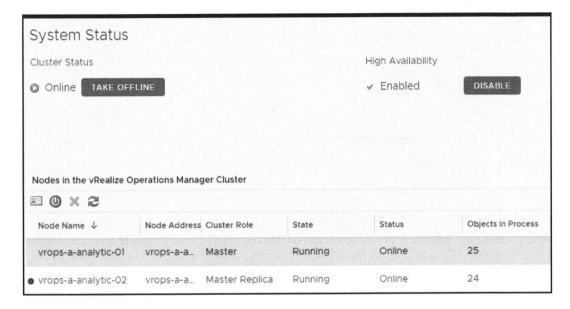

System Status

Cluster Status

⊙ Online TAKE OFFLINE

High Availability

✓ Enabled DISABLE

Nodes in the vRealize Operations Manager Cluster

Node Name ↓	Node Address	Cluster Role	State	Status	Objects In Process
vrops-a-analytic-01	vrops-a-a...	Master	Running	Online	25
● vrops-a-analytic-02	vrops-a-a...	Master Replica	Running	Online	24

> The master and master replica nodes should have resolvable names. To ensure complete protection, the two nodes should not share hardware.

The HA cluster is now up and running, data is being sharded across the two nodes, and a copy of the configuration data is also replicated.

As we mentioned earlier, before enabling HA or making decisions on the size of your cluster, make sure to refer to the sizing guide first. Enabling HA will double the data stored in both the GemFire cache and persistence, compared to a non-HA configuration.

Additionally, a load balancer can be placed in front of the two nodes and balance the web UI traffic between the two of them.

vRealize Operations 6.6 supports the following load balancer solutions:

- HAProxy
- F5 Big-IP
- Citrix NetScaler
- VMware NSX

An example of the custom send and receive strings that vRealize Operations uses when load balanced with VMware NSX is as follows:

Name	Type	Method	URL	Receive
vROps_Monitor	HTTPS	GET	/suite-api/API/deployment/node/status	ONLINE (upper case)
EPPOS_Monitor	HTTPS	GET	/epops-webapp/health-check	ONLINE (upper case)

For more information about which load balancers are supported with what configuration, visit the VMware vRealize Operations Load Balancing configuration guide at `http://pubs.vmware.com/vrealizeoperationsmanager-65/topic/com.vmware.ICbase/PDF/vrealize-operations-manager-load-balancing.pdf`.

Finalizing the new installation

At this point, we have installed two nodes in the vRealize Operations cluster and configured them for HA. If you remember your installation workflow, you are at the state where you can perform the final task of a new installation.

Here, you can again provide licensing information, if you haven't done that already. Here is also where you configure your solutions:

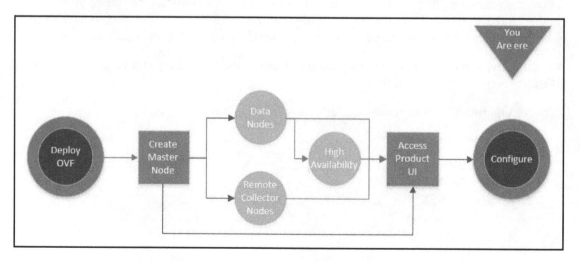

Configuring user access control

vRealize Operations offers several ways you can authenticate users:

- Use an identity source that uses the **Lightweight Directory Access Protocol (LDAP)**.
- Use VMware vCenter Server® users. Users must already be valid users in the vCenter Server system.
- Use local user accounts that are created by using the vRealize Operations user interface.
- Use a single sign-on server so that users can use their single sign-on credentials to log in to vRealize Operations and vCenter Server
- **VMware Identity Manager (vIDM)**.

It is recommended to use an LDAP source authentication method for the following reasons:

- If your company already uses, for example, Active Directory, then you can leverage the existing identity source
- Active Directory can be leveraged by single sign-on
- An LDAP user can access VMware vSphere® and other objects including third-party objects, provided the user has the appropriate privileges

Authentication is delegated to an identity source that is being used.

> Except for SSO, you can configure multiple instances of an identity source, for example, multiple vCenter Server instances and multiple LDAP servers.

The identity source provides the authentication for its users. For example, vCenter Server users can use their vCenter Server credentials to log in to vRealize Operations. The vCenter Server instance authenticates the user for vRealize Operations.

If an LDAP source is used, LDAP users can use their LDAP credentials to log in to vRealize Operations. Users and user groups are imported from the LDAP database to vRealize Operations.

When you create local users, vRealize Operations stores the credentials for those accounts in its Global Postgres database and authenticates the user account locally. A single vRealize Operations instance can use multiple instances of identity sources, for example, multiple vCenter Server instances and multiple LDAP servers.

Each user must have a unique account with one or more roles assigned to enforce role-based security when they use vRealize Operations.

A role is a collection of privileges that grants a user or user group the permission to access objects. Using a privilege, a user can perform a certain function, or action, in the vRealize Operations user interface. The roles associated with a user account determine the features that the user can access and the actions that the user can perform.

A given privilege can be included in multiple roles. You do not assign privileges directly to users. Rather, you apply roles to users.

The **Authentication Module** and **Authorization Module** in vRealize Operations are illustrated in the following diagram:

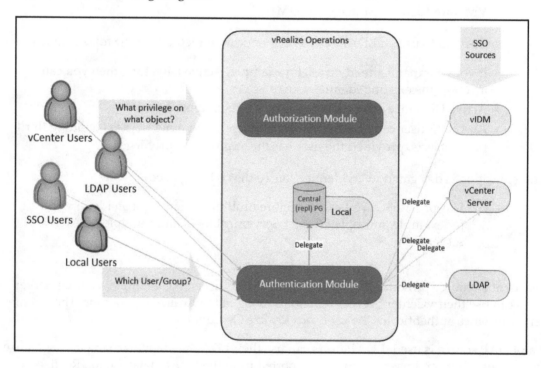

For the purpose of this example, we will be configuring LDAP as identity source and configure roles for our users and user groups.

Perform the following steps to configure the LDAP as an identity source in vRealize Operations:

1. Go to the **User UI** on the master replica node by navigating to the following URL: `https://<FQDN or IP of the master replica Node>/ui`. Navigate to the **Administration** section and select **Access**, and then **Authentication Sources**. Click the plus (+) button to add authentication sources:

2. Fill in the information required to add LDAP as a source for user and group import:
   - **Source Display Name**: Give a name for the identity source
   - **Source Type**: Select type of the identity source, for this example, select LDAP
   - **Integration Mode**: Select either **Basic** or **Advanced** integration mode, which will allow you specify the search criteria with finer control (Base DN)
   - **User Name** and **Password**: Provide credentials to authenticate to the identity source

3. Click **Test** to verify the information and test the connection, and then click **OK**:

4. Click **Synchronize User Groups** to trigger and initial synchronization with LDAP.
5. Navigate to **Access**, and then to **Access Control**. Go to **User Groups** and click **Import Group** to add user groups to vRealize Operations and assign roles to them.

6. On the **Import User Groups** page, search for and select the group(s) you want to add and click **Next**.

7. On the **Roles and Objects** page, select the **Role and Objects** you want to assign to the group, as shown in the following screenshot, and click **Finish**. For this example, we are assigning **Allow access to all objects in the system** to the **Administrator** role to the user group:

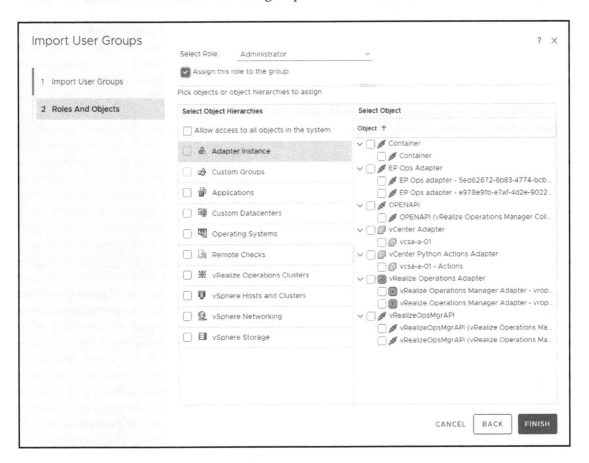

8. As you can see from the following screenshot, we have added an LDAP user group called vRealize Operations Admins to vRealize Operations, and we have assigned administrator role permissions to it to access all objects:

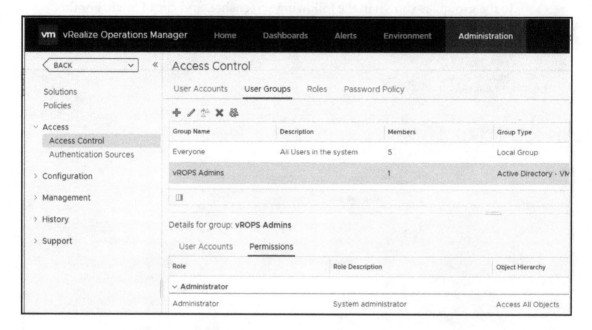

9. To verify successful LDAP Identity source configuration, log out of from the UI and log back in again with a user member of the LDAP user group you've added.

 Make sure to select the correct LDAP identity source on the login UI.

If you want to go the extra mile, in addition, you can explore the options to create custom roles and set Password Policies in vRealize Operations. As these are self-explanatory, we will not be covering them in this book.

Configuring your first solution

Now that you have installed vRealize Operations and configured user access control, it's time to configure what we want to monitor.

As we discussed in previous chapters, management packs extend vRealize Operations capabilities to third-party products and technologies. We will be discussing further management packs later in this book, but for now, we will just mention that a management pack includes data adapters. A data adapter is a software component that collects data from an external data source and transforms the data into a format that vRealize Operations can process.

By default, the vSphere solution is installed when you install vRealize Operations. This is the first solution that you must configure. Perform the following steps to configure the solution:

1. Go to the **User UI** on the master replica Node by navigating to the following URL: `https://<FQDN or IP of the Master Replica Node>/ui`. Navigate to the **Administration** section and **Solutions**.

2. Under **Solutions**, select VMware vSphere and click **Configure**. The VMware vSphere adapter polls a vCenter Server system to collect data for vSphere objects. To configure the VMware vSphere, specify a name and description. Specify the vCenter Server system that you want to manage. You must also specify the credentials, such as root or administrator credentials, to access the vCenter Server system as shown in the following screenshot. You can select those from the Credentials drop-down menu, or create a new credential configuration by clicking on the plus button. The new credential configuration can be reused for other VMware vSphere adapters. Click **Save Settings**. On the **Review and Accept Certificate** window, review the certificate information and click **Accept**. Click **Close**:

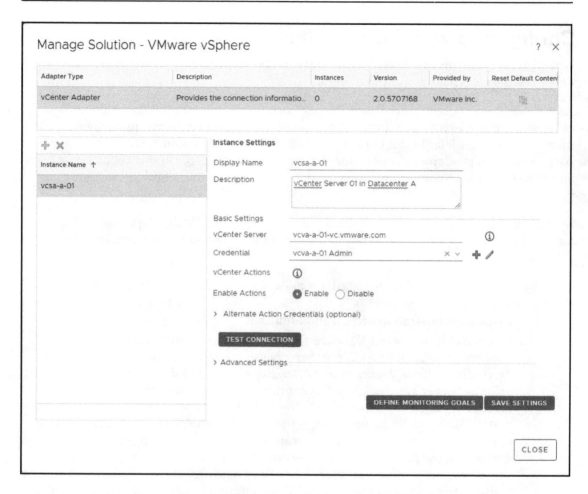

A few advanced settings exist. For example, you can choose a specific collector (a specific cluster node) to be used by this adapter. The **Auto Discovery** option determines when new objects are added to the monitored system (in this case, the vCenter Server system) are discovered and added to vRealize Operations after the initial configuration of the adapter.

You can also define monitoring goals. Based on your monitoring goals, a default policy is created for the solution that you installed and configured.

We will not be configuring any advanced settings or defining monitoring goals at this point.

Under **Configure Adapter Instances**, you should now see the configured vCenter Adapter with **Collecting** collection state and **Data Receiving** connection status, as shown in the following screenshot:

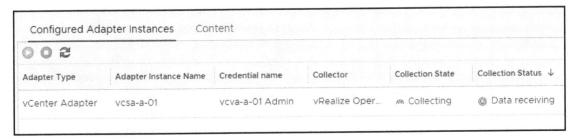

Optionally, you can continue and configure other solutions and adapters. For the purpose of this example, this will be the only solution we will configure. Later on, we will discuss some of the most commonly used solutions.

Upgrading vRealize Operations

Sooner or later, you have to deal with upgrading vRealize Operations, as you do with any other software in your environment. The good news is that upgrading to vRealize Operations 6.6 is a breeze. It's done by simply performing a software update.

Before proceeding with an example upgrade, there are a few important things to note:

- vRealize Operations version 6.5 was the final one to support installation on RHEL operating systems. If you fall in this group, you can upgrade to vRealize Operations 6.6.
- You can upgrade the standalone version of vRealize Operations on **Red Hat Enterprise Linux** (**RHEL**) 6.5, 6.6, and 6.7 operating systems.
- If you are upgrading from vRealize Operations 6.0.x or 6.1 you must use a two-step upgrade process: You must upgrade to vRealize Operations 6.3.1 first and then upgrade to vRealize Operations 6.6.
- If you are upgrading from vRealize Operations versions 6.5, 6.4,6.3.1, 6.3, 6.2.1, or 6.2, you can upgrade directly to vRealize Operations 6.6.

Upgrading from vRealize Operations 6.2.x or later

Performing an upgrade is a pretty straightforward process and involves performing only a few steps.

The following is an outline of the steps you will typically go through when performing a vRealize Operations upgrade:

1. Download the PAK files containing the upgrade from the VMware page.
2. **Back up the existing vRealize Operations content**: If you have customized parts of the vRealize Operations content, it is recommended to clone the content before the upgrade. As part of the upgrade, reset and provide new content without overwriting and customizing it. Backing up is simple. Just clone the content and give it a new name, as shown in the following screenshot:

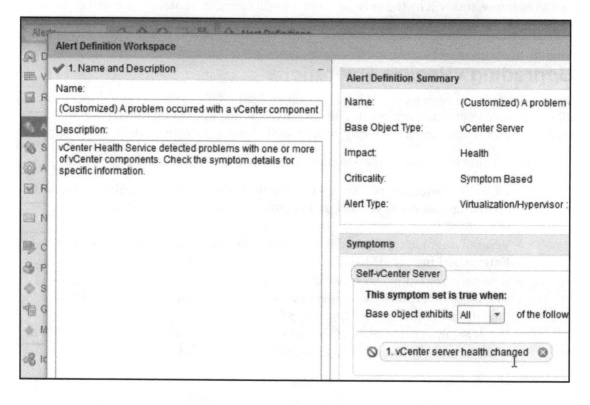

3. **Snapshot the cluster**: Before performing an upgrade, you do a snapshot of the vRealize Operations cluster, including all nodes.

 Note: The cluster can be online or offline when running the upgrade.

4. **Update the cluster**: You trigger the upgrade by logging in to the vRealize Operations Master node, navigating to **Software Update**, and clicking on **Install a Software Update...** Here is where you will be asked to provide the .pak files you obtained earlier:

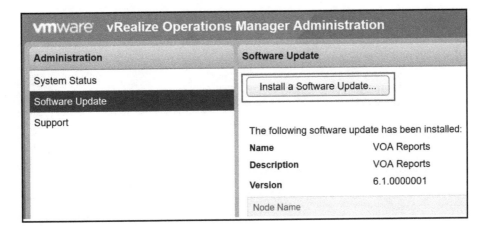

 Installation might take up to a couple of hours, depending on the size of your cluster. During that time, do not refresh the screen. After completing the installation, vRealize Operations will log you out of the user interface.

5. **Log in to the Admin UI**: When the installation completes and the cluster comes back online, the web page is redirected to the new vRealize Operations login page. We are ready to log into our new vRealize Operations 6.6 cluster.

Summary

In this chapter, we learned how to perform a fresh install of a vRealize Operations 6.6 instance and subsequently add additional nodes. We learned how to configure HA and what load balancer settings need to be implemented for the vRealize Operations cluster. After that, we configured user access control to vRealize Operations. We installed our first solution and started monitoring our environment. We showed how to configure notifications to send out emails when an alert gets generated. We also covered how to upgrade from vRealize Operations 6.2.

In the next chapter, we will cover the iconic vRealize Operations badge systems.

4
Extending vRealize Operations with Management Packs and Plugins

vRealize Operations has always supported adapters for other sources, other than just vSphere. This gives it the ability to pull in metrics from other data and metric collectors such as HP Business Availability Center and **Microsoft System Center Operations Manager** (**SCOM**), but also allows direct connections with other systems, such as storage arrays and network switches.

Since vRealize Operations 6.0, all adapters are now referred to as solutions, including the VMware vSphere adapter.

VMware supplies, out-of-the-box, a number of these solutions for other products, such as VMware vRealize Log Insight, VMware vRealize Business for Cloud, VMware vRealize Automation, and VMware vSAN.

In this chapter, we will cover the following topics:

- vRealize Operations solutions
- Overview of popular solutions
- Installing solutions
- Importing data with a REST API

Collecting additional data

Why would an administrator want to import data from other monitoring systems or data sources into vRealize Operations, especially when the data for those systems is already being managed by an existing monitoring solution? This is a fair question. The obvious advantage is to have all the data in one place, accessible via a single pane of glass. The real power of vRealize Operations is in how it handles relationships, and the benefits that this provides to the administrators out there.

Say we have installed vRealize Operations and we are successfully importing vSphere data and providing various types of useful information and reports. When an incident ticket is created and reports that there is a performance problem in a VM or a number of VMs, we can look at that VM in vRealize Operations and see what cluster it belongs to, what host it is currently sitting on, and what datastore the VM's disks are located on. We can see the overall health of the VM collected from the hypervisor and rule out any anomalies or bottlenecks that might be occurring.

Then the ticket starts its journey to the SAN team, to the network team, and to the application team, with generally everyone saying everything is fine at their end.

But what if we could go deeper than the logical datastore, further than the physical NIC or up into the application in the guest OS of the VM? Well, we can, and this is done through solutions.

Picture for a moment what can currently be seen when looking at the health relationship objects of a VM. We get stopped at the datastore level. But if we were using **EMC Storage Analytics (ESA)** solutions we could then break through the datastore and keep moving down to see the array that the datastore belongs to, then to the disk pool the LUN belongs to, then finally hit the physical disks themselves. All the while we would have access to all the metrics, logs, and alerts for all of these objects.

Then onto the networks—what if we could see the upstream switch and port the NIC is plugged into and all the metrics and data that goes along with it? Then, using new features like **End Point Operations (EPO)** monitoring, we could go into the guest and see the services that make up the application and all the relevant application-level metrics. For example, for Microsoft Exchange, we'd be able to see the number of incoming and outgoing messages, number of people logged in, response times, and so on.

In the 6.1 release of vRealize Operations, VMware merged the Hyperic Monitoring solutions into vRealize Operations. This is now known as the **End Point Operations (EPO)** monitoring feature in vRealize Operations.

Having all this data on a single pane of glass is great, but having a full end-to-end view of the infrastructure supporting a virtual machine and the applications within it allows for the service desk or the server administrator to more accurately pinpoint where the problem most likely is in the stack.

While solutions can take advantage of different vRealize Operations analytics such as dynamic thresholds and capacity management, relationship linking is the key to making a big difference in the day-to-day operational running of the environments.

Defining a vRealize Operations solution

vRealize Operations solutions extend the capabilities of vRealize Operations by integrating with external management tools.

Some solutions are delivered with vRealize Operations. Other solutions can be added as management packs. Solutions that are delivered as management packs include dashboards, reports, alerts, and data adapters. Data adapters are used by vRealize Operations to manage communication and integration with other products, applications, and functionalities:

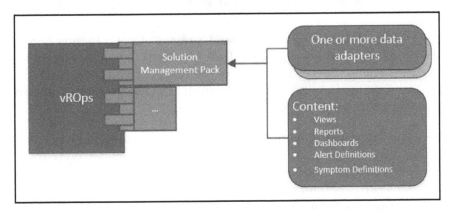

Once the solution management pack is installed and data adapters are configured, you can use vRealize Operations analytics and alerting tools. To download a solution for vRealize Operations, go to the VMware Solution Exchange web portal.

Let's take a deeper look into it as an example of the out-of-the-box solutions in vRealize Operations. The VMware vSphere solution manages the connection between vRealize Operations and your VMware vCenter Server instances, and provides the ability to run actions on those instances:

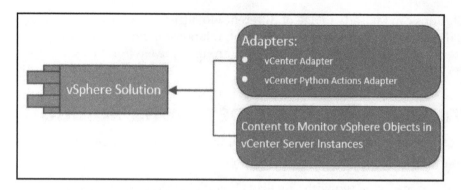

This solution consists of two data adapters:

- **The vCenter adapter**: Using the vCenter adapter, you can monitor the vSphere objects, such as clusters, hosts, virtual machines, datastores, resource pools, and so on.
- **The vCenter Python Actions adapter**: Using the vCenter Python Actions adapter, you can perform actions from vRealize Operations to modify objects on your managed vCenter Server instance. For example, you can power on or off virtual machines, set the CPU resources for a virtual machine, or delete unused snapshots from a virtual machine.

Adapters connect to and collect data from external sources in multiple ways:

- API calls
- Command-line interface
- Database queries (relational database, CSV, XML, and so on)

This vSphere solution also provides content to monitor vSphere objects, such as inventory trees, metrics, dashboards, views, reports, alert definitions, and symptom definitions.

Overview of popular solutions

As we mentioned before, vRealize Operations comes with some preinstalled solutions. In vRealize Operations 6.6, you can find the following solutions out of the box:

- VMware vSphere
- VMware vSAN
- VMware vRealize Log Insight
- VMware vRealize Business for Cloud
- VMware vRealize Automation
- Operating System/Remote Service Monitoring (End Point Operations monitoring)

Other popular solutions that you can download and install from VMware Solution Exchange include:

- Storage devices
- Network devices
- VMware vSphere for NSX
- VMware vCloud Air
- VMware Horizon
- VMWare vRealize **Service Discovery Management Pack (SDMP)**

 There is also a management pack for **Amazon Web Services (AWS)**. The preferred way to integrate vRealize Operations with AWS is through the VMware vRealize Business for Cloud solution. This is the solution that is being actively developed.

Let's take a deeper look into some of these solutions and what functionalities they offer.

Service Discovery solution

The VMware vRealize Operations **Service Discovery Management Pack (SDMP)** is a service awareness adapter for vRealize Operations that provides continuous dependency mapping of applications.

The solution offers an application context to virtual infrastructure administrators for monitoring and managing virtual infrastructure inventory objects and actions. Administrators can use the management pack to understand the impact of the change on the virtual environment in their application infrastructure. Administrators can discover services running on each virtual machine. The management pack also shows dependencies between different virtual machines:

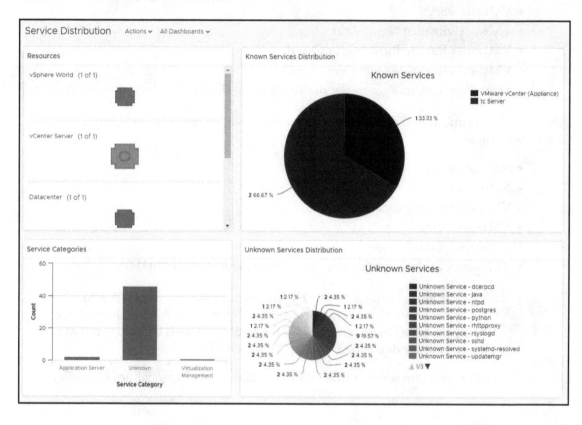

The functionality this solution brings into vRealize Operations was earlier provided by VMware vRealize Infrastructure Navigator. It leverages the **Virtual Infrastructure eXtension (VIX)** for service discovery by executing commands in the guest OS. In vSphere 6.5, the VIX API was removed and this led to the birth of the SDMP solution. While the vRealize Infrastructure Navigator works with all previous vSpheres prior to vSphere 6.5, SDMP is the solution of choice for vSphere 6.5 and later versions. vRealize Infrastructure Navigator will continue to be maintained as long as prior versions of vSphere are maintained.

Mixed environments are supported with both solutions installed.

The following is an illustration of how the solution integrates:

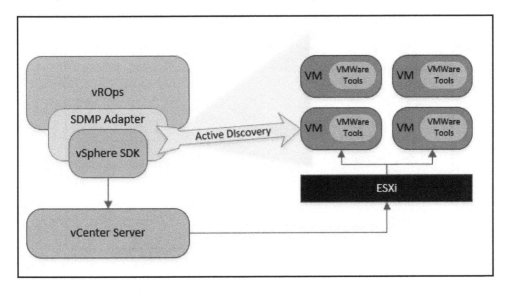

Note: The solution requires VMware tools 10.1 or higher be installed in the guest VMs to operate.

As you will see, when configuring the solution, it also needs guest **operating system** (**OS**) credentials for Windows or Linux OS. For the Service Discovery adapter to be able to discover the services that are running in the VMs, the adapter has to be able to execute scripts on the VMs. vCenter 6.5 allows this operation only if the guest credentials are authenticated and mapped in vCenter. As shown here, these are entered during the solution configuration:

Manage Credential   ?

Credential name	SDMP Creds
vCenter User Name	administrator@vsphere.local
vCenter Password	••••••••••••••••••••••••••••••
Default Windows User Name	administrator
Default Windows Password	••••••••••••••••••••••••••••••
Default Linux User Name	root
Default Linux Password	••••••••••••••••••••••••••••••
SRM Username	srm_admin@vmware.com
SRM Password	••••••••••••••••••••••••••••••
Guest User Mapping CSV Password	••••••••••••••••••••••••••••••

After discovery, all the known services are grouped and shown as one service type. You can expand the inventory tree to see all the VMs where the corresponding services are running:

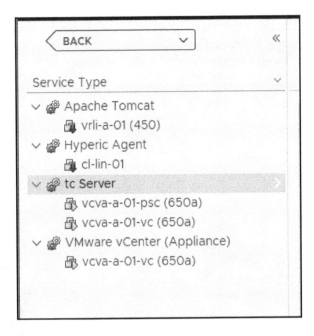

When configuring the solution, you also have two options to choose between for the Discovery Plan: **shallow discovery** and **deep discovery**.

Shallow discovery discovers known services only. It will not show relationships unless services are known.

Deep discovery discovers all known and unknown services. Known services will be shown with their name. Unknown services will be shown with the process name and unknown will be prefixed to it.

 Unknown services can be converted to known services.

You can also enable or disable a dynamic application group for automatically creating dynamic application groups. When activated, it will discover and group applications with UUID in the name, but you can rename it afterwards as shown here:

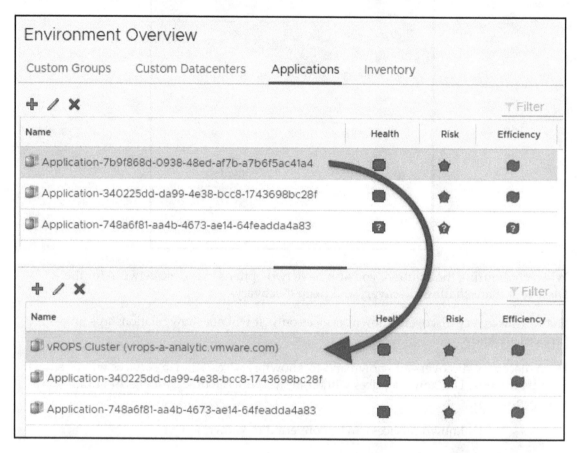

Log Insight solution

When vRealize Operations is integrated with vRealize Log Insight, you can view the vRealize **Log Insight** page, the troubleshoot with logs dashboard, and the **Logs** tab. You can collect and analyze log feeds. You can filter and search for log messages. You can also dynamically extract fields from log messages based on customized queries.

From the **Log Insight** page, you can create queries to extract events based on timestamp, text, source, and fields in log events. vRealize Log Insight presents charts of the query results:

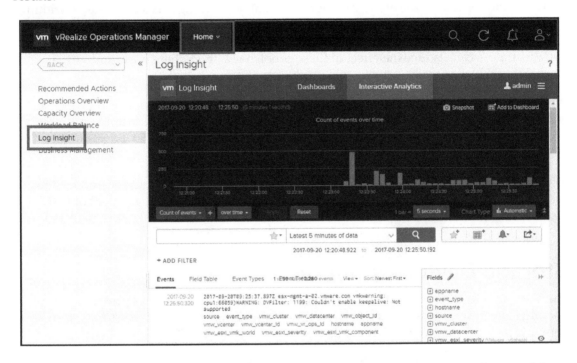

To access the vRealize **Log Insight** page from vRealize Operations, you must do one of the following:

- Configure the vRealize Log Insight adapter from the vRealize Operations interface
- Configure vRealize Operations in vRealize Log Insight

This integration also gives you access to the vRealize **Log Insight** dashboards through the vRealize Operations interfaces. You can access these by going to the **Dashboards** section.

You can view the logs for a selected object from the **Logs** tab, and can troubleshoot a problem in your environment by correlating the information in the logs with the metrics. You can then most likely determine the root cause of the problem.

vSphere NSX solution

The VMware vRealize Operations Management Pack for VMware vSphere NSX discovers, analyzes, and represents the broad number of virtual networking services available within vSphere NSX graphically. Administrators can view this data for quickly identifying configuration, health, and capacity problems within their virtual VMware NSX networks. Administrators can also see the effect of these problems with vSphere hosts and virtual machines.

When a configuration or health problem is detected as per five-minute interval checks, an event is posted in vRealize Operations with recommendations about how to correct the problem. The NSX services include logical switching or routing. The NSX Edge services include load balancing, firewalls, SSL VPN, DHCP, DNS, NAT, and IPsec.

vRealize Operations reports on abnormalities, resource depletion, and underused resource conditions. These reports enable better optimization and proactive management of NSX virtual networking functions.

Storage Devices solution

The VMware vRealize Operations Management Pack for Storage Devices provides an end-to-end view of topology, statistics, and events at every affected level of the storage area network, including network-related information for NFS and iSCSI.

This solution enables a vSphere administrator working with a virtual environment to isolate problems that are caused by elements in the physical storage stack. The physical storage stack might include the **Host bus adapter** (**HBA**), storage switches, and array. The vSphere administrator uses this information to hand off the problem to the domain administrator for further analysis.

This solution discovers the storage switches and applies credentials required to collect data from objects in the storage network. This solution uses the **Common Information Model** (**CIM**) to exchange information with objects that are managed by the following management systems:

- Cisco Data Center Network Manager
- Brocade Network Advisor

The Management Pack for Storage Devices adapter discovers objects in your storage topology. This adapter also maps the path of the data between virtual machines on the ESXi host, through the storage network switches, and out to the storage array.

 Note: As of the writing of this book, the Storage Devices solution is not yet compatible with vRealize Operations 6.6.

vCloud Air solution

The VMware vRealize Operations Management Pack for VMware vCloud Air extends vRealize Operations capabilities to vCloud Air, providing a consistent user experience across clouds. This solution collects metrics, change events, and resource topology information from vCloud Air and displays this information in prebuilt dashboards.

The solution provides the following features:

- Visibility of all the resources deployed on vCloud Air including vCloud Air Clouds, Virtual Data Centers, Virtual Machines, vApps, vApp Templates, Edge gateways, and gateway services such as firewalls, SSL VPN, IPsec VPN, load balancers, and so on.
- Search and drill down capability for obtaining the operations health of deployed vCloud Air resources.
- Exhaustive list of symptoms and alerts for the detection of misconfiguration, connectivity, and health problems. All alerts are consolidated in a VMware vRealize Operations alert interface.
- Extension of the core vRealize Operations health and risk analytics engine for the inclusion of vCloud Air object key performance and health indicators.
- Detailed capacity analysis for all the resources deployed in vCloud Air.

The list of solutions goes on and on, and unfortunately, we cannot cover them all in this book. Feel free to go to the VMware Solution Exchange and explore the vast majority of management packs being offered today.

Installing solutions

Let's now have a look at installing a solution. Just like in previous versions of vRealize Operations, solutions are simple to install. The solution we are installing here is the vSphere NSX Solution:

1. The first step to install a solution is to navigate to the **Administration** section and select **Solutions**. There we will be able to see the installed solutions. At the top of the page, we will find a green plus ( ) icon. Click it to add a solution:

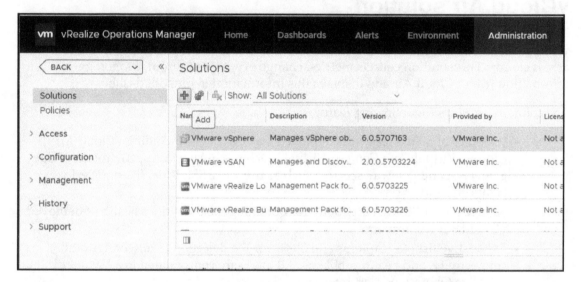

2. This will open up the **Add Solution** window. In the **Select Solution** section, click browse navigate to browse, and select a solution. This will be a PAK file. We have the option to select force install. This is used if the solution already exists and we need to overwrite it completely.

If you are installing a new version of an already existing solution, you have the option to override any changes to the default **Alert Definitions**, **Symptoms**, **Recommendations**, **Policies Definitions**, **Views**, **Dashboards**, **Widgets**, and **Reports**. If you decide to reset the default content, make sure to write down and redo any user changes after you install the solution. When ready, click **Upload** and click **Next**:

1. In the **End User License Agreement** section, we are then presented with the EULA; **Accept** this and click **Next** again.

2. Once the **Next** button is clicked, the installation will instantly start. It's important to remember that this is installing the solution for every node in the cluster and the logs will reflect that.

3. When the installation is complete, click **Finish** and you are then directed to the solutions page where you will be able to see the newly installed solution.

The solution is now installed. This installation process will be identical for all solutions. However, before a solution starts collecting data it needs to be configured.

Solution configurations will vary greatly between solutions; some will require license keys, and others will require connections to multiple servers or devices. For example, the universal storage solution requires authentication and connection to vCenter(s) and Fabric Switch(es), while the vSphere NSX Solution requires connection to the NSX Manager as well as certificate and additional advanced setting configurations.

All solutions will vary, and it is recommended that you follow the solution documentation from the supplying vendor.

Let's now go through the configuration of the solution we just installed:

1. While having the solutions highlighted in the solutions windows, click the little gear icon to open up the configuration window for that solution.

2. After filling in all the details, the solution requires you hit the **TEST CONNECTION**; this will tell us if everything is configured correctly. Once you are happy, click on **Save** settings:

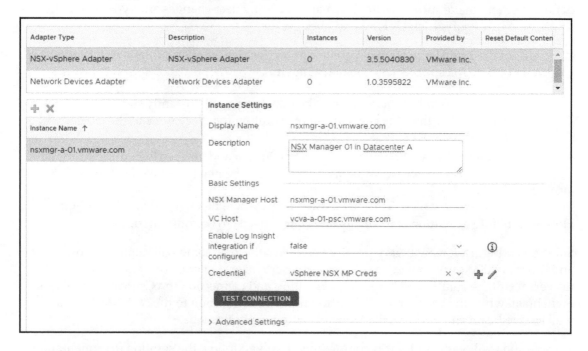

Adapter Type	Description	Instances	Version	Provided by	Reset Default Conten
NSX-vSphere Adapter	NSX-vSphere Adapter	0	3.5.5040830	VMware Inc.	
Network Devices Adapter	Network Devices Adapter	0	1.0.3595822	VMware Inc.	

Instance Settings

Instance Name ↑

nsxmgr-a-01.vmware.com

Display Name — nsxmgr-a-01.vmware.com

Description — NSX Manager 01 in Datacenter A

Basic Settings

NSX Manager Host — nsxmgr-a-01.vmware.com

VC Host — vcva-a-01-psc.vmware.com

Enable Log Insight integration if configured — false

Credential — vSphere NSX MP Creds

TEST CONNECTION

> Advanced Settings

3. Click on **Close** after the settings have been saved and you will now be looking at the solutions page again, but there is a small difference. With the newly installed solution selected in the lower solution details pane, we will see its status. Give it a single cycle (5 minutes by default) and you should see that data is being collected.

As shown in the screenshot, the rainbow (semi-circle) icon under the **Collection State** column is the data collection state, and the ball icon under the **Collection Status** column shows whether the data is being received correctly. Both should be green if everything in the solution is configured correctly:

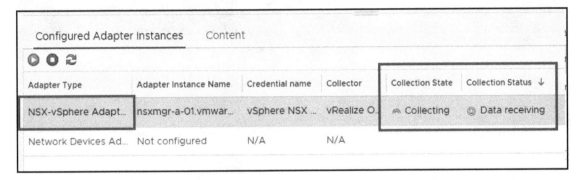

The solution is now installed and collecting data. The solution we covered here is the vSphere NSX solution. As explained at the start of this chapter, what a solution provides will vary, but at the very least they will generally be providing new object types and new attribute types. A more feature-complete solution also provides a good selection of out-of-the-box dashboards, and the most mature solutions, for example, will take advantage of other features such as the opened capacity management framework.

It is very important to resize vRealize Operations accordingly, to accommodate for new object types after a solution pack is installed.

Let's now take a look at what dashboards this vSphere NSX solution has given us. To do this, navigate to the **Dashboards** section in the UI. By default, the new ones will be placed on the **Dashboards** home screen.

Here, we can see the default **NSX-vSphere Main** dashboard that the vSphere NSX Solution creates, which is showing the health of the key NSX components and the open active alerts, among other things:

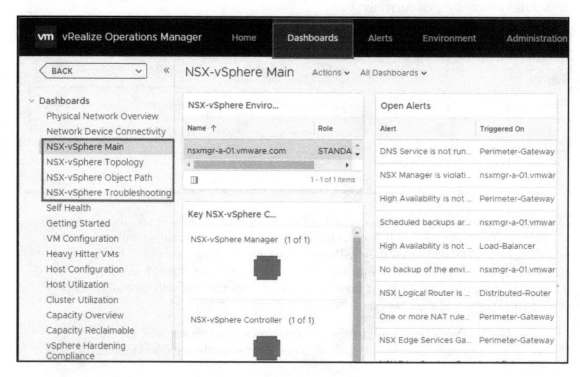

Importing data with a REST API

What if there is information we would like to import into vRealize Operations but there is no solution available? This is fine as vRealize Operations supports multiple ways to import any data we like, but it will require some scripting if it's a regular import.

Prior to vRealize Operations 6.0 in 5.x, we had the HTTP POST adapter and the TEXT adapter. Both could import data into vCenter Operations Manager 5.x. In vRealize Operations 6.6, we still have access to the HTTP POST adapter; this adapter has remained unchanged from vCenter Operations Manager 5.x for legacy support, and any current scripts importing data that is configured should still work using this adapter.

The new and preferred way to import our own data is through the new vRealize Operations REST API. This is a highly-functional API. Most GUI tasks can also be done through the API if required. The vRealize Operations nodes we have deployed all have a detailed REST guide built in; this can be found by navigating to `https://<vRealizeOperations_FQDN/IP>/suite-api/docs/rest/index.html`. Here we can find sample code and information on all the rest functions. If you currently don't have anything importing via the HTTP `POST` adapter, it would be highly recommended that anything new be done through the new REST API, or as its commonly referred to, the Suite API solution.

The Suite API is the only officially supported API for vRealize Operations. As you might have seen in the previous screenshot, the Suite API is broken down into two parts:

- Public API
- Internal API

 Note: The Internal API may not be supported in future releases. Use it at your own risk.

In this example, we will be importing a Recommendation into vRealize Operations using the REST API:

1. Open your favorite REST tool. Anything that can make standard REST calls will work, like curl in Linux or even a browser with the right plugins. In this example, I'm using Postman.
2. Select `POST` as the method, and type the `https://<vRealizeOperations_FQDN_OR_IP/suite-api/api/recommenda tions` URL.
   - Create authorization for requests by supplying a username and password for vRealize Operations

3. Create an `application/XML` header:

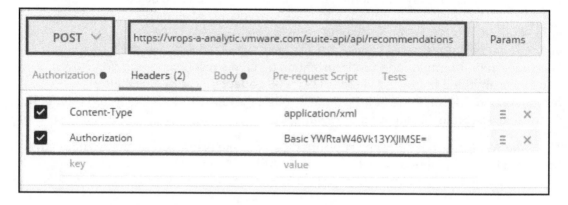

4. Paste the following code in the body of the request:

```xml
<?xml version="1.0" encoding="UTF-8" standalone="yes"?>
<ops:recommendation
xmlns:ops="http://webservice.vmware.com/vRealizeOpsMgr/1.0/"
xmlns:xs="http://www.w3.org/2001/XMLSchema"
xmlns:xsi="http://www.w3.org/2001/XMLSchema-instance">
  <ops:description>My REST imported recommendation (USR)</ops:description>
</ops:recommendation>
```

In Postman the request body would look similar to this:

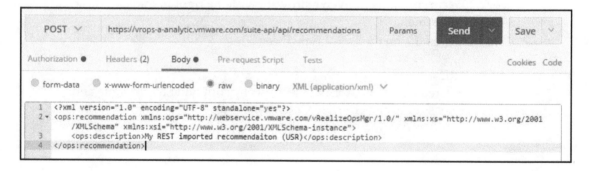

For reference, the JSON for the above XML code would be as follows:

```json
{
  "description" : " My REST imported recommendation (USR)",
  "others" : [ ],
  "otherAttributes" : {
  }
}
```

5. After posting this to vRealize Operations, navigate to the
    Recommendations section within the UI. You should see the imported
    recommendation listed:

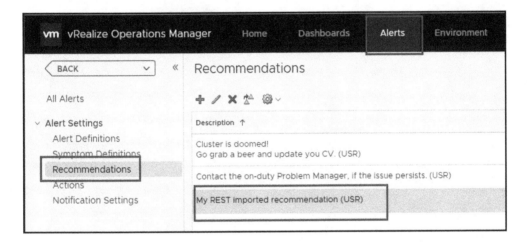

This is a very basic example of what can be achieved if there is no official solution for the data we would like to import. Most of what people want to import will be IT-related in some way, but vRealize Operations is definitely not limited to computer data; we can import data on weather, power usage, parcel deliveries, and anything we can apply relationships and metrics to.

Summary

In this chapter, we learned about solutions and how helpful they can be to an organization, and especially the team on the ground who are monitoring and supporting your infrastructure. We learned how to install and configure solutions. We then moved on to importing our own data when no solution was available.

5
Badges

This chapter discusses in detail the critical concept of vRealize Operations 6.6 badges and how they assist in effectively managing your vSphere and non-vSphere environments. This will include the following topics:

- What is the concept of badges?
- What the major badges and their corresponding minor badges are

What are vRealize Operations badges?

A vRealize Operations badge is a graphical representation of the state of the current environment or object. A badge can range from using a few metrics, to millions of metrics, providing a summarized piece of useful information that would sometimes take an administrator hours or even days to collocate manually in the vCenter Performance tab or similar monitoring system.

Badges are seen as an important source of information rather than just data. If at any time an administrator wishes to understand more about a certain badge state or score, they can review the metrics or events that are behind the badge to get a more in-depth understanding of the environment.

One of the most unique and powerful aspects of badges is that they allow an administrator to view the same important information from the VM or Datastore level all the way up to the vCenter (or even higher) level. This is because all objects can have the same set of badges applied to them, it is just how they are calculated that may slightly differ. As all objects can have the same set of badges, this allows for badges to be rolled up to higher levels by leveraging parent-child relationships. For example, the Workload badge of an ESXi host includes all the workloads of its children virtual machines in its score. Similarly, the Workload badge of a vSphere Cluster includes all the workloads of its children ESXi hosts and virtual machines. This is not the case, though, for some badges such as the Health badge.

The badges in vRealize Operations 6.6 can be split into two distinct categories: major or minor. The major badges are Health, Risk, and Efficiency. Unlike the minor badges, the major badges do not contain a score (we will discuss this is the next section).

The Health badge indicates that current issues exist that need to be resolved immediately.

The Risk badge indicates that potential issues exist that might eventually degrade performance.

The Efficiency badge helps identify optimization opportunities in your environment.

The badges in vRealize Operations 6.6 are also represented by a color from red, to orange (amber), to yellow, and finally to green (red indicating an issue or alert). As we will be discussing later, minor badges also contain a score that determines their color representation.

Badge color	Icon	Description
Green colored badge		The object is in normal state, based on the set thresholds. For example, by default, the green infrastructure Workload badge indicates a score above 76.
Yellow colored badge		The object is experiencing some level of problems. For example, by default the infrastructure yellow Workload badge indicates a score between 80 and 89.
Orange colored badge		The object might have serious problems or is approaching its capacity. For example, by default, the infrastructure orange Faults badge indicates a score between 50 and 74.
Red colored badge		The object is either not functioning properly or will stop functioning soon. Most of the metrics are beyond their thresholds. For example, by default, the infrastructure red Risk badge indicates a score 100.
Gray colored badge		No data is available for this object or the object is offline. For example it this may indicate that there is no data for the Capacity Remaining of the object.

Badges on the **Analysis** tab provide specific information and guidance for when you troubleshoot issues encountered by an object:

The color of a badge on the **Analysis** tab is determined by its badge score. Badges change color based on badge score thresholds. These thresholds are defined in the policy used by the object.

A policy is a set of rules and base settings that apply to an object, such as threshold values that are used to evaluate badge scores.

 A vRealize Operations administrator can change the badge score thresholds. For example, a green Workload badge can indicate a score below 50 instead of 80, which is the threshold set in the default policy.

As shown in the following table, several badges exist on the **Analysis** tab, identified by their icon. Like Health, Risk, and Efficiency badges, the color of these badges indicates the severity of an issue:

Name	Icon	Description
Workload		The Workload badge combines metrics that show the demand for resources on an object as a single value. These metrics include CPU utilization, memory usage, and so on.
Anomalies		The Anomalies score is calculated using the total number of threshold violations for all metrics for the selected object. A low Anomalies score indicates that an object is behaving according to its established historical parameters.
Faults		The Faults score is calculated based on events published by the vCenter Server. The scores are computed based on the severity of underlying problems. When more than one fault-related problem exists on the resource, the Faults score is based on the most severe problem.
Capacity		The Capacity badge represents the capability of your virtual environment to accommodate new virtual machines. vRealize Operations calculates the Capacity score as a percentage of the remaining virtual machines count compared to the total number of virtual machines that can be deployed on the selected object.

Time Remaining		The Time Remaining score indicates how much time is remaining before the resources of the object exhaust. It takes into account the configured provisioning buffer in days. The Time Remaining score allows you to plan the provisioning of physical or virtual resources for the selected object, or reorganize the workload in your virtual environment.
Stress		The Stress score indicates the historic workload of the selected object. The Stress score is calculated as a ratio between the demand for resources and the usable capacity for a certain period.
Reclaimable Capacity		The Reclaimable Capacity score indicates over-provisioning in your virtual infrastructure or for a specific object. It identifies the amount of resources that can be reclaimed and provisioned to other objects in your environment.
Density		The Density score indicates consolidation ratios, such as virtual machines per host, virtual CPUs per physical CPU, virtual memory per physical memory, and so on. You can use the Density score to achieve higher consolidation ratios and cost savings.
Compliance		The Compliance badge value is a score based on one or more compliance templates that you run in vRealize Operations against the data collected from vRealize Operations. You can use the alert-based compliance that is provided, or, if you also use **VMware vRealize Configuration Manager** (**VCM**) in your environment, you can add the adapter that provides Configuration compliance information in place of the alert-based compliance. With vRealize Configuration Manager, the Compliance badge value is a score based on one or more compliance templates that you run in vRealize Configuration Manager against the data collected from vSphere objects that are managed by vRealize Operations and by vRealize Configuration Manager.

Each major badge also has associated minor badges that are part of the same discipline. The relationship of the major and minor badges is as follows:

- Health:
    - Workload
    - Anomalies
    - Faults

- Risk:
    - Capacity Remaining
    - Time Remaining
    - Stress
    - Compliance
- Efficiency:
    - Reclaimable Capacity
    - Density

Alert and symptom definitions define the state of a badge for a particular object type. This, in turn, allows for more intelligent alerting based on key symptoms that can be observed from multiple sources providing an informed recommendation to administrators.

This symptom-based approach, which was introduced in vRealize Operations 6.0, allows solution pack creators to define a series of alerts on particular observed Metrics, Messages, Faults, and so on and then link them to an overall alert and possibly even an automated remediation action to resolve the issue.

Although the badges were originally introduced in Operations Manager 1.0, they were limited to the vSphere UI and therefore to vSphere objects. There were a few exceptions, such as the Health badge for certain objects; however, as a general principle badges were for vSphere only.

One of the major aspects of vRealize Operations 6.0 and later versions is that all objects are treated as first-class citizens, or in other words, all solutions and adapters are treated and respected equally. This concept of equal weighting for all solutions is one of the driving factors behind the merged UI. This has allowed all objects to support the badges, allowing a consistent reporting and troubleshooting experience, no matter what the source of the data is.

The ability for non-vSphere objects to provide data to the full badge set will vary depending on the maturity level of the associated solution (adapter). In most cases, this will allow administrators to create dashboards that display common badge dashboards, no matter the context of the object.

Understanding the Health badge

The Health badge is the first high-level indicator for the overall status of your environment. This is the first badge that should be looked at by an administrator and acted upon as soon as possible. The Health badge shows how your environment or object is right now. This helps in identifying issues that need immediate attention.

As previously mentioned, all major badges in vRealize Operations 6.6 are now based on Alert and symptom definitions that determine the overall badge state. The minor badges are still driven by analytics, with the color bands defined within the effective policy.

For example, in the following screenshot, we can see a host system has lost connection to vCenter. This alert is also a symptom that has led to an alert being applied to the major Health badge:

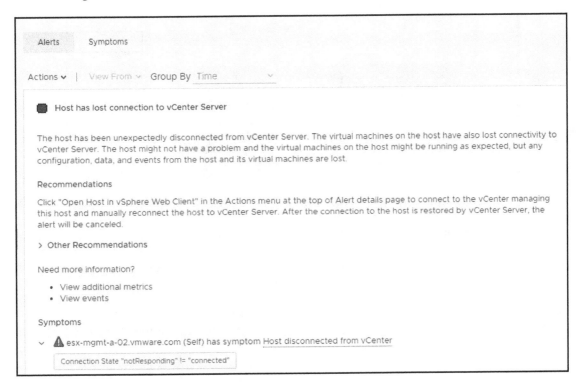

The Workload badge

The Workload badge indicates how hard an object is working. The score for the workload badge ranges from 0 being good to 100 being bad.

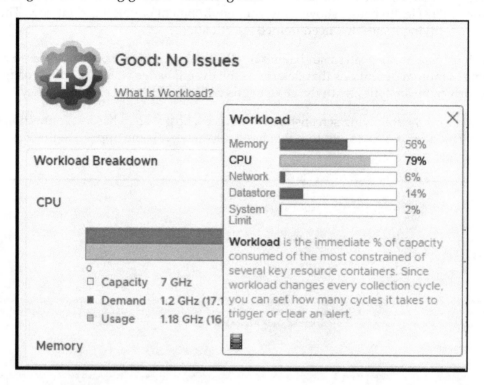

Workload is most commonly measured against CPU, Memory, Network I/O, Storage I/O, and vSphere configuration limits for a particular object, with the score based on the most constraining resource. There are exceptions, such as Datastores, as well as other vSphere objects that may have different factors that contribute.

Workload is calculated by taking the demand of a resource and dividing it by the effective capacity of that resource. If Workload is near, at, or above 100%, then the object has a high likelihood of having performance problems.

Workload can be greater than 100%, as demand can be greater than 100% of its currently—assigned capacity.

Badge colors indicate the state of the object's workload:

- **Green (<= 80)**: The workload on the object is not excessive
- **Yellow (> 80)**: The object is experiencing some high-resource workloads
- **Orange (> 80)**: The workload on the object is approaching its capacity in at least one area
- **Red (> 95)**: The workload on the object is at or over its capacity in one or more areas

 The default thresholds (80, 90, and 95) for the Workload badge are defined by the policy settings for the object type, and they are configurable.

The following screenshot shows an example breakdown of the Workload badge with a score of 49 shown previously. As you can see, the most constraining resource is the memory with 49.06% demand, which in turn determines the badge score:

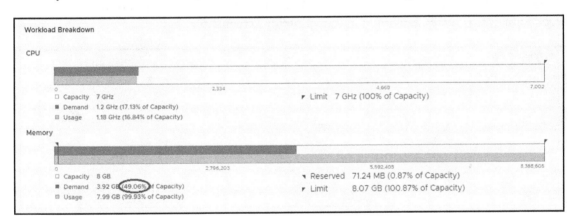

Capacity refers to the amount of resource that an object, such as a virtual machine, is configured with.

Demand refers to the amount of resource that a virtual machine requests due to its guest operating system and application workload. Usage is the amount of resource that a virtual machine gets.

The Workload Breakdown panel shows capacity, demand, and usage for each of these resources: CPU, memory, network I/O, and Datastore I/O. Reservations and limits are also shown for CPU and memory.

Network I/O and Datastore I/O resources are not shown by default and have to be activated first.

The Further Analysis panel provides links to one or more views. These views give you information that might provide further insight into the object's workload.

If the selected object is a virtual machine, the virtual machine Resources panel gives you general information about this virtual machine. This information includes the amount of disk space, memory, and virtual CPUs configured, and the guest operating system name.

Host, virtual machine, and Datastore objects will have workload calculated directly from their own raw metrics, while cluster and data center objects will be derived from an average of all the children being both vSphere hosts and virtual machines.

vRealize Operations 6.6 offers an out-of-the-box dashboard called Heavy Hitter VMs. The **Heavy Hitter VMs** dashboard provides information about the VMs that generated the highest CPU Demand, Memory Demand, IOPS, and network throughput during the last week for a given cluster, as shown in the following screenshot:

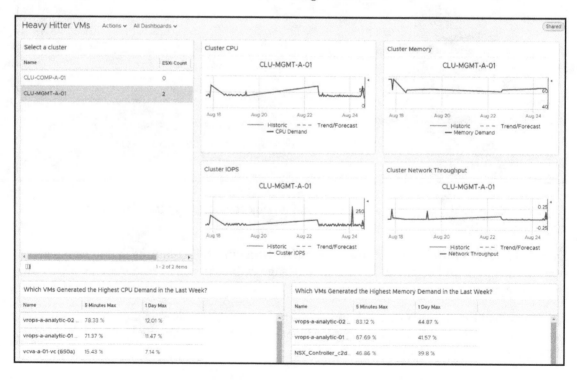

This can be useful when trying to determine which VMs are eating up resources in your environment.

We will be covering dashboards in more detail later in this book.

The Anomalies badge

The Anomalies badge is a measurement of how abnormal an object is behaving. The score for the Anomalies badge is scored from 0 being good and `100` being bad.

Anomalies are based on the most powerful feature of vRealize Operations, Analytics. Analytics allow vRealize Operations to understand the normal behavior of any performance metric, no matter the resource or metric type. They are incredibly useful in generating alerts without the need to hard set static thresholds, and in the discovery of hidden metric relationships. Anomalies use dynamic thresholds to create an upper and lower boundary for a metric in a particular time period. If a metric leaves this dynamic threshold, it is considered an active anomaly.

Anomalies will not be available as a metric or alerting source until vRealize Operations has been monitoring the resource for four weeks. This is the amount of time that it takes to learn the normal behavior of the resource. The object's dynamic threshold is calculated and is visible in the UI after one week (or one cycle) of data collection. It then takes a further three cycles for vRealize Operations analytics to learn the normal behavior of the resource. During this time, the dynamic thresholds become more refined to more accurately reflect the normal operating range of the metrics.

The Anomalies badge itself is based on a noise line or problem threshold. The noise line is required, as some level of noise (abnormality) in the data center is normal. Once the amount of anomalies is greater than the noise line, the score starts to increase. This is shown in the following analogy:

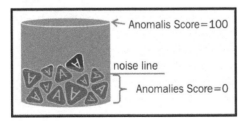

The noise line is dynamically calculated and it's based on Analytics and observed data.

The Anomalies score is the percentage of all metrics that have abnormal behavior. The Anomalies score ranges between 0 (good) and 100 (bad).

The badge changes its color based on badge score thresholds:

- **Green (<= 50)**: The Anomalies score is normal.
- **Yellow (> 50)**: The Anomalies score exceeds the normal range.
- **Orange (> 70)**: The Anomalies score is very high.
- **Red (> 95)**: Most of the metrics are beyond their thresholds. This object might not be working properly or might stop working soon.

 The default thresholds (50, 70, and 95) for the Anomalies badge are defined by the policy settings for the object type, and are configurable.

The Anomalies score is represented by the blue area in the **Score** graph. Yellow, orange, and red lines indicate the badge score thresholds, as follows:

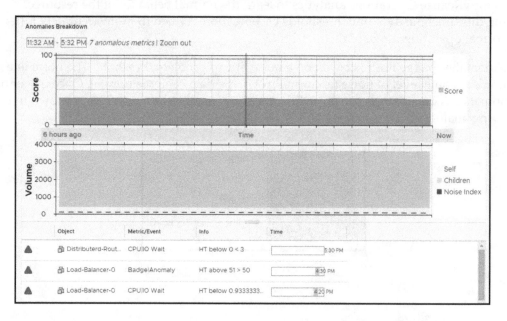

Normally, when an issue occurs, many metrics change in response to the issue. A single abnormal statistic should not drastically affect health, because some level of noise (abnormality) in the data center is normal. Anomalies consider trends of the average noise level for an object, and degrade health only when the number of abnormalities exceeds the noise level.

The Fault badge

The Fault badge is a measure of immediate problems the object has. The score for the Fault badge is scored from 0 being good to 100 being bad.

The Fault badge is mapped against events of the object. This could be loss of a storage path event from the vCenter server or CPU temp or memory DIMM failure retrieved from the ESXi hosts CIM providers. The Fault badge usually highlights issues that require immediate action. The Fault badge is also the only badge that is solely event-driven and is not derived from any metrics.

The badge changes its color based on the severity of the faults:

- **Green (<= 25)**: No faults are registered on the selected object
- **Yellow (> 25)**: Faults of low importance are registered on the selected object
- **Orange (> 50)**: Faults of high importance are registered on the selected object
- **Red (> 75)**: Faults of critical importance are registered on the selected object

Each issue generates its own alert, and resolution of the issue both clears or cancels the alert, and lowers the badge score.

> The default thresholds (25, 50, and 75) for the Faults badge are defined by the policy settings for the object type. These thresholds are configurable.

The Health badge summary

In summary, the Health minor badges can be considered as follows:

- Workload is how hard your object is working
- Anomalies are how normal is your object is right now
- Faults are what's wrong with your object right now

Understanding the Risk badge

Since Health is looking at the current issues in the environment, the Risk badge is looking at future issues and health of the environment or object. If there are no immediate issues to address from the Health badge, Risk should be looked at next.

As was the case with the Health badge, the Risk badge is now derived from Alert and symptom definitions.

There are four minor badges that relate to Risk; Capacity, Time Remaining, Stress, and Compliance.

 The accuracy of Risk, Capacity Remaining, and Time Remaining for your environment are heavily affected by what policies are in effect. Capacity Management will be discussed in detail in `Chapter 7`, *Capacity Management Made Easy*.

The Capacity Remaining badge

The Capacity Remaining badge shows the percentage of usable capacity that has not yet been consumed, therefore an object with a score of `100` has all of its Capacity Remaining, and vice versa; an object having a score of `0` would indicate that there is no capacity available at that moment. For every cluster, virtual machine, or Datastore, Capacity Remaining allows you to determine which resource (CPU, memory, disk, network) might run out first. The Capacity Remaining can be calculated based on average consumption, or consumption at peak times.

For example, average consumption might be 48% of total capacity. The capacity used for vSphere HA and buffers might be 10% of total capacity. So, the Capacity Remaining is 42% *(100 - (10 + 48))*. You can replace average consumption with peak consumption in the equation. For example, if peak consumption reached 60% of total capacity, then the Capacity Remaining is 30% *(100 - (10 + 60))*.

In vCenter Operations, Manager 5.x, Capacity Remaining was based on the number of Virtual Machines as the unit of capacity. In vRealize Operations 6.0, the unit of capacity varies depending on the object type. This is primarily due to the fact that capacity management has been opened up to non-vSphere objects.

It is important to note that Capacity Remaining is based on the resource that is the most constrained. For example, in the following screenshot, we see a vSphere Cluster with CPU, Memory, Disk Space, and Configuration Limits selected as resources to include in Capacity Management as the currently—applied policy.

The badge changes its color based on the badge score thresholds:

- **Green (>= 10%)**: The Capacity Remaining for the object is at a high level
- **Yellow (< 10%)**: The Capacity Remaining for the object is at a medium level
- **Orange (< 5%)**: The Capacity Remaining for the object is at a seriously low level
- **Red (= 0%)**: The object is expected to run out of capacity soon or has already run out of capacity

The default thresholds (10, 5, and 0) for the Capacity badge are defined by the policy settings for the object type, and they are configurable.

Looking at the four selected resources, memory is the most constrained at 64.53% remaining after buffers are taken into account, therefore this is where the Capacity Remaining score is derived from for this object:

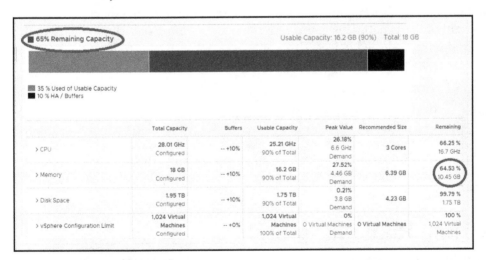

	Total Capacity	Buffers	Usable Capacity	Peak Value	Recommended Size	Remaining
> CPU	28.01 GHz Configured	-- +10%	25.21 GHz 90% of Total	26.18% 6.6 GHz Demand	3 Cores	66.25 % 16.7 GHz
> Memory	18 GB Configured	-- +10%	16.2 GB 90% of Total	27.52% 4.46 GB Demand	6.39 GB	64.53 % 10.45 GB
> Disk Space	1.95 TB Configured	-- +10%	1.75 TB 90% of Total	0.21% 3.8 GB Demand	4.23 GB	99.79 % 1.75 TB
> vSphere Configuration Limit	1,024 Virtual Machines Configured	-- +0%	1,024 Virtual Machines 100% of Total	0% 0 Virtual Machines Demand	0 Virtual Machines	100 % 1,024 Virtual Machines

65% Remaining Capacity · Usable Capacity: 16.2 GB (90%) Total: 18 GB

35 % Used of Usable Capacity
10 % HA / Buffers

Capacity Manager data is now provided with five-minute granular samples.

For each resource, the Capacity Breakdown panel provides the following details:

- Total capacity configured for the resource
- Percentage of resource capacity used for buffers
- Amount of usable capacity consumed by the object
- Percentage of usable capacity consumed during peak times
- Percentage of usable capacity demanded during non-stress times (stress accumulates when a workload exceeds the stress line)
- Percentage of usable capacity remaining for the resource

The Capacity Breakdown panel also indicates the number of average, small, medium, and large virtual machine profiles that can fit into the capacity remaining for this object. In addition to the default profiles, you can create custom profiles based on specific sizing requirements in your environment. Custom profiles show how many more of a specified object can fit in your environment given the available capacity and object configuration.

When creating capacity projects, you can use custom profiles in addition to the default profile. We will cover capacity projects later in this book.

The vSphere Configuration Limit row shows the remaining virtual machine count (at the bottom–right of the panel). This count represents the number of virtual machines that can be deployed on the selected object. This value is based on the current amount of unused resources in a cluster and the average virtual machine profile.

The Capacity Remaining badge is only calculated once a day with the overnight batch processing. This process occurs at 22:00. Keep this in mind that although changes to policies for Capacity Management will take effect straight away in terms of breakdowns and trending, the badge itself will only update overnight. One small exception to this rule, if a project is committed, the Time Remaining badge will update soon afterward.

The Time Remaining badge

The Time Remaining badge is the amount of time before an object runs out of capacity. The score for the Time Remaining badge ranges from 0 being bad and 100 being good. The most restrictive compute resource will be the one that makes an impact to the badge score. The score is based on the number of days minus your provisioning time buffer based on the current rate of consumption or forecast.

As shown in the following figure, data points collected over a period of time are used to build a trend line. This line is then used to forecast capacity into the future, both for demand and allocation of each relevant resource, for example, CPU, Memory, Disk Space, and so on.

The first component of the forecast is the provisioning buffer that is set in the associated policy. This buffer (30 days by default) is used as a value that administrators set to reflect how long it will take to add additional capacity to the object. If this object is a vSphere cluster, for example, this setting should reflect how long it would take to provision another ESXi host that may even include procurement time.

The time after the provisioning buffer is used to provide the score to the Time Remaining badge. If the estimated time remaining is equal to or less than the provisioning buffer the time remaining score will be 0. Each day after this point will add to the time remaining scale, with a maximum score of 100.

The following figure shows a graphical example of how the Time Remaining score is calculated:

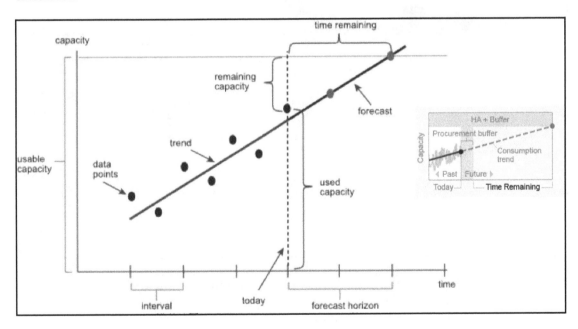

The badge color represents the Time Remaining for the most constrained resources:

- **Green (>= 50%)**: The number of days that remain is much higher than the provisioning time buffer

- **Yellow (< 50%):** The number of days that remain is higher than the provisioning time buffer, but is less than twice the size of the time buffer
- **Orange (< 25%):** The number of days that remain is lower than the provisioning time buffer
- **Red (= 0%):** The number of days that remain is zero

The default thresholds (50, 25, and 0) for the Time Remaining badge are defined by the policy settings for the object type, and these thresholds are configurable.

The following figure is an example breakdown of the Time Remaining badge with a score of 98:

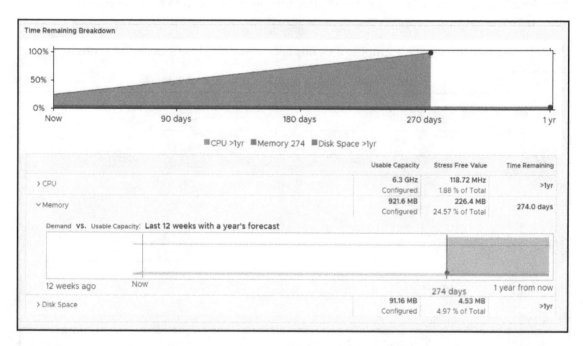

The amount of Time Remaining is calculated for each resource type and is based on historical data for the use pattern for the resource type. The amount of time remaining for each resource is shown in the graph and in the table below the graph.

In this example, the time remaining for CPU is 274 days. The time remaining for the other resources is over one year.

As with the Capacity Remaining badge, the Time Remaining badge is only calculated once a day with the overnight batch processing.

The Stress badge

The Stress badge is an early warning view of upcoming provisioning needs. An object that is experiencing stress is experiencing high usage of a resource over a period of time.

The stress score accumulates when workload exceeds the stress line. The stress score is the percentage of the stress zone area with stress in the selected time sample. By default, the stress zone is 70%+ and is observed in any 60-minute peak period.

The following screenshot shows an example breakdown of the Stress badge:

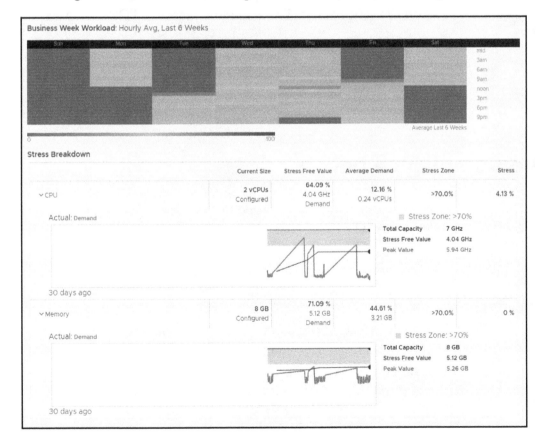

The Stress score helps you to identify clusters, hosts, and virtual machines that do not have enough resources allocated. This score also helps you to identify clusters and hosts that are running too many virtual machines.

The Stress badge changes its color based on the badge score thresholds:

- **Green (<= 25)**: The Stress score is normal.
- **Yellow (> 25)**: Some of the object's resources are not enough to meet the demands.
- **Orange (> 35)**: The object is experiencing regular resource shortage.
- **Red (> 50)**: Most of the resources on the object are constantly insufficient. The object might stop functioning properly.

A high Stress score does not imply a current performance problem, but does highlight the potential for future performance problems.

In this example, the stress score for the object is 4. This score means that the object has been using 4% of its workload capacity, which is below the stress threshold (25%) for a six-week period.

The default thresholds (25, 35, and 50) for the Stress badge are defined by the policy settings for the object type, and these thresholds are configurable.

The Compliance badge

The Compliance badge value is a score based on one or more compliance policies that you run in vRealize Operations against the data collected from vRealize Operations. Compliance policies are set of rules which your environment must comply to meet corporate or industry standards.

The compliance score is based on the number of violations against those policies.

The Compliance badge displays one of the following values:

- 100 if there are no triggered standards. The badge color is green.
- 75 if the most critical triggered standard is a warning. The badge color is yellow.
- 25 if the most critical triggered standard is immediate. The badge color is orange.
- 0 if the most critical triggered standard is critical. The badge color is red.

The alert details provide information on the compliance violation.

vRealize Operations 6.6 now offers **Payment Card Industry Data Security Standard (PCI DSS)** and **Health Insurance Portability and Accountability Act (HIPAA)** compliance for vSphere. vRealize Operations 6.6 also offers the **vSphere Hardening Compliance** dashboard, which measures your environment against the vSphere Hardening Guide and shows you the results along with affected objects, as shown in the following screenshot:

In the dashboard, you can see the trend of high risk, medium risk, and low risk violations and see the overall compliance score. The dashboard also allows you to drill down into various components to check compliance for your ESXi hosts, Clusters, Port Groups, and virtual machines using heatmaps.

The Risk badge summary

The easiest way to look at the minor badges that are related to Risk is as follows:

- Capacity Remaining is the percentage of capacity you have left on this object
- Time Remaining is how long you have until you are out of resources
- Stress is how much pressure a given object is under, as it's demanding most of or more than its currently–assigned resources
- Compliance is how many violations there are against corporate policies

Understanding the Efficiency badge

The Efficiency badge is the last major badge, and it advises us on how efficient we are being with our resources in terms of right-sizing and target density ratios.

Issues relating to efficiency are rarely issues that you would need to be alerted on, however, they are useful for reporting and ensuring that you are getting the most out of your infrastructure.

The Reclaimable Capacity badge

The Reclaimable Capacity badge is a graphical representation of the amount of unused compute resources currently assigned to your virtual machines.

In vSphere, Reclaimable Capacity is only applied to virtual machines, as it is seen that VMs are fairly straightforward to right-size as requirements change in the environment. The same could not be said for hosts, for example, as adding or removing resources from physical hosts based on demand would not be seen as a common task.

Although Reclaimable Capacity only applies to virtual machines, objects such as Clusters, Hosts, Datastores, and other containers still have a badge (and associated score) due to the relationship of children VMs.

Reclaimable capacity has four specific items that impact the score. These are:

- Oversized virtual machines
- Idle virtual machines
- Powered-off virtual machines
- Unused file capacity

The Reclaimable Capacity score is based on the resource that has the highest percentage of Reclaimable Capacity divided by its total capacity. This score ranges from 0 (good) to 100 (bad), and for virtual machines this score filters up to the objects, parent containers.

The following screenshot shows an example breakdown of the Reclaimable Capacity badge with a score of 37. You can see that the CPU has the highest reclaimable capacity of 36.63%, which determines the badge score:

Reclaimable Capacity Breakdown		
How Much Can Be Reclaimed	**Reclaimable Breakdown** Based on current top offenders	
37 vCPUs	Memory Idle 2 GB	Disk Space Reclaimable - VMDK Usage Idle 3.21 GB
CPU **22.72 GB** Memory	Memory Oversized 20.72 GB	Disk Space Reclaimable - VMDK Usage Powered Off 75.32 GB
198.73 GB Disk Space Reclaimable	CPU Idle 4 vCPUs CPU Oversized 33 vCPUs	Disk Space Reclaimable - Snapshot Space Idle 0 GB
		Disk Space Reclaimable - Snapshot Space Old Data 80.2 GB
		Disk Space Reclaimable - Snapshot Space Powered Off 0 GB

Reclaimable capacity values based on last computation time

	Provisioned	Reclaimable	% Reclaimable
> CPU	101 vCPUs	37 vCPUs	36.63 %
> Memory	130.5 GB	22.72 GB	17.41 %
> Disk Space Reclaimable	3.46 TB	198.73 GB	5.61 %

The **Reclaimable Capacity Breakdown** panel shows you how much of each resource can be reclaimed, also shown as a percentage of the provisioned resource.

In this example, CPU is the resource type that has the highest percentage of reclaimable capacity (about 36%).

Reclaimable Capacity might be in contrast to Health and Stress. An ideal environment without wasted resources creates stress, so it is important to balance the proper size of the virtual machine based on Stress and Reclaimable Capacity recommendations. Normally, the same virtual machine shows up as stressed from a memory perspective, but it is oversized from a CPU perspective.

The Reclaimable Capacity badge color indicates the following states:

- **Green (<= 50%)**: No resources are wasted on the selected object
- **Yellow (> 50%)**: Some resources can be used better
- **Orange (> 75%)**: Many resources are underused
- **Red (= 100%)**: Most of the resources on the selected object are wasted

The default thresholds (50, 75, and 100) for the Reclaimable Capacity badge are defined by the policy settings for the object type, and these thresholds are configurable.

vRealize Operations 6.6 offers an out-of-the-box dashboard called **Capacity Reclaimable**. From the Capacity Reclaimable dashboard, you can select a vCenter, Datacenter, or Cluster object to review for a top-down approach to gain resource efficiency:

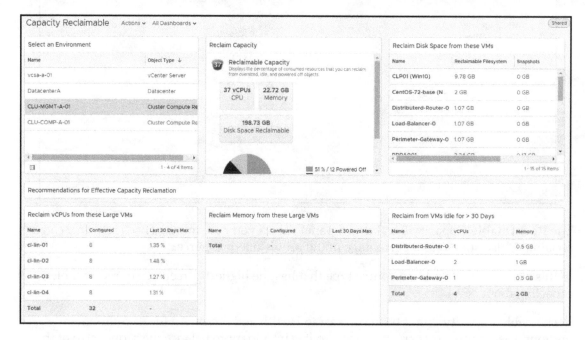

A thumbnail view shows the total capacity that can be reclaimed in CPU, memory, and disk space. Disk space is the easiest to reclaim, since it is due to old snapshots and powered off virtual machines.

For CPU and memory reclamation, the dashboard offers some best practices. Removing CPU and memory often involves approvals and maintenance windows, so it is best to focus on larger VMs first where there is more benefit for the efforts.

In either case, all of the lists provide a set of totals that serve as an estimate of resource gains for reclamation efforts.

We will be covering dashboards in more detail later in this book.

Idle VMs

Idle virtual machines are exactly as the name suggests; how many virtual machines in your environment that are idle. How is a virtual machine considered idle? The idle calculation is directly related to the threshold settings that are set in policy for virtual machines under Reclaimable Capacity. Idle virtual machines are virtual machines with a compute usage less than the configured threshold. The settings that you would change are shown as follows.

By default, a virtual machine must spend 90% of its time consuming less than:

- 100 MHz CPU
- 20 I/O Operations of Disk I/O
- 1 KBps of Network I/O (Both VM and Host)

As per the preceding diagram, the Time interval (T) is the same value as used for Stress and other non-trended analytics.

> Some resource containers may need to be excluded from analysis to accurately detect idle VMs. Consider scheduled activities such as Anti-Virus scans and possibly disabling Disk I/O analysis to compensate.

Powered off Virtual Machines

This is the simplest part of Reclaimable Capacity. By default, if a virtual machine is powered off for 90% of the time, then it is considered powered off and included in the Reclaimable Capacity. The percentage can be changed in the settings. This will include CPU, RAM, and DISK capacity from the powered off virtual machines.

> If using the default Data range (Time) of 30 days or longer, it is recommended to adjust this value to 100%. This will ensure that VMs that are flagged as reclaimable due to being powered off were not used at all in the time period.

Oversized virtual machines

Oversized VMs will generally be the bulk of the Reclaimable Capacity in your environment.

By default, a virtual machine is flagged oversized when the amount of CPU, Memory, or Disk Space demand is below 50% for the selected Data Range (time period).

For a production environment, it is recommended to use Stress to account for spikes and peaks setting is checked. This will ensure that VM peaks are taken into account when determining if a VM is oversized.

A common question that arises with oversized VMs is what is the right-sizing value based on what is shown in the VM optimization report. The right-sizing recommendations are calculated from *Demand + HA + Buffers*. Therefore, it is important to consider what buffers are appropriate for your environment to ensure accuracy in these reports.

 In VMware vSphere, when you enable VMware vSphere High Availability for a cluster, resources are set aside so that you can meet the requirements for failover. Also, VMware vRealize Operations sets aside capacity for buffers, used for capacity planning and management purposes.

The Density badge

The Density Badge score is the ratio of current density to calculated ideal density. Ideal density is calculated using demand that is being generated, the amount of virtual capacity that is provisioned, and the amount of actual physical usable capacity deployed.

The goal of density is to calculate the amount of resources that can be provisioned with minimal contention and therefore maximize the **Return** of **Investment** (**ROI**) you can receive from your infrastructure. There are three parts to density that are calculated. These are:

- VM to Host
- vCPU to pCPU
- vMem to pMEM

The Density score ranges from 0 (bad) to 100 (good), as it takes the resource type with the highest density score as the badge score.

The following image is an example breakdown of the Density badge with a score of 90. You can see that, in this example, the virtual machine host system and memory density score are the same. This score in turn determines the badge score:

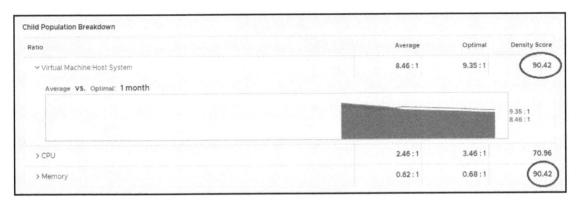

The density graph shows the average versus optimal values over one month of trend data for the various consolidation ratios.

Density information includes the following consolidation ratios:

- Ratio of virtual machines to physical hosts
- Ratio of virtual CPU to physical CPU
- Ratio of virtual memory to physical memory

Density is a badge that is useful for understanding your workloads at a macro level in terms of what ratios your environment is actually achieving. It is also important that, as the Density score of a host or cluster increases over time, its Capacity Remaining score will decrease.

The Efficiency badge summary

The best way to sum up the Efficiency badge is:

- **Reclaimable Capacity**: This determines which *resources* you have assigned that are not being used at all or used very little
- **Density**: This determines how close you are to an ideal density based on all your resources and what's being used

Summary

In this chapter, you learned what each major badge is and how it relates to your environment. We covered each badge (major and minor) and looked at how they are calculated, to give you a better idea of how the resultant numbers are generated and how to interpret them in your own environment.

In the next chapter, we will cover what vRealize Operations alerts are, how symptoms can affect Alerts, and how recommendations and actions can help us resolve Alerts. We will also discuss and configure alert notifications for some alerts.

6

Getting a Handle on Alerting and Notifications

This chapter discusses in detail the building blocks of alerts in vRealize Operations and the notification settings we can configure for them. We will discuss what symptoms are and how they affect alerts. We will also look at how we can define recommendations for alerts and apply actions when necessary.

What are symptoms, recommendations, and actions?

Symptoms, recommendations, and actions combine to give alerts. In the following diagram, we can see where they all fit in relation to alerts:

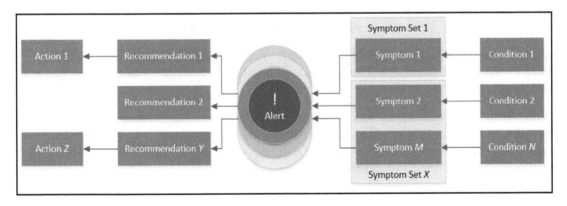

What are symptoms?

Symptoms are made up of a single condition of an object. Conditions can be metric-based conditions, such as CPU usage greater than 90%, or property-based conditions, such as DRS equals Fully Automatic.

Within an alert, multiple symptoms can be grouped into symptom sets. For example, you may group symptoms such as Cluster CPU contention at critical level and cluster compute resource anomaly is critically high when evaluating the health and availability of a cluster.

The symptoms in each symptom set are evaluated for being true (valid). You can select a matching criterion of **Any** or **All** for each symptom set.

If you select **Any** as a matching criterion for a symptom set, at least one symptom in the set must evaluate to true in order for the whole symptom set to evaluate to true.

If you select **All** as a matching criteria for a symptom set, all symptoms in the set must evaluate to true in order for the whole symptom set to evaluate to true.

This can be illustrated as follows:

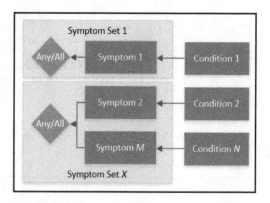

Symptoms can be used as just highlighting an issue that then, through an alert, directly affects the score of the associated badge, such as health. Or a symptom can be a part of a greater problem, which in this case is an alert.

A symptom doesn't necessarily have to be caused by an issue. For example, if HA is enabled, which has criticality type Info, combines two symptoms to an alert: DRS is enabled for a cluster and DRS is configured to Fully Automatic. Alerts will appear within the vRealize Operations UI under the related badge and object.

Symptoms have a severity value called **criticality**. Criticality controls the color of the symptom in the user interface:

- **Info**: gray
- **Warning**: yellow
- **Immediate**: orange
- **Critical**: red

Alerts and symptoms come from the following sources:

- Prebuilt, included in vRealize Operations
- Management packs
- End users

Many prebuilt symptoms are included with the product. Often, these symptoms describe incremental levels of concern. For example, Volume nearing capacity limit might have a severity value of warning, while Volume reached capacity limit might have a severity level of critical. The first symptom is not an immediate threat, while the second one is an immediate threat.

What are alerts?

Alerts are made up of one or many symptoms. Alarms can be configured in such a way that either all symptoms must be true or only a single symptom must be true to activate the alert:

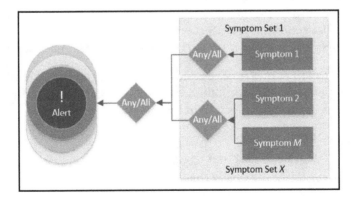

As we said before, this can be broken up further by creating multiple symptom sets, where either one or all symptoms in that set must be true to activate the symptom set, and then the alert can be if one symptom set or all must be true to activate.

Triggering an alert can be illustrated as follows:

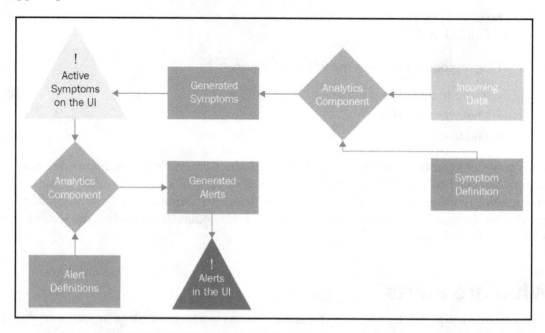

The **Analytics Component** checks for symptom conditions at the end of each polling cycle (every 5 minutes). Data is collected from the monitored objects and sent to the **Analytics Component**. The **Analytics Component** then compares the data to the conditions in the symptom definition. If a condition is true, then the symptom is triggered. The triggered (or active) symptom is displayed in the appropriate areas of the product user interface.

One or more symptoms are part of an alert definition. If one or more symptoms are triggered (based on the alert definition), then the alert is triggered. The triggered (or active) alert is shown in the product user interface in the following places:

- The **Alerts Overview** page
- The **Alerts** tab of the object that triggered the alert
- The **Summary** tab of the object that triggered the alert

A symptom can be triggered, but this event does not necessarily mean that the alert is triggered. The alert definition defines what combination of symptoms needs to be triggered for the alert to be triggered.

The **Alerts** page provides details about each triggered alert, such as the following information:

- Alert criticality
- A descriptive alert name
- Alert status (active or inactive)
- Object on which the alert was triggered
- Object type
- Alert impact (health, risk, or efficiency)
- Assigned owner
- Date and time at which the alert was triggered
- Date and time at which the alert was canceled:

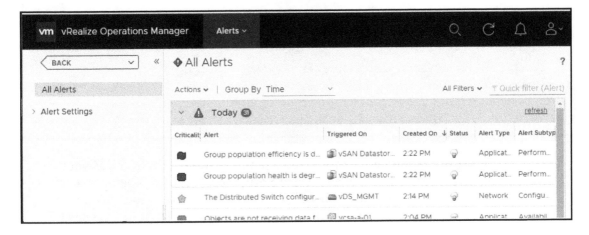

The urgency of an alert is determined by the alert impact, which in turn determines which badge will be affected by this particular alert.

On the **Summary** tab of the alert, you can find additional information, such as the object affected by the alert and the current state. When you are looking for ways to resolve an alert, the **Summary** tab is where you should start:

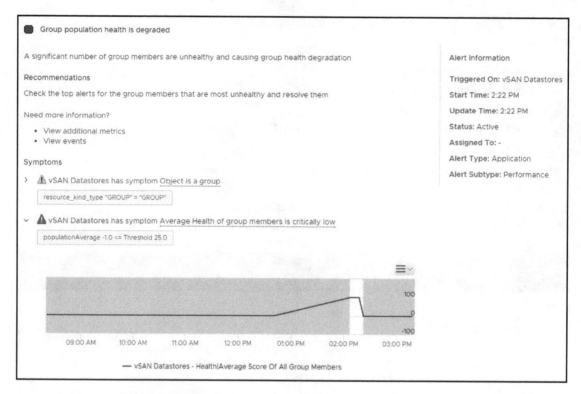

 vRealize Operations 6.6 comes with compliance alerts to cover VMware vSphere Hardening Guide versions 5.5 and 6.0. This means being able to achieve compliance for vSphere 5.5 and 6.0 objects. The next version of vRealize Operations should include hardening compliance for vSphere 6.5 objects.

What are recommendations?

Recommendations are used to supply information on how to fix the alert that has been triggered:

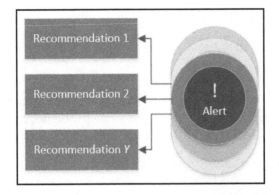

There are plenty of built-in recommendations but these can be created manually based on your organization policies and procedures; KB links and contacts can be included as well. A recommendation can be a single line of text or can be pages on how to fix the issue at hand.

When assigning recommendations to an alert, they are given priorities. This is because, as any administrator knows, there could be a number or issues that represent the same symptoms so we can prioritize which recommendation would be more likely to be the fix, all based on environment knowledge.

What are actions?

Actions are the new feature that first came out in vRealize Operations 6.0. An action provides a method for fixing the issue that you are trying to resolve. Only a single action can be assigned to a recommendation but this is completely optional:

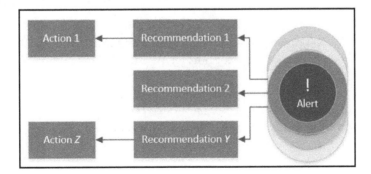

Actions come from the following sources:

- Built into the product
- Installed management packs

The number of actions is fixed and additional ones cannot be created currently. The out-of-the-box actions offer simple actions to remediate some problems, for example, remove snapshot, add vCPU, add memory, and remove vCPU.

 vRealize Operations actions used to require the vCenter Python solution to be configured. This is now part of the vCenter Adapter and can be enabled via the **Enable** actions option from in the adapter configuration.

The following diagram shows an example scenario of how this would fit together:

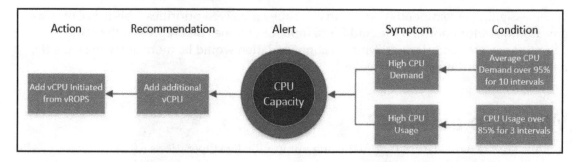

With all these pieces coming together, they create one neat way for troubleshooting in an environment, especially when a good catalog has been created or modified to fit in with the environment.

Think about it: we have a known issue in the environment and we know the signs. It could be something like when Microsoft Cluster Service raw device mappings are set to Round Robin and are not using Dell EMC PowerPath/VE, which means the storage latency will peak in bursts as it switches paths and waits for the switch back. Or it could be we notice when the server's BIOS power settings have not been correctly configured, and we get specific CPU performance issues.

We can supply all the data needed to fix the issue as well as additional suggestions within a recommendation so that when an alarm is triggered when the SME of the environment is not there, the lone junior server engineer can fix the issue as the resolution is right there in black and white.

Creating symptoms, recommendations, and alerts

Now that we have a good understanding of what symptoms, recommendations, actions, and alerts are, let's see how we can create new ones and tie them together.

 As mentioned earlier, actions are predefined and new actions cannot be created in vRealize Operations.

Creating symptoms

First, let's see how we can create a symptom definition. vRealize Operations comes out of the box with more than 600 symptom definitions. I recommend you first spend some time getting yourself familiar with them as much as possible. Before creating a new one, make sure an existing definition doesn't exist that matches your needs, by using the symptom definition search and filter options vRealize Operations provides. Otherwise, you may end up creating new definitions when there is an already existing one which can satisfy your requirements.

For the purpose of this example, let's say we have a company policy which states that we should be alerted if a VM is configured with more than 16 GB of memory. Let's see how we can create a symptom definition to match that policy.

Perform the following steps to create a new symptom definition:

1. Go to the vRealize Operations User UI on the Master Replica node by navigating to the following URL: `https://<FQDN or IP of the Master Replica Node>/ui`. Navigate to the **Alerts** section and select **Alert Settings**, and then **Symptom Definitions**. Here we can see the symptoms on the right-hand side. Here is where we can tweak existing ones or create our own. Let's create our own so we can see what goes into a symptom definition. Click on the little green plus (+) icon, as shown in the following screenshot:

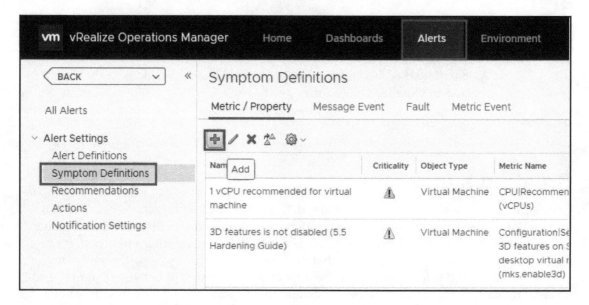

2. From the **Base Object Type** drop-down menu, navigate to **vCenter Adapter** and select **Virtual Machine**. Select **Properties** from the next drop-down menu. Navigate to **Memory** and select the **VM Limit (KB)** property.
3. Type a name for the definition. For example, `Virtual Machine maximum memory configuration is violating corporate policies`. From the **Criticality** drop-down menu, select **Warning**. From the matching criteria drop-down menu, select **is greater than or equal to**. Enter a value of `16384`. Click **Save**:

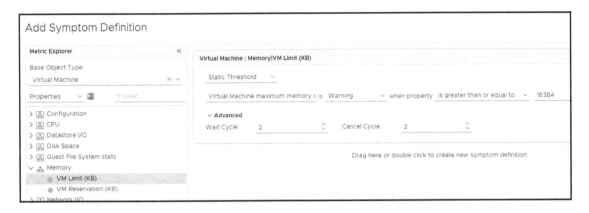

This completes the process of creating a symptom definition.

Creating recommendations

For the purpose of this example, let's say we want to create a recommendation that will inform the **Network Operation Center** (**NOC**) engineers monitoring our environment that if they are not able to resolve a given alert, they should always contact the on-duty problem manager.

Perform the following steps to create a new recommendation:

1. Go to the vRealize Operations user UI on the master replica node by navigating to the following URL: `https://<FQDN or IP of the Master Replica Node>/ui`. Navigate to the **Alerts** section and select **Alert Settings**, and then **Recommendation**. Here we can see the defined recommendations on the right-hand side. Here is where we can edit the existing ones or create our own. Let's create our own so we can see what goes into a recommendation. Click on the little green plus (+) icon.

2. In the **Edit Recommendation** window, enter the recommendation text, for example, `Contact the on-duty Problem Manager if the issue persists`. Here is where, optionally, you can select an action for this recommendation. We will not be selecting one. Click **Save**.

This completes the process of creating a recommendation.

Creating alerts

As shown at the beginning of this chapter, alerts are a combination of symptom definitions. Any single symptom being true can cause an alert to activate, or all the symptoms need be true for the alert to then activate. This is completely up to how we configure it. For the purpose of this example, we will be creating an alert that will include symptoms concerning cluster computer resource health.

Perform the following steps to create an alert:

1. Go to the vRealize Operations user UI on the master replica node by navigating to the following URL: `https://<FQDN or IP of the Master Replica Node>/ui`. Navigate to the **Alerts** section and select **Alert Settings**, and then **Alert Definitions**. Here we can see the alerts on the right-hand side. Here is where we can tweak existing ones or create our own. Let's create our own so we can see what goes into an alert. Click on the little green plus (+) icon.

2. This then opens up the **Alert Definition Workspace**, which is very similar to the policy creation window. We need to first enter the **Name** and **Description**.

3. Now we click on the **Base Object Type** bar. There is only a single thing to select here, which is the base object to which this alarm will be associated. **Cluster Compute Resources** was selected but could be **Host** or **VM** or **Datastore**; any object from any solution can be chosen.

4. Next, we click on the **Alert Impact** bar. In this section, we choose the following:
   - **Impact**: Which major badge this will affect: health, risk, or efficiency.
   - **Criticality**: This is the type of alert: info, warning, immediate, critical, or symptom-based. The last one mentioned there will take the criticality of the symptoms to make up the alerts value.
   - **Alert Type and Subtype**: There are quite a number of values in here to select. In this example, we've selected **Virtualization/Hypervisor**. This will give the alert a category it fits into.
   - **Wait Cycle**: How many cycles in which the symptoms need to be triggered, for the alarm to be triggered as well.
   - **Cancel Cycle**: This is the opposite of the **Wait Cycle**: how many cycles the alert remains active when the conditions are not met.

The following screenshot illustrates how it could be configured:

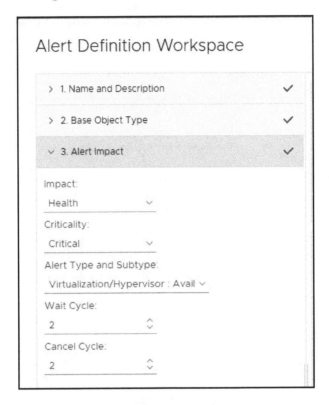

5. Click on the **Add Symptom Definitions** bar—this is where the magic happens. In this section, we can choose the level at which we want the symptoms to apply; we have selected **Self**. We could also select a child, which in this case is a host, or a parent, which would be a Datacenter.

We then need to choose a symptom or 10. From the drop-down list, select the **Symptom Definition Type** and then, below that, select a symptom and drag it over to the right. We can drag and drop symptoms on top of each other to nest them, which is called a symptom set, in which case we will see multiple numbered symptoms in one box, or we can drag and drop into the dotted outlined area to create a new symptom set.

From the following screenshot, we can see all the previous data we entered at the top of the right-hand side and the metric symptoms we dragged over below. Each symptom set has the drop-down option to say whether **All** or **Any** of the symptoms need to be true to make the symptom set true. At the top of the symptom sets, we have a **Match** value, which can be set so that **All** or **Any** of the symptom sets must be true to activate the alert:

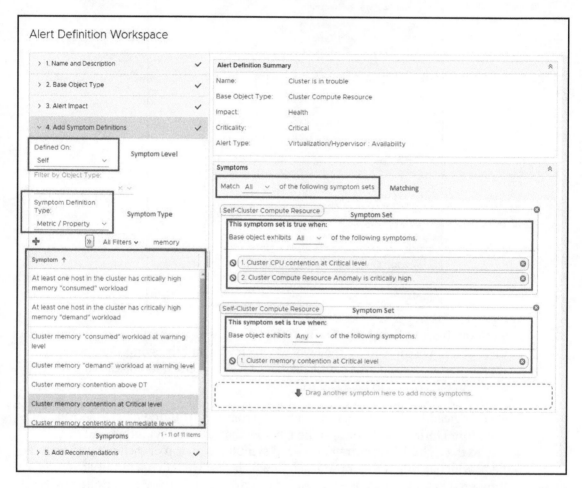

6. Recommendations are the last step. This is optional when creating an alarm but I would highly recommend it, as it can save time, especially when you're not there to fix it. Click on the **Add Recommendations** bar and search for the recommendation we require and drag and drop it from the left to the right.

What we can also do is drag multiple recommendations over and give them a priority, so if we know a particular symptom we have chosen could have multiple courses of action, we can put them in here and all the information will help. This is shown in the following screenshot:

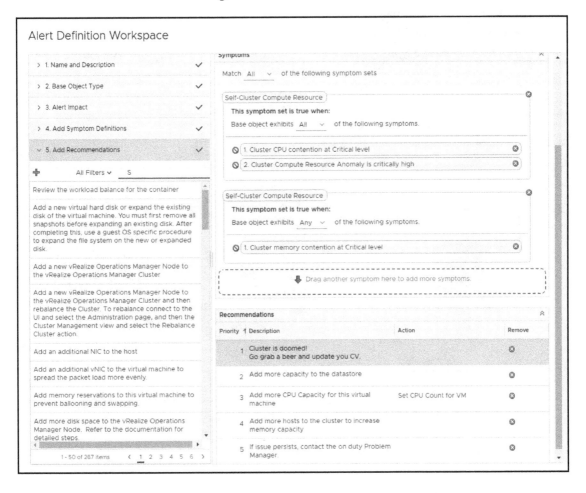

Click on the **Save** button and we have just created an alert. From this very simple example, we can see just how powerful the new alerting system is, as it's made up of multiple items. It allows us to become very specific with the alerts we want while providing guidance on how to fix the issue.

Now let's take a look at few examples on using multiple conditions, symptoms, symptom sets, and matching options.

Consider the following example:

- We have defined three conditions.
- We have mapped three symptoms to those conditions.
- We have two symptom sets. The first symptom set has only one symptom. The second symptom set has two symptoms.
- We have a matching condition (**Any/All**) for each set.
- We have a matching condition (**Any/All**) for the whole alert.

In general, those settings can be illustrated as follows:

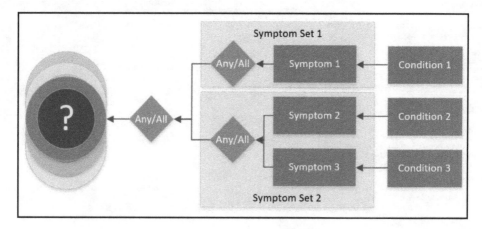

The alert definition example we gave earlier can be illustrated as follows:

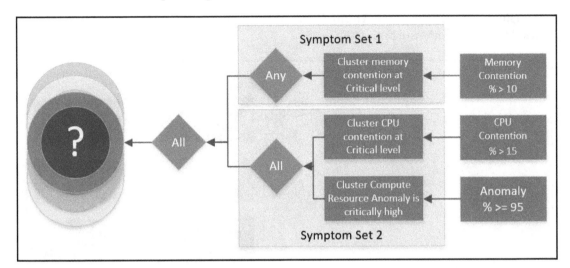

As you can see, we have selected the following matching criteria:

- **Symptom Set 1**: Symptom set is true when **Any** of the symptoms is true. In this example, we have only one symptom: **Cluster contention at Critical level**.
- **Symptom Set 2**: Symptom set is true when **All** of the symptoms are true. In this example, we have two symptoms: **Cluster CPU contention at Critical level** and **Cluster Compute Resource Anomaly is critically high**.
- **Alert**: The alert matching is set to **All**. This means all symptom sets must return true in order for an alert to be generated.

Now let's play out few examples.

Example 1

The **Cluster Compute Resource Anomaly is critically high** and **Cluster contention at Critical level** symptoms are both true:

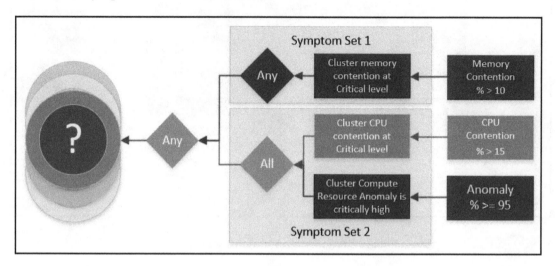

In this example, an alert will not be generated for the following reasons:

- **Symptom Set 2** requires all symptoms in the set to be true. In this example, only one symptom in the set is true.
- An alert requires all symptom sets to return true. In this example, only one symptom set is returning true.

Now, if the second symptom in the **Symptom Set 2** returns true, and therefore the whole set returns true, this will generate an alert as all of the matching criteria in the alert are fulfilled:

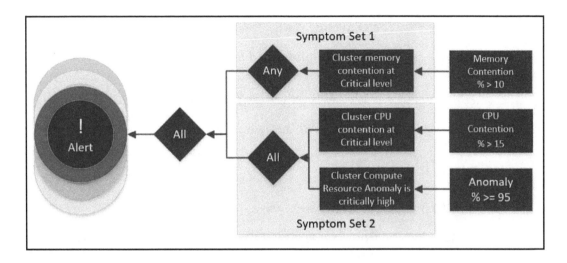

Example 2

Let's change the matching criterion for this example as follows:

- **Symptom Set 2**: Symptom set is true when **Any** of the symptoms are true

Again, as in the previous example, the **Cluster Compute Resource Anomaly is critically high** and **Cluster contention at Critical level** symptoms are both true:

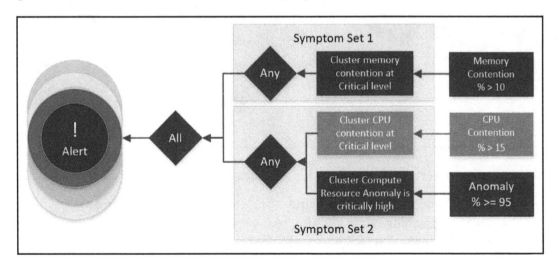

In this example, **an alert will be generated** for the following reasons:

- The matching criterion for **Symptom Set 1** is **Any** and we have at least one symptom returning true
- The matching criterion for **symptom Set 2** is **Any** and we have at least one symptom returning true
- The alert matching criterion is **All**, and we have all symptom sets returning true

Example 3

Let's change the matching criteria for this example as follows:

- **Alert**: Matching criterion is set to **Any**. The criterion will return true when any of the symptom sets returns true.

The **Cluster Compute Resource Anomaly is critically high** returns **true**:

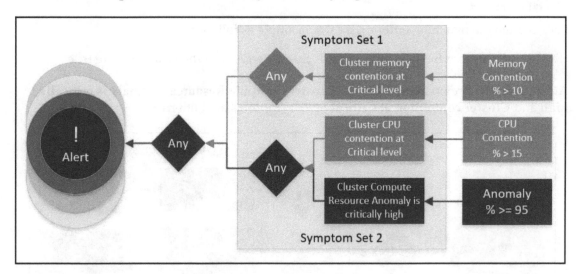

In this example, an alert will be generated for the following reasons:

- The matching criterion for **Symptom Set 1** and **Symptom Set 2** is **Any**
- The alert matching criteria is **Any**, and we have we have at least one symptom in at least one symptom set returning true

What are policies?

A policy allows you to modify the way that vRealize Operations analyzes and presents data in the dashboard and in various views and reports. A policy allows you to adapt the appearance and operation of vRealize Operations to your environment and preferences.

A policy includes the following settings:

- Metrics or properties for different object types (such as virtual machine, host, or Datastore)
- Symptom and alert definitions
- Badge threshold definitions
- Buffers, such as provisioning time buffers, and VMware vSphere® High Availability buffers

A comprehensive set of content is readily available when you install and configure vRealize Operations. You might have to customize some of the content to satisfy certain business requirements or to adhere to your company's policies.

For example, you can create custom policies to support service-level agreements and business priorities. vRealize Operations allows you to modify existing content and create content if necessary.

You can customize the following content:

- **Policies**
- **Dashboards**
- **Dashboard views**
- **Reports**
- **Alert Definitions**
- **Symptom Definitions**
- **Recommendations**
- **Super Metrics**

Policies can be found by navigating to the **Administration** tab and then selecting **Policies**. Here you will find two tabs: **Active Policies** and **Policy Library**. Policy Library is a repository of standard policies delivered with vRealize Operations, policies installed with management packs, and policies created by a user or the installation wizard.

Let's take as an example vSphere Solution's Default Policy and look closer at its settings.

On the **Policy Library** tab, select **vSphere Solution's Default Policy** and click **Edit**. The **Edit Monitoring Policy** window opens:

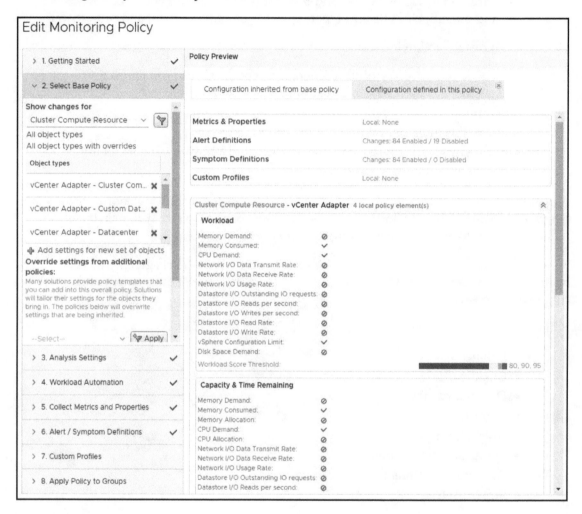

In the left-hand side pane, you can find the steps you must go through when creating a policy.

On the **Select Base Policy** page, select a base policy from which your new custom policy can inherit settings:

- The **Start** with drop-down menu allows you to choose which policy is to be used as a starting point. All settings from the starting point policy are inherited as default settings in your new policy.
- The **Policy Preview** pane displays tabs for the inherited policy configuration, and the configuration for the policy that you are creating. From this pane, you can view the number of enabled and disabled alert definitions, symptom definitions, attributes (metrics and properties), and the number of local changes. A local change is a change made to a setting in the policy that you are building which overrides the same setting in the parent policy.
- You typically apply a default policy to most of the objects in your environment.

Create a separate policy for each object group and make only minor changes in the settings for that policy so that vRealize Operations can monitor and analyze dedicated groups of objects:

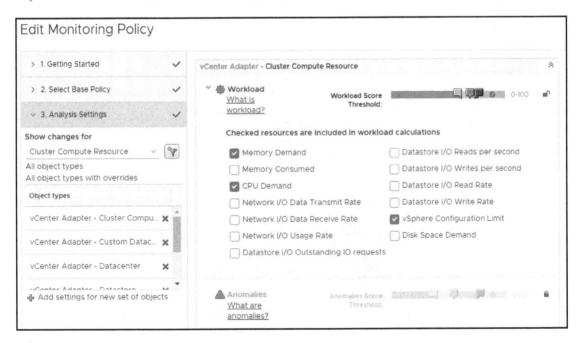

On the **Analysis Settings** page, you can override settings for badge calculations. You need to click the padlock icon to the right before you can edit. In this example, I'm editing the **Workload** badge calculation. If you want to change the settings for an object defined in a management pack, you need to click the green plus sign next to **Add settings for new set of objects** and choose it from the drop-down list.

On the **Workload Automation** page, you can edit the **Consolidate Workloads**, **Balance Workloads**, and **Cluster Headroom** workload policies. Here is also where you can select whenever to prioritize virtual machines with the lowest or highest demand during balancing and whether to allow Storage vMotion or not.

The **Override** settings from additional policies drop-down menu enable you to select policy templates that you can add into the overall policy.

Built-in policies are provided for you to configure settings such as overcommit ratios, buffers, alerts, time periods, and peak usage periods. Choose from the built-in policies, policies provided by installed management packs, or policies that you created:

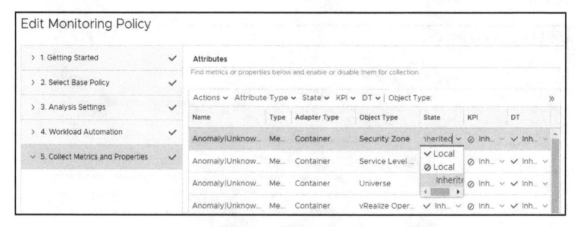

On the **Collect Metrics and Properties** page, you can find all the metrics and properties available in vRealize Operations. In your policy, you can enable or disable the collection of attribute types, which include metrics, properties, and super metrics.

These attribute settings are used by symptom definitions, specifically the metric-based and property-based symptom definitions. Since these settings affect the alerts that are generated and the results that are reported in dashboard scores, you must be aware of which symptoms are available that use the metrics and properties that you are customizing.

You can identify whether a metric, property, or super metric attribute is considered to be a **Key Performance Indicator (KPI)** when vRealize Operations reports the collected data in the dashboards. For example, you might identify disk command latency to be a KPI on a datastore cluster object. KPIs can be inherited from the starting point policy:

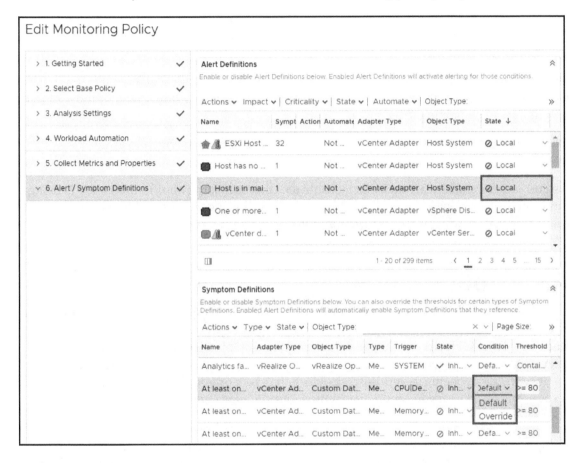

On the **Alert/Symptom Definitions** page, you can suppress a smart alert from an adapter that is not useful to you. You do this by changing the state of the adapter to **Local**. For example, out-of-the-box alerts are disabled for the **Host is in maintenance for at least 72 hours** alert definition.

Here is where you can also change a symptom definition threshold. You can do this by selecting **Override** from the **Condition** column.

You can only change the symptom definition if a threshold is defined in the last column and not a dynamic condition.

For example, you can override at least one cluster in the custom data center has high CPU demand workload symptom definition and change the default threshold value that will generate an warning alert.

On the **Custom Profiles** tab, you can specify setup profiles of typical objects and the resources they consume, then vRealize Operations can show you how many of those objects will fit in your remaining capacity.

On the **Apply Policy to Groups** tab, you can select the groups to which to apply the policies.

As you can see, policies are an indispensable tool that can help you fine-tune what is being monitored in your environment and at what threshold value alerts should be generated for each and every metric in vRealize Operations.

Alert notifications

Unless you have a very small IT footprint, you probably can't go through your environment often enough to make sure everything is performing as expected. And if you have high **Recovery Time Objective** (RTO) and **Recovery Point Objective** (RPO) objectives hanging over your head, it's even more difficult. That's where alert notifications can help. Once you identify the components in your infrastructure that you, or your business unit, are responsible for, it's easy to set up alert notifications to warn you of potential problems in your environment.

Using a notification, you can send triggered alerts to an external alert notification system. For example, you can send alerts by using email. You connect vRealize Operations to the external alert notification system by configuring an outbound alert plugin.

The outbound alert plugin has different use cases, as shown in the following table:

Alert plugin	Usage
Standard Email	Email alert notifications
SNMP Trap	Log alerts on an SNMP Trap server
Log File	Log alerts to a file on a vRealize Operations instance
REST API	Send alerts to another REST-enabled application
Smarts SAM	Send alert notifications to EMC Smarts Server Assurance Manager

To create an outbound alert plugin instance, you have to perform the following steps:

- Select the plugin type
- Provide a plugin instance name
- Configure the communication settings for the plugin type that you select

 The plugin instance is automatically enabled after it is created.

Configuring alert notifications

For the purpose of this example, we will configure the Standard Email plugin. We will be triggering a notification alert when a host loses its connection to the vCenter Server and raises a critical alert.

Perform the following steps to configure the SMTP Relay:

1. Go to the User UI on the Master Replica node by navigating to the following URL: `https://<FQDN or IP of the Master Replica Node>/ui`. Navigate to the **Alerts** section and **Alert Settings**. Select **Notification Settings** and click the plus (+) sign to add a new notification rule.

2. First, you need to configure the SMTP Relay options for the Standard Email plugin. Select **Standard Email Plugin** from the drop-down menu. In the **Add/Edit Outbound Instance** window, fill in the information required:

3. In the **Edit Rule** window, fill in the following general information:
    - **Name**: Name for the rule, for example, ESXi Host System is Down
    - **Method**: Select **Standard Email Plugin** from the drop-down menu. Select the **SMTP Relay** you configured earlier. Configure **Recipient(s)** and optionally enter values for **Notify again**, **Max Notifications**, **Delay to notify** and **Description** fields.

Under **Filtering Criteria**, fill in the following information: **Notification Trigger**: Select **Alert Definition** from the drop-down menu. Select the **Host has lost connection to vCenter Server** predefined alert.

    - **Criticality**: Select **Critical** from the drop-down menu.
    - Under **Advanced Filtering**, you can optionally define advanced filtering criteria. We will not be defining any for this example.

Your rule configuration should look similar to the following one. Click **Save** to save the rule:

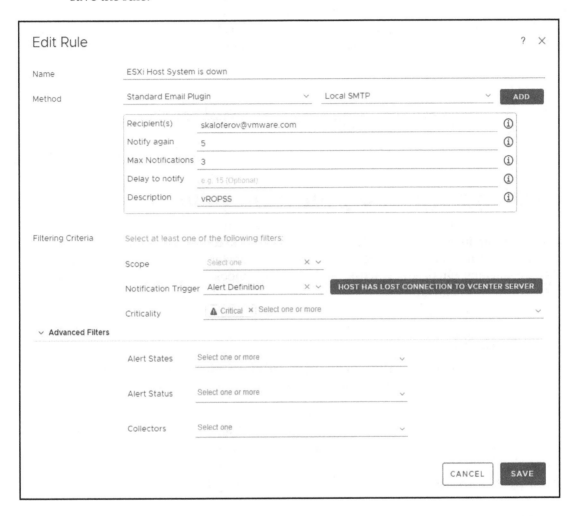

4. Now when a host system goes down, it will trigger an critical health alert. This in turn triggers a notification alert which will send an email to the recipients defined in the rule.

Now that you have vRealize Operations up and running, it's a good time to gather the different business groups and teams responsible for the different parts of the infrastructure, such as storage, networking, virtualization, and applications, and discuss for which alerts in vRealize Operations you should be sending email notifications. It's not recommended to send out notification emails for every alert vRealize Operations generates, but rather filter out only the important and critical ones.

 Since vRealize Operations 6.4, you can now also filter SNMP alert notifications at the source by Scope, Trigger, and Criticality just like with SMTP or Rest Plugin rules.

Pushing alerts into your ITSM solution

If your company has a preferred **IT Service Management** (**ITSM**) solution, there is a good chance you can integrate it with vRealize Operations and forward events to it. Most popular integrations include custom Representational State Transfer (REST) integration with VMware vRealize Orchestrator workflows, using Webhooks, or an already existing plugin that offers that functionality.

Using REST

Developers can use the API to build interactive clients of vRealize Operations. The API follows the REST style and is available since vRealize Operations 6.0 to all licensed users.

Building vRealize Orchestrator REST workflow to integrate between vRealize Operations and your ITSM solution can be a time-consuming job. Still, if your service management solution doesn't have an out-of-the-box integration with vRealize Operations, that may be the only way to go. Another drawback of this method is that, as you are pulling information on scheduled intervals, you may not be notified right away that an alert has been generated.

Using Webhooks

vRealize Operations also has support for Webhooks. These allow for an integration with any API-capable software product. In essence, Webhooks are HTTP callbacks. Compared to custom REST workflows, this will notify you right away that an alert was generated.

VMware vRealize Log Insight 3.3 and newer has support for Webhooks.

The problem with Webhooks is that the output per product is proprietary and the incoming format per product is also proprietary. These means that, by default, two different products cannot communicate with each other.

VMware offers an open source shim for both vRealize Operations and vRealize Log Insight to convert between proprietary formats. This shim covers common integrations with products such as Jenkins, vRealize Orchestrator, ServiceNow, and Bugzilla.

You can configure shims in vRealize Operations by navigating to the **Administration** tab and then to **Outbound Settings**, and configuring the **Rest Notification Plugin**. The following screenshot shows an example configuration:

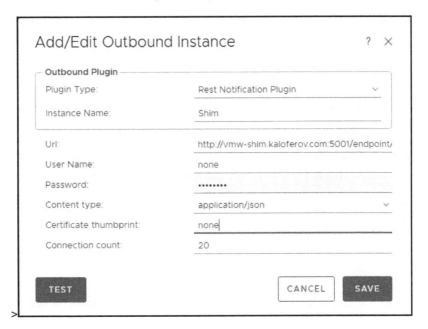

All fields are required even if you are not using them.

The shim can be downloaded from GitHub at the following address: `https://github.com/vmw-loginsight/webhook-shims`.

Using ITSM plugins

Some ITSM solutions offer out-of-the-box plugins to integrate with vRealize Operations.

For example, **ServiceNow** offers integration to vRealize Operations through its **Event Management** plugin.

For this integration to work, you have to configure a **Management, Instrumentation, and Discovery** (**MID**) server in ServiceNow and connect it to a vRealize Operations instance to obtain event information. Events are collected from vRealize Operations using a pull operation. Events will start to be received from the vRealize Operations server according to the pull interval schedule.

Refer to the ServiceNow IT Operations Management documentation online for more info.

Summary

In this chapter, we have looked at what symptoms, actions, and recommendations are, and how to create and bundle them together to create fine-tuned granular alerting that meets the environment's needs. After that, we examined what policies are made of and how they can affect alert generation. At the end, we showed how to configure alert notifications and the possible ways to push alerts to an external system, such as an ITSM solution.

In the next chapter, we will cover vRealize Operations Capacity Management functionality and see how we can define proper policies to meet your environment's needs.

7
Capacity Management Made Easy

The capacity management components of vRealize Operations are vital tools that should be in every administrator's tool shed. A poor understanding of capacity management leads to remaining capacity values or reports that do not seem realistic and are hence ignored.

In this chapter, we will dive into the details of vRealize Operation's capacity management. We will also cover the capacity management policies in detail and understand how they need to be tuned for your environment to ensure the recommendations are of the highest quality.

Resource capacity

Many enterprises have chosen to embrace a private cloud model for running their IT infrastructures. These organizations face specific capacity management challenges.

Capacity planning enables you to ensure that sufficient resources exist in your environment and that your infrastructure is working efficiently.

Capacity planning has the following benefits:

- Ensures the performance of service-level agreements
- Increases use and reduces costs
- Plans better by performing what-if modeling

Before we talk about capacity in more detail, let's go over some of the basic resource capacity concepts and terms used.

Overview and concepts

The following table lists terms that are used to understand resource capacity usage in a virtual environment:

Term	Definition
Total capacity	All the configured capacity
Limit	User-defined capacity limit (maximum limit)
Reservation	User-defined capacity that is booked (reserved)
Entitlement	Determined by the system based on shares, reservation, and limit
Overhead	Small amount of resources used to manage the hypervisor and virtualized workloads
Usable capacity	Capacity available after setting aside the capacity for high availability requirements and buffer reservations
Demand	Amount of capacity a workload asks for
Usage	Amount of capacity a workload receives
Contention	Capacity that a workload asks for but does not receive

Total capacity refers to the amount of resources that an object, such as a virtual machine, is configured with.

Entitlement is determined by the number of shares, the reservation value, and the limit value. Shares specify the relative priority or importance of a virtual machine's access to a given resource.

Demand refers to the amount of resources that a virtual machine requests due to its guest operating system and application workload. **Usage** is the amount of resources that a virtual machine gets.

In VMware vSphere®, when you enable VMware vSphere® High Availability for a cluster, resources are set aside so that you can meet the requirements for failover. Also, vRealize Operations sets aside capacity for buffers, used for capacity planning and management purposes.

Contention occurs when a workload needs more resource capacity than it receives. For example, a virtual machine workload needs 8 GB of memory to perform properly, but receives only 3 GB. **Demand** refers to usage plus contention.

The following diagram illustrates the resource capacity concepts and shows the relationships of these concepts with each other:

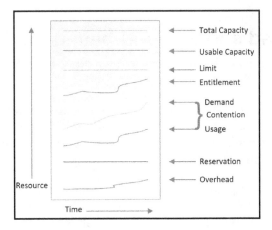

Resource capacity is measured over time. The top line represents total capacity. Usage represents the amount of resources which have been consumed, which varies over time.

A limit can be set on the amount of resources that an object can use. Entitlement, which varies over time, is calculated based on shares, limits, and reservations. Entitlement falls between the limit and the reservation.

Demand and usage vary over time. If demand is higher than usage, then resource contention occurs.

Resource capacity models

You can use one of the following resource capacity models in your environment:

- Consumed
- Allocation-based
- Demand-based
- Combination of models

The consumed model is based on the amount of physical resources that are allocated to the virtual machines. With the allocation-based model, a static amount of resources is allocated to an object, regardless of whether the object uses all of these resources.

With the demand-based model, resources are dynamically allocated to the object, based on the object's demand.

Allocation-based and demand-based models

Many organizations want to be able to optimize their capacity better, and to assess risks in their data centers based on their varying business needs.

Organizations might have varying business needs across their production, test/development, and infrastructure IT environments. For example, in production environments, businesses might want to optimize for performance, but in test/development environments, businesses might want to optimize for higher density.

If you adopt a demand based policy, the capacity planning engine will only consider the resources that are actually being used, or demanded, as consumed. So, if your 2x vCPU, 2 GB RAM, 20 GB disk VM is only using 0.5 vCPU, 1.2 GB RAM, and 4 GB disk space, the remaining resources are reported as having some capacity still available.

The following VMware Management Policies contain settings that monitor for demand and allocation models:

- **VMware Production Policy (Demand only)**: Optimized for production loads, without using allocation limits, to obtain the most capacity
- **VMware Production Policy (with Allocation)**: Optimized for production loads that require the demand and allocation capacity models
- **VMware Production Policy (without Allocation)**: Optimized for production loads that require demand capacity models, and provides the highest overcommit without contention
- **VMware Test and Dev Policy (without Allocation)**: Optimized for Dev and test environments to maximize capacity without causing significant contention, because it does not include capacity planning at the virtual machine level

We will be discussing policies again later in this chapter.

Memory consumed model

The memory consumed model is the default resource capacity model. It demonstrates the consumption of memory from a guest point of view, in contrast to the memory demand model, which is based on active memory usage from a vSphere perspective. The memory consumed model becomes relevant when applications such as Microsoft SQL Server claim all available memory at the virtual machine level, and thus report higher memory usage than the active memory used.

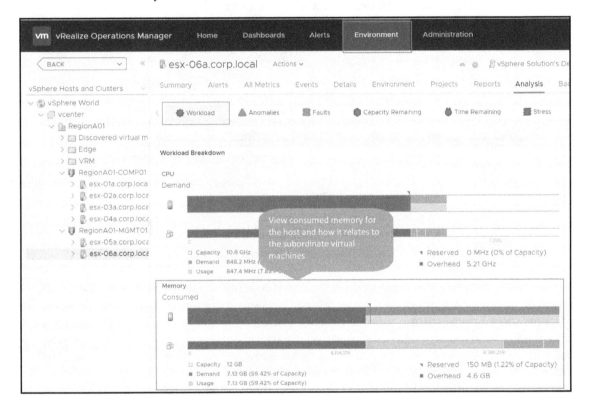

If an environment is relatively conservative in respect to capacity planning without memory over allocation, then turn on the allocated, consumed, and demand memory models. This action enables you to see how much memory you can safely get back if you relax your capacity planning policy. vRealize Operations helps ensure that you never run out or use the consumed and demand memory models for more aggressive workload deployment on hosts.

To stop vRealize Operations from reporting that your thin-provisioned storage is out of capacity, turn off the disk allocated model and only leave the demand mode active.

Preparing for capacity planning

Here are some questions that can get you started with your capacity planning discussion:

- Is your focus today on demand, allocation, or both?
- Do you overallocate the following resources on your host systems and virtual machines?
  - CPU
  - Memory
  - Storage
- If you do overallocate resources, by what percentage do you overallocate them?
- Do you use VMware vSphere High Availability?
  - If so, what percentage of hardware have you reserved for High Availability?
  - Do you use a buffer?
- Where do you place your workload types?
  - Are production workloads in their own clusters?
  - Are test/development workloads in their own clusters?

Know your priorities for managing capacity and risk across your environments. For example, performance might be the top priority for your production workloads, whereas resource use might be the top priority for your test/development workloads. You can fine-tune your capacity analysis to account for your varying business needs by using policies. Built-in policies are available for you to configure overcommit ratios, capacity buffers that are used by vRealize Operations, alerts, time periods, peak usage periods, and so on. Thus, you can make accurate and intelligent decisions in day-to-day operations.

All of these topics will be covered in more detail later in this chapter.

For now, we will only use a simple example of capacity planning for a production and a test/dev workload:

Capacity planning for a production workload	Capacity planning for a test/dev workload
Flag risk when 60 percent capacity is allocated.	Flag risk when 85 percent capacity is in demand.
Overcommit CPU 2:1.	Overcommit virtual CPU 4:1.
Do not overcommit memory.	Overcommit memory by 20 percent.
Ensure capacity for peak usage.	Allow a stress score of 10 percent.
Allocate a high percentage of capacity buffers.	Allocate a low percentage of capacity buffers.
Enable alerts.	Disable alerts.
Set a business time period to monitor and collect data.	Do not set a business time period to monitor and collect data.

Monitoring capacity

A few badges can be used to monitor capacity.

The Risk badge is an indicator of potential performance issues that might affect your environment in the near future.

In addition to the **Risk badge**, the **Capacity Remaining**, **Time Remaining**, and **Stress badges** are often used to assess whether an object is experiencing resource capacity risks.

The **Compliance badge** is often used to assess a security risk.

The **Capacity Remaining badge** represents the capability of your environment to accommodate new virtual machines.

We covered all of these badges in great detail in earlier chapters. Before continuing, make sure that you understand each of them and what they represent. If necessary, go back and review what we've already covered.

Capacity management for vRealize Operations policies

The first and most important aspect to cover with capacity management in vRealize Operations is all about policies. Policies are the King. The calculations and recommendations for all areas of capacity management are directly related to what policy options are configured and currently active on the selected resource.

It is highly improbable that one policy is suitable for all workload types such as a server, VDI, production, dev/test, and so on. It is important to understand when defining policies that the configuration is usually a trade-off of performance vs. utilization. An example of this is shown in the following diagram:

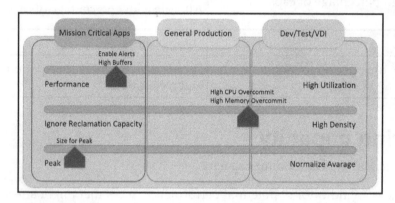

Defining the correct capacity management policies for your environment

As just discussed, the accuracy and value of capacity management views and reports relies on an administrator's ability to correctly translate their environmental requirements into policies. Although it is important to understand that capacity management in vRealize Operations is no longer limited to vSphere instances, for the purposes of this chapter, vSphere will be the primary focus. The ability for capacity management to extend to non-vSphere components is based on the associated Solution (also known as the Management Pack), and as such will not be covered in detail in this chapter. It is important to note, however, that many of the concepts in this chapter relate to capacity management in general, and as such may also be useful for non-vSphere solutions.

Resource containers

One of the first decisions that needs to be made in relation to capacity management is what resource containers are going to be selected. A resource container is a set of metrics from an object type that gives capacity data for one particular aspect of an object. The resource containers for a resource are usually quite predictable and are defined in the Capacity/Time Remaining section of a vRealize Operations policy. The solution provider will use metrics that would commonly be used for capacity management within that field. In vSphere, for example, the most common options are containers such as CPU, Memory, Network I/O, Disk Space, and so on. Although an administrator cannot define what metrics are used for resource containers or define their own resource containers, they can select which of the available resource containers for a given resource kind are used to calculate capacity.

There are two important points to take away from this:

1. Even within the same adapter type (for example, the vCenter Adapter) different object types will have different resource containers available to choose from. For example, a vSphere Cluster allows Memory, CPU, Network I/O, Disk I/O, and Disk Space as containers to choose from, whereas a vSphere Datastore only supports Disk I/O and Disk Space. Although this may be quite obvious why this is the case in this example, it is important to keep this in mind for other resources.
2. Only select the resource containers that you believe should contribute to capacity management for the selected environment. By default, most adapters have all available resource containers enabled.

The second point also leads to a very important design decision when creating your capacity policies. vRealize Operations will always calculate the remaining capacity of an object based on the most constrained resource. Although this seems very practical in most use cases, it requires the administrator to be aware of how each container is calculated and if they really want to use that container type for everyday capacity management.

Let's go through a few quick scenarios to explain the aforementioned. Both of these scenarios will be based on the commonly used vSphere Cluster as the object type. To keep things simple, we will just use total capacity, used capacity, and remaining capacity for calculations.

vRealize Operations also allows us to apply virtual machine profiles to this remaining capacity to give us an idea of how many more VMs we could provide with this remaining capacity. These profiles reflect common sizes, as well as your environment's average VM profile. For this example, an Average VM profile has been provided.

Scenario 1 – CPU and memory-enabled only

Looking at the following table, we can see that since only the CPU and memory containers are enabled, the most constraining resource is the memory, with a remaining capacity of 12.5 percent:

	Used	Average VM Usage	Total Capacity	Used Capacity	Remaining Capacity
CPU	Yes	3.0 GHz	560.0 GHz	300.0 GHz	260.0 GHz (46.4%)
Memory	Yes	7.0 GB	800 GB	700 GB	**100 GB (12.5%)**
Disk I/O	No	2.6 MBps	760 MBps	260 MBps	500 MBps (65.7%)
Network I/O	No	3 Mbps	20,000 Mbps	300 Mbps	19,700 Mbps (98.5%)
Disk Space	No	195 GB	20.0 TB	19.5 TB	500 GB (2.5%)

This results in an overall remaining capacity value or score of 12.5 percent. As per our Average VM profile, only another 14 VMs could fit (assuming we were filling to 100 percent) based on their memory usage. However, hypothetically, another 86 VMs could fit based on CPU alone, but this fact is largely irrelevant as you can't provision VMs with CPU and zero memory.

Scenario 2 - CPU, memory, disk I/O, and disk space enabled only

Looking at the following table, we are using exactly the same figures, but we have also selected Datastore disk space to be included as a container for capacity management. This has had quite a dramatic effect on the capacity remaining score, as we are now down to 2.5% remaining capacity (or 2 VMs, based on disk space):

	Used	Average VM Usage	Total Capacity	Used Capacity	Remaining Capacity
CPU	Yes	3.0 GHz	560.0 GHz	300.0 GHz	260.0 GHz (46.4%)
Memory	Yes	7.0 GB	800 GB	700 GB	100 GB (12.5%)
Disk I/O	No	2.6 MBps	760 MBps	260 MBps	500 MBps (65.7%)
Network I/O	No	3 Mbps	20,000 Mbps	300 Mbps	19,700 Mbps (98.5%)
Disk space	Yes	195 GB	20.0 TB	19.5 TB	**500 GB (2.5%)**

Initially, your immediate thought might be, "Well this container should be enabled or else we are excluding important data from the capacity calculations". However, this all varies based on the target environment and what principals are in place.

In most environments, unless you are provisioning all your SAN storage to your vSphere clusters upfront, the total capacity value for Disk Space is misleading as your storage administrators provision new LUNs as required. This is because what the total capacity is to a vSphere administrator, is actually used/allocated capacity to a SAN administrator. In most cases, vRealize Operations has no actual visibility of how much unallocated storage remains on the physical array.

Now, there are exceptions to this example, such as pre-allocating all your storage to vSphere clusters or using a technology such as VSAN, where one large pool of storage is simply created at creation time. However, generally, you will need to rely on a partner solution pack such as EMC Analytics to provide the capacity data metrics required to properly analyze the storage array. As such, you would disable the Disk Space container at the vCenter Adapter layer and enable % Free FAST VP Pool capacity at the EMC Analytics Adapter layer.

 As vRealize Operations will always calculate the remaining capacity based on the most constrained resource container of an object, ensure that only the required containers are selected in the applied policy.

Observed versus configured metrics

Another important factor to consider when choosing what resource containers should be used is where the data supporting the resource container originates and how it is calculated. With vSphere data, each container's total capacity is either configured or observed, as shown in the following screenshot:

	Total Capacity
⌄ CPU	28.01 GHz Configured
> Demand	28.01 GHz Configured
> Allocation	64 vCPUs Configured (Includes overcommit) · Overcommit 8.0:1
> Memory	68 GB Configured
> Network I/O	200 MBps Observed
> Datastore I/O	485.33 MBps Observed
> Disk Space	5.55 TB Configured (Includes overcommit) Overcommit 0.0%
> vSphere Configuration Limit	2,048 Virtual Machines Configured

The configured total capacity is a hard, factual piece of data that vRealize Operations has access to or is able to directly derive from other data. A good example of this is host or cluster CPU and memory capacity. Through vCenter, vRealize Operations knows exactly how much GHz and GB of memory an ESXi host has.

Conversely, the observed total capacity is a value that vRealize Operations has had to estimate based on observed historical maximums. Although this is not necessarily ideal, it is necessary for certain data sources. For example, Datastore I/O capacity can be a useful capacity management metric, however, there is no way for vRealize Operations to know exactly what the maximum I/O of a Datastore is when little is known about the underlying storage. Even if vRealize Operations did have a detailed understanding of underlying disk pools and RAID groups, there are just too many variables in the equation to give a definitive maximum.

Observed containers also usually suffer from the trade-offs of using infrastructure. When a shared resource is used by more and more vSphere objects, its initial total capacity estimate becomes less and less accurate. A good example of this is if a new array is commissioned and one LUN is presented as a Datastore to vSphere for performance testing. vRealize Operations will observe the I/O during the performance testing and determine that a very high total capacity is available on that Datastore. However, as more LUNs and Datastores are provisioned from the same Array/Disk Pool/RAID group, they are all sharing the same backend total pool of performance. As such, the original observed total capacity for the original Datastore will be too high for normal operation.

Policy recommendations for containers

Selecting the right containers to include in capacity management depends greatly on the adapter (source of the data), the target environment, and any organizational policies. Continuing on from the current focus of a vSphere Compute Cluster, since it is the most common object, administrators would be required to perform capacity management reporting. We will quickly cover some common recommendations for what containers we enable on our generic production vSphere Cluster policy:

- **CPU (Enabled)**: CPU should generally be enabled when assessing capacity for virtual machines, hosts, and clusters. CPU is a configured container and is probably the most accurate container used on vSphere objects. As a general rule, when administrators are sizing vSphere clusters or deciding what type of new hardware should be procured, CPU and memory are usually at the top of the list. This is because CPU and memory are the two most common constraining factors of capacity in virtualized environments.

- **Memory (Enabled)**: In similar circumstances to CPU, memory is usually always enabled and generally a critical container for capacity management of virtualized environments. Memory is also a configured container, however, the accuracy of memory demand (which will be discussed shortly) varies based on workload and right-sizing. In most production server virtualization environments, memory is the constraining resource for capacity management. It is also often the most wasted resource, and as such is critical for capacity management reporting.
- **Network I/O (Disabled)**: Due to some of the drawbacks of observed containers and the fact that most administrators will use a separate solution pack for network and storage, these containers are commonly disabled for capacity analysis in many environments. It is also rare that Network I/O is a constraining factor in most environments since the common adoption of 10 GB Ethernet.
- **Datastore I/O (Disabled)**: In similar circumstances to Network I/O, Datastore I/O is commonly disabled due to the constraints of observed containers. However, unlike Network I/O, Datastore I/O and storage performance, in general, is a highly important area of capacity management for vitalized environments. As such, it is recommended that an administrator is keeping an eye on the performance capacity of their storage (not just the storage capacity), but this is commonly performed using a vendor-provided solution pack.
- **Disk Space (Situational)**: The use of disk space as a capacity management container depends on your target environment and procedures. As a general rule, disk space can be extremely useful as a capacity management metric if your storage is pre-provisioned or you are using thin provisioning at the VMDK level. As such, there are some situations where you may or may not enable disk space.

We would recommend enabling disk space when:

- All storage from the physical array is pre-provisioned to the vSphere environment
- Using Datastore-level thin provisioning (thin VMDKs)
- Using VSAN or local storage

We would recommend another solution when:

- Storage capacity is managed at the array level and LUNs (Datastores) are provisioned on demand

- Array-level thin provisioning is being used, such as FAST VP, and your environment has targeted overallocation ratios at the array level

  As mentioned previously, in the case where storage is being provisioned on demand, or array-based thin provisioning is being used with over-commitment, it is recommended that a vendor-provided solution pack be used to pull in capacity metrics from the array directly.

- **vSphere configuration limits (Enabled)**: The use of vSphere configuration limits as part of capacity management is a new feature of vRealize Operations 6.0. In most cases, it is unlikely that there will be a concern, however they still provide useful information, so it is recommended to leave them enabled. vSphere configuration limits for capacity management can be particularly useful when looking at the ESXi host level, for example.

Demand versus allocation

Now that we have discussed the importance of containers, it is time to move on to an equally important discussion on demand vs. allocation. Demand and allocation are different methods for calculating the capacity on containers, and are set in the same location as enabling the containers themselves, as shown as follows.

Before we dive into specific containers, you can simply think of demand as how much of a resource is being used, where allocation is how many resources the object has been configured with or given.

If both demand and allocation are enabled for a container, it results in two different calculations being performed on the resource, and just like overall capacity, the most constraining result will be used. Therefore, it is important to understand where these calculations are derived from to ensure the capacity estimates match your real-world environment.

Demand and allocation calculations and recommendations

The following are the demand and allocation calculations and recommendations.

CPU demand

CPU demand is a derived metric that is made up of multiple sub-metrics (in this case CPU usage, CPU ready, and so on), and is used to estimate the amount of CPU an object actually wants to consume. Although demand and usage are often identical, it is possible for demand to exceed usage; this would indicate resource contention. Demand is a useful way to manage capacity, since a virtual machine will rarely use all the CPU it has been configured with; this is the basic principle of over commitment. You will also find that demand usually matches the Usage % metric, which is observed inside the vCenter web client.

Recommendation for CPU demand:

As CPU demand accurately reflects the amount of CPU the workloads in your environment are requesting, regardless of what they have been allocated, we recommend enabling this container in nearly all situations.

CPU allocation

From a host or cluster perspective, CPU allocation is the ratio of virtual machine CPUs (vCPU) to physical ESXi host cores (pCPU). Ignoring buffers and overcommitment (which will be discussed shortly) allows an administrator to manage capacity simply based on this one to X mapping. Using CPU allocation as a capacity container is usually based on environment design or special use cases. For example, if an administrator had a cluster dedicated to mission-critical applications and there was an associated organizational policy that CPU overcommitment should not exceed 2:1 (2 vCPUs to every pCPU), that administrator could then use the allocation model in combination with overcommitment to ensure that this ratio was never breached.

Recommendation for CPU allocation:

As a general rule for generic production server clusters, it is recommended to either disable this container altogether or ensure that you have an overcommitment ratio high enough so that this container does not become the most constraining resource unnecessarily.

Memory demand

Memory demand is often the least understood metric in vRealize Operations, and as such it causes a great deal of confusion and often leads to incorrect capacity management data. Memory demand, like CPU demand, is derived from a variety of metrics to easily show the administrator how much memory a virtual machine requires or is asking for.

The difference between CPU and memory demand is that CPU demand is based on CPU usage, which is a very accurate metric that vSphere is easily able to record. Memory demand, on the other hand, is primarily based on the metric's Active Memory.

Active Memory is defined as the "amount of memory that is actively used, as estimated by VMkernel based on recently touched memory pages." This concept is well-described in a VMware vSphere Blog called *Understanding vSphere Active Memory,* by Mark Achtemichuk . To read the full article, visit:

https://blogs.vmware.com/vsphere/2013/10/understanding-vsphere-active-memory.html

For the purposes of capacity planning, Active Memory is a counter that can help an administrator understand how aggressively memory is being used inside a virtual machine. The Active Memory counter is based on an estimation of how much memory has been accessed in a 20 second period (vCenter sampling period) and then averaged into a 5-minute value for vRealize Operations. Due to the nature of the short sampling period, it often does not reflect the full memory requirement of an application. This is because there is no guarantee that the memory accessed within the sample periods is unique. This can especially be the case if another layer of memory management is involved above the OS, such as Java virtual machine or database engines.

With the issues surrounding active memory as a capacity planning metric, it often begs the question, "why does vRealize Operations not use memory consumed for capacity planning instead?" This is because the memory consumed metric also has its shortcomings. With the introduction of large pages and **Address Space Layout Randomization (ASLR)**, it is very common that a guest consumed memory will quickly match its configured memory shortly after boot. This, in turn, essentially results in the memory consumed matching that of the allocation model.

It is important to consider that the memory demand model does have its advantages and should not always be quickly dismissed as irrelevant. Memory demand is very useful in determining undersized virtual machines as well as playing a vital role in making recommendations for VM right sizing. For the purposes of capacity planning, vRealize Operations is also analyzing memory demand over a long period of time (30 days, by default), and periods of high usage are used as the baseline for demand rather than the raw average over that period.

Recommendation for memory demand:

As a general rule for generic production server clusters, it is recommended that the memory demand model is left enabled as a container, since although, it's accuracy can vary, it is often too aggressive rather than conservative. This, in turn, results in memory demand rarely being the constraining container when memory allocation is also used.

Memory allocation

Memory allocation is very straightforward and often well-understood. Memory allocation is simply how much memory each virtual machine is configured with in vSphere. Although this allows for a simple metric to perform capacity analysis with, it suffers from the obvious weakness of oversized workloads being used to judge the amount of remaining capacity. Simply because a VM is configured with 24 GB of RAM does not imply that it actually requires this amount of resources. This, in turn, results in overly conservative capacity planning, unless right-sizing is regularly undertaken.

Recommendation for memory allocation:

We recommend using memory allocation as an enabled container, mostly due to the issues surrounding memory demand. Using memory allocation as a capacity metric will imply what resources a virtual machine is configured with in terms of memory it requires. As such, workload right-sizing will not be automatically taken into account.

The primary purpose behind this recommendation is that due to the effects of large pages, as previously mentioned, VMs now generally consume all the memory they are configured with, regardless of their normal demand. Therefore, unless large pages are not being used (such as in a VDI environment), the memory allocation model most accurately reflects the memory that is consumed at the vSphere host level.

Setting overcommitment

Overcommitment is a basic principle and benefit of virtualization, and it plays an important role in capacity planning. As discussed in the section *Demand versus allocation*, overcommitment is only applicable to the allocation model, and allows either a percentage or ratio of overcommitment to be set for CPU, memory, and disk space. Overcommitment is set as part of the usable capacity section of a policy, as shown in the following screenshot:

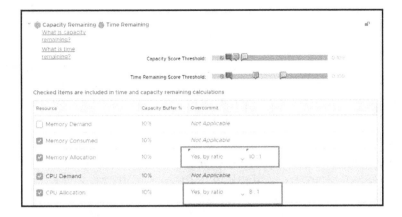

CPU overcommitment

As discussed in the *CPU Allocation* section, CPU overcommitment allows a ratio or percentage of CPU overcommitment to be set, affecting the amount of total capacity. The following screenshot shows the effect that CPU overcommitment has on the total capacity. The cluster shown in the following screenshot has 8 pCPUs configured. However, with an 8:1 overcommitment ratio in place, we now have a total cluster capacity of 64 vCPUs:

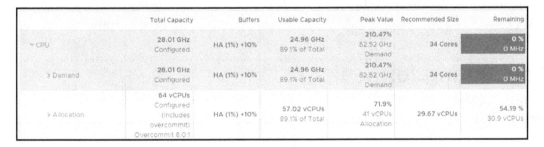

When using the CPU allocation model, it is generally the case that some level of CPU overcommitment should be set. If you do not have a specific level of CPU overcommitment in mind for an environment, this can often be set at a fairly aggressive level such as 6:1 or 8:1.

Memory overcommitment

Memory overcommitment is relatively straightforward since the introduction of large pages and other factors which affect **Transparent Page Sharing** (**TPS**). Memory overcommitment is built on the age-old vSphere principal that due to VMs not requiring all the amount of memory they are configured with, as well as leveraging TPS to share common memory blocks, we can overcommit memory on a host or cluster relatively safely.

We have already touched on this with the introduction of large pages with 64-bit operating systems and hardware-assisted memory virtualization; virtual machines now generally consume all the memory they are configured with. Also, combine this with a recent change to combat a rare security edge case inter-virtual machine; TPS is now disabled by default as per VMware KB 2080735.

Unless inter-VM TPS is re-enabled and large pages are disabled (which can be common for dev/test or VDI environments), memory overcommitment should generally be set to zero.

Disk space overcommitment

Disk space overcommitment is relevant if using vSphere Thin provisioning (Thin VMDKs) on VMFS Datastores. This allows administrators to set a target overcommitment percentage on the storage to benefit from thin provisioning. This percentage should be based on the organizational policy and in line with the associated risks of overcommitting storage.

Accounting for peaks

With the big topics covered, it is time to move on to the relatively simpler (however just as important) topic– peak consideration.

Peak consideration was originally introduced in vCenter Operations Manager 5.6, and allows the stress metric to be used to account for capacity spikes and peaks. The use of this setting has two main effects:

1. Virtual Machine demand is now based on peak demand rather than average
2. Right-sizing recommendations are based on peak demand rather than average

The first key takeaway is that this setting only effects demand; allocation is unaffected. Therefore, this setting is most relevant to CPU demand (as this is more than often a constraining resource) and right-sizing recommendations for both CPU and memory.

The second key takeaway is that it changes the way demand is calculated and therefore the remaining capacity calculation. Let's go through an example to see its effect. The following screenshot shows a vSphere cluster with peak consideration disabled. As capacity is now calculated on an average, we can see that we have 43.78% remaining capacity.

The following screenshot shows cluster capacity with peak consideration disabled:

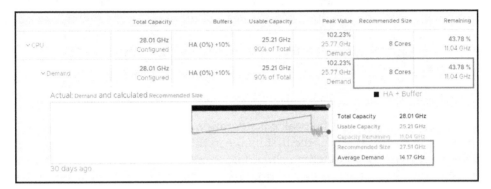

Now, let's show the same cluster's remaining capacity with peak consideration enabled. As capacity is now calculated based on peak demand rather than average, we can see that we have only 1.78% remaining capacity due to some short spikes in the demand.

The following screenshot shows cluster capacity with peak consideration enabled:

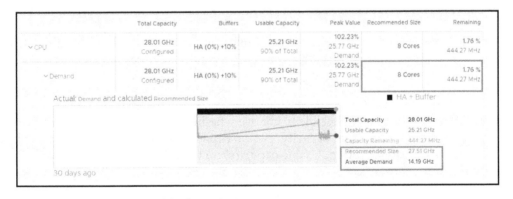

With peak considerations enabled, the remaining value is now showing the amount of used capacity based on the maximum observed in the time period.

The end result is a far more conservative estimate of used capacity, which is based more on peak than average.

As mentioned previously, peak considerations also play a role in right-sizing recommendations. The effect is similar to the one seen at the cluster level, however, generally the difference between the two options is less extreme. This is primarily due to the fact that the right-sizing recommendations are looking at an individual VM rather than the whole cluster level. As such, a right-sizing recommendation is already taking workload peaks into account to some degree. This is based on the principle that only a few would have the need of a right-sizing report for virtual machines that only looked at average usage and could not cater for workload peaks.

Recommendations:

At the end of the day, the use of the peak consideration option comes down to your environmental requirements as per the first image in this chapter. For mission-critical and production-type workloads, this setting should be enabled to ensure a conservative capacity management model that caters for peak workload. For Dev/Test or VDI clusters however, you may choose to disable this setting and simply work off average workload for capacity demand. Although this may sound like you are setting yourself up for failure, remember that not all workloads peak at the same time, and, in certain environments, consolidation and cost may be more important than guaranteed performance.

High Availability and buffers (usable capacity)

Now, we reach the final component of capacity management policies, **High Availability (HA)** and buffers. The concept of usable capacity is not new to vRealize Operations 6.0, but there are some great improvements, especially around virtual machines.

First and foremost, we need to discuss usable capacity vs. actual capacity. In vCenter Operations Manager 5.x, it was possible to choose whether your remaining capacity was based on usable capacity or actual capacity. Actual capacity is the raw capacity of an object based on its physical configuration. Usable capacity, on the other hand, is the physical capacity minus buffers to reflect a real-world environment.

Since vRealize Operations 6.0, you now no longer have the option to select actual capacity, only which buffers effect usable capacity. This is a far better outcome, because I cannot think of one use case where an administrator would want the capacity to be based on physical raw capacity. Even in an environment where HA was not required, without any CPU or memory buffer, you do not want your ESXi hosts filled up to 100% where swapping and unresponsiveness are occurring.

High Availability and buffers affect your capacity estimates by removing a percentage of total capacity and therefore basing the capacity and time remaining badges using the smaller, usable capacity value. This is a common practice that administrators would previously do, since running any hypervisor (or workload, for that matter) at 100% usually encounters issues. An example of this is when memory becomes critically low on an ESXi host; the memory states progress to the state where memory compression and hypervisor swapping is occurring.

The following image is based on the vRealize Operations Time Remaining example diagram that shows the buffer's effect on capacity:

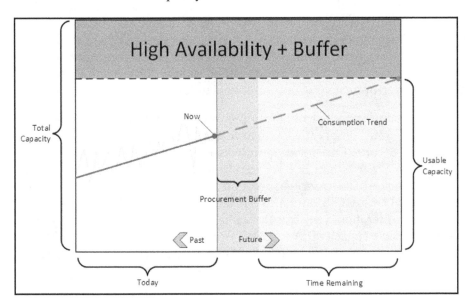

High Availability

Asking vRealize Operations to take vSphere High Availability into account is as simple as enabling the checkbox. This is probably one of the best features of vRealize Operations capacity management as it is often something that people forget to asses when judging cluster capacity, or are under the disbelief that HA Admission Control will do this for you.

Although vRealize Operations does check what admission control policy is in effect and its value for each cluster, this inventory is only updated every 24 hours. Keep in mind that changes to HA (including enabling or disabling it completely) won't be reflected in usable capacity until the next day.

Without discussing vSphere HA in too much detail, I have a quote from the vSphere Availability Guide:

> *"vCenter Server uses Admission Control to ensure that sufficient resources are available in a cluster to provide failover protection and to ensure that virtual machine resource reservations are respected."*

What is important from the above statement that specifically relates to capacity management is that HA Admission Control is ensuring machine resource reservations are respected. Although the 'host cluster tolerates' and percentage models differ in the calculate capacity, by default both models are based on reservations to either determine the percentage, remaining capacity, or the slot size. Where this becomes an issue for administrators is the common practice of only using reservations where required. When using the percentage of cluster resources model, for example, a large number of VMs are estimated at the default of size 32 MHz and 0 MB + Memory Overhead. This usually results in administrators over-provisioning environments unless reservations are used extensively.

vRealize Operations implements a much simpler model of accounting for vSphere HA, which although far more conservative, will save administrators the headache of commonly over-provisioning. vRealize Operations simply assess which admission control in is effect and removes that total percentage of resources from the total capacity accordingly. For example, the percentage of a cluster resources admission control policy that is in effect with a 10% reservation on cluster CPU and a 15% reservation on cluster memory will be taken into the buffer's consideration. vRealize Operations will only take HA buffers into consideration for usable capacity if Admission Control is active. If HA is enabled but Admission Control is disabled, vSphere HA will have no effect on usable capacity.

Buffers

Buffers, like HA, remove a percentage of total capacity to help define the usable capacity value which is used for analysis. An important point to be aware of is that buffers are applied to total capacity after the HA buffer is taken into account.

Although most administrators would simply set both CPU and memory buffers at 10%, for example, it is important to understand that buffers need to be set accordingly for your model (demand or allocation), and, more importantly, based on your workload types.

When using the demand model, for example, buffers become critical, ensuring sub-hour peaks can be handled that are too short to affect stress and therefore the demand calculation. It is recommended that, in conservative mission critical or production environments, large buffers be set to cater for sub-hour spikes in interactive server workloads or other workloads that are sensitive to user response time.

Projects

Projects are a new feature that first appeared in vRealize Operations 6.0 and replaced the old 'what-if' functionality from vCenter Operations Manager 5.x. A project is an upcoming change to your environment that either affects the supply or demand (or both) of capacity. Projects allow capacity modeling to help an administrator set up hypothetical scenarios, such as adding or removing virtual machines and hosts from a cluster. These scenarios can then be used to determine how a pipeline of incoming organizational projects will affect the time remaining calculation. An image of the Projects screen is shown as follows:

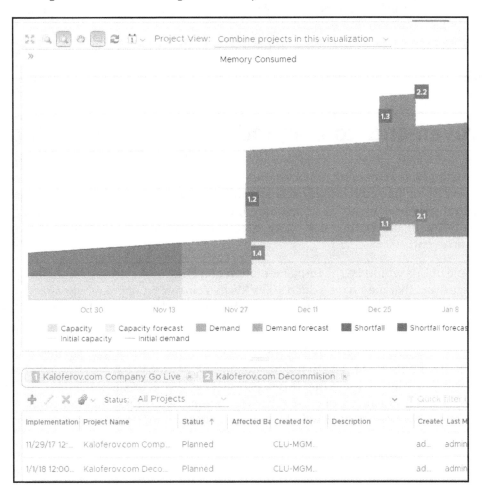

Although projects may be similar to the what-if scenarios, it is not just a small upgrade. Projects are a complete overhaul of the scenario modeling capability, and their features and improvements include:

- Projects are persistent and can be saved so that they are no longer removed when you log out
- Projects can be shared among different users in vRealize Operations
- Project can be set to occur at a future date and time, not simply applying from now
- Projects can be set to be either planned or committed, and, as such, permanently effect time remaining
- A single project can have multiple scenarios that affect demand and capacity

The detail on how to create projects can be found in the vRealize Operations User Guide.

Improvements to demand or capacity trending

Although previously vRealize Operations did a good job of reporting capacity remaining and forecasting time remaining, this was under the requirements that demand and/or supply were changing at a relatively steady and predictable rate. However, if sudden changes to supply or demand weren't counted, vRealize Operations would often readjust violently, throwing off the time remaining calculation completely for what could potentially be a one-off event.

An example of this would be the implementation of a large VM commissioning or migration project that may have added 100 VMs to a cluster on one day. vRealize Operations would then adjust the trend line to compensate for the dramatic growth, rather than analyzing if this growth was a common event.

Capacity trending has been greatly improved, with new algorithms that can detect major changes in the environment. The first time vRealize Operations observes a major change in the environment, it will assume that this is part of a cycle, and as such, the time remaining will not be affected. However, once vRealize Operations determines that this event was not a cyclical environment change, it will then be considered an offset, and the time remaining will be accurately updated accordingly.

Pipeline management

One of the big reasons for the changes from what-if to projects is to allow administrators to have an increased focus on pipeline management and capacity forecasting. Although previously the 'what-if' scenarios were useful for determining the impact of an upcoming project or change without the ability to save them, they could not be used for pipeline management. As such, administrators often had to keep separate spreadsheets to keep track of how many incoming projects had been given capacity approval but were still to be deployed.

Projects capability in vRealize Operations allows administrators not only to see the impact of the upcoming project, but also to keep track of all projects that have been given approval and combine their result. This, combined with the fact that different implementation dates can be set on different projects, allows administrators to keep track of how much capacity they have committed to other teams but have not actually delivered yet. By default, as per the image at the start of the *Projects* section, vRealize Operations combines all projects into one display that has been dragged into the active project bar. It also shows the most constraining resource, however, administrators can also select to view other resources or compare projects rather than combine them.

Planned versus committed projects

Before we end the chapter, let's quickly discuss the difference between planned and committed projects. The major difference between planned and committed projects is that committed projects affect the time remaining, assuming that this policy option is enabled as per the recommendation in this chapter. The difference between the two project types also allows an administrator to see, at a glance, what projects are definitely going to occur vs. what projects are in the maybe category.

Planned projects are useful for analyzing the impact of future projects or changes in your environment that have not yet been confirmed. They are also useful for modeling different scenarios, such as changes to supply. It is common that most committed projects will start their lives as planned projects. Once it is confirmed that the project will occur, an administrator can change it to committed.

Committed projects, on the other hand, and designed to reflect that a project is now confirmed and the associated changes to its capacity have been committed to external stakeholders. For example, large upcoming projects will require a number of machines in a week's time. The client has confirmed the deployment is going ahead and requires that capacity be available for the deployment.

Custom Datacenter

A **Custom Datacenter** (**CDC**) can be used to perform capacity management and planning across disparate groupings of capacity providers.

You can associate all the analysis Badge data for these groupings. Using custom data centers, you can group various capacity provider objects, such as hosts, clusters, virtual data centers, and VMware vCenter Server® instances. These objects might span multiple vCenter Server instances.

For example, if you have an SQL Server environment that is made up of two clusters, but each cluster is in different vCenter Server environments, you can use a custom data center to track performance and capacity of this environment as a holistic SQL Server environment.

Creating a Custom Datacenter

You can create a custom datacenter from the **Custom Datacenter** tab of the Environment page.

A list of the objects in your environment appears in the CDC wizard. You can select objects to add to your custom data center:

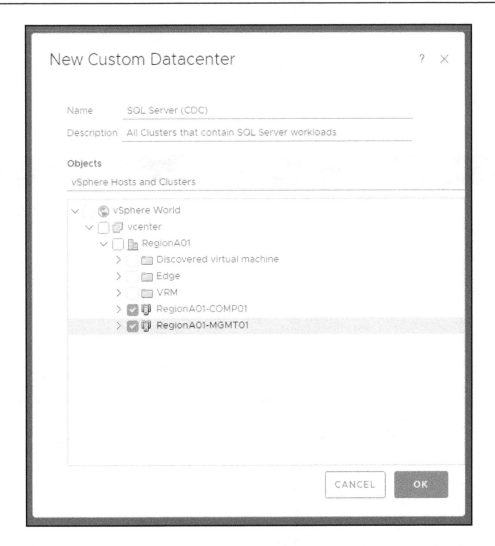

When you add an object, its children become part of the custom data center. An object can belong to multiple custom data centers. The objects that you can add are vCenter Server, vSphere data center, vSphere cluster, and VMware ESXi™ host.

You can clone a custom datacenter and use it as a template.

Profiles

vRealize Operations uses profiles to calculate how many virtual machines with the specified memory demand model can fit in your environment. You can see this calculation in the **What Will Fit** panel of the **Capacity Remaining** tab on a container object.

By clicking on each profile, you can see the profile's properties:

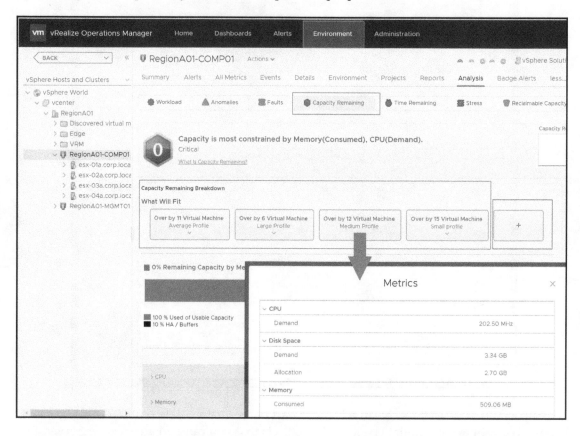

In addition to the default profiles, you can create custom profiles based on specific sizing requirements in your environment:

- Custom profiles show how many more of a specified object can fit in your environment given the available capacity and object configuration
- When creating capacity projects, you can use custom profiles in addition to the default profile

Creating custom profiles

You can create custom profiles by navigating to **Administration**, **Configuration**, and then the **Custom Profiles** workspace.

When you create a profile for an object, you define its metrics configuration. Calculations for the object are based on the metrics that you specify. You can create new metrics or populate metrics from an existing object or profile by clicking the **Populate Metrics From the** button, and modify them for this profile if necessary.

Summary

In this chapter, we have covered the detailed yet important topic of capacity management in vRealize Operations 6.6. We discussed what the resource capacity models are. We have also discussed how to set vRealize Operations 6.6 capacity management policies, and more importantly, why a certain policy should be set over another, based on your environment. At the end, we covered how projects, custom datacenters, and profiles further help us perform capacity management and planning in our environment.

In the next chapter, we will see how we can use vRealize Operations Tags, application groups, and custom groups in conjunction with Super Metrics to create dashboards that provide business-oriented value to stakeholders.

8
Aligning vRealize Operations with Business Outcomes

In this chapter, we will discuss how we can meet business-oriented reporting needs by using vRealize Operations tags, application groups, and custom groups with super metrics, and subsequently using those super metrics in dashboards before reporting back to stakeholders with any necessary business information.

What is business-oriented reporting?

While vRealize Operations is an excellent forensic analysis and near-real-time virtual infrastructure monitoring solution, it is a poor solution with regard to business-oriented reporting, even with its additional performance and capacity planning capabilities. Building reports around logical business structures such as services, applications, departments, business groups, organizational units, and so on, as well as providing visibility, utilization, consumption, and performance insights to key business and application stakeholders throughout an enterprise doesn't come out of the box in vRealize Operations.

Providing compute performance, utilization, and consumption reporting for workloads, or groups of related workloads, is a frequent and painful task for storage, network, virtualization, cloud, and application administrators, as well as general IT administrators.

Because of this, questions that IT must seek to answer include:

- How many vCPUs have been allocated to all VMs in Application *Y*, and how much of the allocated CPU power are those VMs utilizing? (This is a commonly asked question when calculating licensing costs.)
- How much resources (storage, network, memory/CPU, and so on) are all of the VMs in Department X consuming?
- What is the current and/or expected number of VMs for Application *X*?
- Which applications or services do not meet company SLAs?
- How much compute power is Cloud Tenant A consuming?

Although the answers to these questions can be found in vSphere's infrastructure level (vSphere instance, cluster, host, or virtual machine), these questions also apply to higher, logical business structures.

Virtual infrastructure objects and their hierarchical relationships with Sphere instances, clusters, hosts, and virtual machines are easily translatable in vRealize Operations. The Cluster Compute Resource object is used within vRealize Operations to roll-up and report performance, utilization, and consumption. This may provide all the necessary information needed by IT staff, but it does not provide the answers that key stakeholders may want from you.

With the advancement of cloud services, it has also become very important to be able to extract metadata from cloud-provisioned workloads. This metadata will not only to be used by IT personnel, but also to provide business-oriented reporting.

This metadata may include information such as the following:

- Who requested the VM
- Who the owner of the VM is
- What business unit the VM belongs to
- Which cloud tenant the VM belongs to
- Whether it is a production, test, development, or infrastructure level VM

Depending on the environment, some of this information may be incorporated in the VM hostname. For example, consider a VM with the vSphere name LVVMDEVAPPX01DBSQL. As we are running an environment with predefined naming conventions, all virtual machine names must match our company standards so that we can decode information from the vSphere VM name alone. For example, we know that:

- The first two symbols notate the datacenter where the VM is deployed: **LV** for **Las Vegas**
- The next two symbols notate if it is a virtual or physical machine: **VM** for **Virtual Machine**
- The next three symbols notate the department the machine belongs to: **DEV** for **Development** department
- The next four symbols notate the application or service abbreviation the machine provides: **APPX** for **Application X**
- The next two symbols notate the application or service instance deployed: **01** for the application's first instance
- The final five symbols notate the role of the server: **DB SQL** for a Microsoft SQL Server database server

Sometimes some of the preceding information may be acquired based on which vSphere cluster the VM belongs to: the development, production, test, or accounting department cluster. We could have also used vSphere folders to logically group VMs together.

With the advancement of virtual infrastructures and the increased adoption of cloud services, it has become less important to follow strict naming conventions with regard to a virtual machine's hostname. It has become more important to be able to identify and address a VM by a unique identification number, for example with the vSphere **Universal Unique Identifier** (**UUID**). This is even more vital when we need to introduce automation engines within an infrastructure, such as VMware vRealize Orchestrator, and start automating tasks and processes. Because of this, there may arise a situation where we cannot extract the necessary information easily; in cases like this, the ability to attach metadata, which can be in the form of tags or attributes, to workloads, and then read that metadata, is crucial.

Let's see how vRealize Operations can address those challenges and help us to provide business-oriented reporting around our virtual infrastructure.

Tags, application groups, and custom groups

vRealize Operations offers the following constructs which allow us to logically group or filter objects:

- Tags
- Application groups
- Custom groups

Tags and application groups are used to logically organize similar objects, for example by application, by an organization, or by location.

 Do not confuse vRealize Operations tags with vSphere tags. These are two different constructs.

Custom object groups logically organize objects in your environment and enable you to customize the operational view of your infrastructure to meet specific business needs.

Using tags

A tag provides a way of grouping objects by logical function, such as departments, organizations, or region.

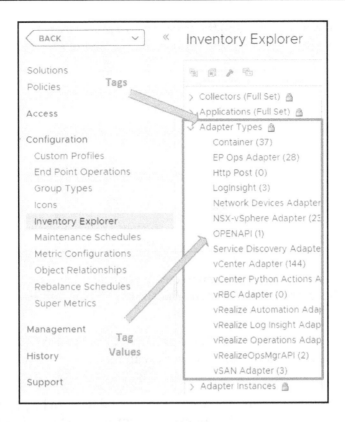

Tags and tag values are listed on the **Inventory Explorer** page. Navigate to the **Inventory Explorer** page from the **Administration** page. You'll see that a tag contains a tag name and tag values. A tag value provides a grouping container function; one or more objects can be added to these tags.

A tag is a type of information, such as adapter types. Adapter types is a predefined tag in vRealize Operations. Tag values are individual instances of that type of information. For example, when vRealize Operations discovers objects using the VMware vCenter adapter, it assigns all the objects to the vCenter adapter tag value under the adapter types tag.

Every tag becomes a root object within the **Inventory Explorer** tree. The tag values become subnodes. The value within parentheses displays the number of assigned objects:

You can use the **Manage Object Tags** icon to create your own tags and tag values. In this example, the tag is **Kaloferov.com Company Locations**. The tag values are **Las Vegas** and **New York**.

A large enterprise can have thousands of objects defined in vRealize Operations. Creating object tags and tag values makes it easier to work with related objects in vRealize Operations.

Tag values are grouping containers. These grouping containers can be populated with one or more objects. These objects might be, for example, virtual machines, hosts, datastores, servers, or application tiers:

An object can be assigned to multiple tags.

 Some tags are prebuilt by vRealize Operations. You cannot add objects to these tags. These tags are indicated with a lock icon.

As new object types, tag values can be used like any other object types:

In this example, we are searching for the object named Las Vegas, which is a tag value. To remove a tag from an object, display the tag values objects in the object list. Drag the desired objects to the Untag tag at the bottom of the tag list.

Using application groups

An application group is a logical grouping of like-functionality objects grouped by tier that represent a business application or service.

Application groups have the following business benefits:

- Application-centric performance
- Visual correlation of impact
- IT socialization via application health

Application groups also have technical benefits, which are as follows:

- Application resources are monitored across IT domains
- The integration of disparate IT data or sources

Generally, the following main drivers determine the approach to application group design: business reasons and technical reasons. Applications that are built for business reasons are used to give better visibility to application owners and line-of-business owners. Usually, this type of design focuses on the application as it is seen by the application owner. A typical scenario would be the health of SAP systems and the relationship of different SAP systems to each other.

A technical application group design creates visibility from a technology perspective. Different application tiers are used in a basic application group definition. The design might incorporate detailed information of technical components like storage and networking into the application group definition. Because an object can be represented in multiple application groups, a mixed approach using technically-driven and business-driven application group designs is often used.

An application group can be used to represent a typical multi-tier application where:

- Each tier includes its own set of virtual machines
- Each tier can have its own thresholds

You can build application group topologies to help the user easily determine how applications are affected when a change occurs across the mission-critical objects contained within the logical tiers of the application. After you have specified an application group topology, you can view the analysis across all tiers and objects that are contained within that application group. Here, you can get an early understanding of any major changes that occur across an application group, which might be an indication of a cascading performance problem.

You create application groups from the **Environment Overview** page, as shown in the following screenshot:

When adding an application, select a template from a list of predefined templates, or create a custom template to define the tiers in the application. The predefined application templates populate the tiers within the application design. However, these templates do not add special functionality or automatic object assignment to the application group; sometimes, the best approach is to select **Custom** and build your own tiers for the application group.

Name your application. You can replace the default tier names with more descriptive names, as shown in the following screenshot:

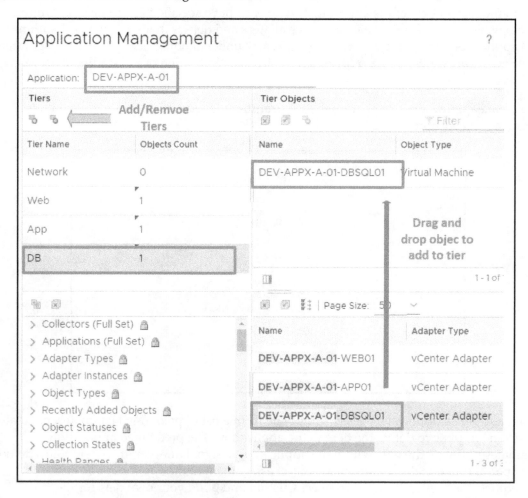

Give your application group a meaningful name. For each of the tiers listed, you can use the default names or provide a descriptive name for each tier.

If you do not need a tier, you can remove the tier from the list. You can also add additional tiers if necessary. You can view your application status on the **Environment Overview** page:

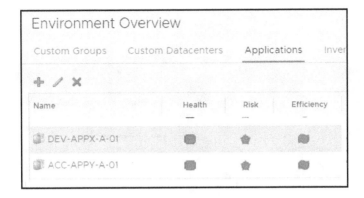

For each application group, information regarding health, risk, and efficiency is displayed, including:

- Badge status
- Status of each tier in the application group

 You might have to wait a few minutes before this information appears.

Using custom groups and types

A custom group is a container that can hold any number of objects and any type of object.

Using custom groups, you can align infrastructure operations with business teams and priorities, such as:

- Lines of business
- Workload types
- Configuration types

Custom groups come from the following sources:

- Built into the product
- Installed management packs
- User-defined

Custom groups are found in the navigation pane on the **Environment** page, as shown in the following screenshot:

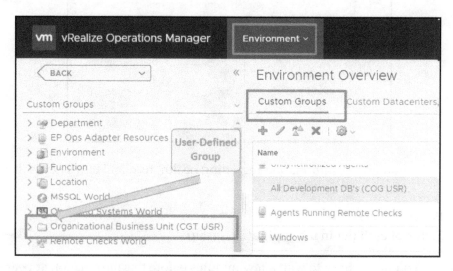

To create a new custom group, click the plus icon at the top of the **Custom Groups** tab.

Custom groups enable you to create your own containers for objects in your environment. The benefit of using custom groups is that you can customize the operational view of your infrastructure to meet specific business needs. For example, a common way to group objects is by application.

vRealize Operations includes a few built-in custom groups. For example, the Universe group is a vRealize Operations custom group that encompasses every object known to the vRealize Operations instance. The vSphere World group is a custom group that is included with VMware vSphere. vSphere World encompasses every vSphere object from every VMware vCenter Server instance that is managed by vRealize Operations.

In this example, the **Organizational Business Unit (CGT USR)** is a user-defined custom group. A custom group type is an identifier that you apply to a specific custom group in your environment to categorize your objects.

Custom group types come from the following sources:

- Built into the product
- Installed management packs
- User-defined

When you create a custom group, you assign an object group type to the new custom group. You can use an existing custom group type, or you can create your own custom group type. You apply a custom group type to groups of objects so that vRealize Operations can collect data from the custom group and display the results, for example, in the dashboards and views.

Each management pack that you add to vRealize Operations might add one or more static groups of objects to group the data received from the adapters, as shown in the following screenshot:

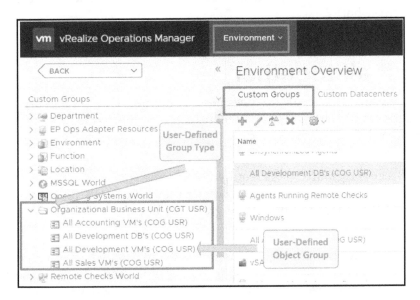

In this example, a user-defined custom group type, named **Organizational Business Unit (CGT USR)**, has been created. The custom groups named **All Accounting VMs (COG USR)**, **All Development DBs (COG USR)**, **All Development VMs (COG USR)**, and **All Sales VMs (COG USR)** have been assigned to this custom group type. These groups are used to group the following objects in the environment together:

- **All Accounting VMs**: All virtual machines that belong to the Accounting business unit
- **All Development DBs**: All virtual machines containing databases that belong to the Development business unit
- **All Development VMs**: All virtual machines that belong to the Development business unit
- **All Sales VMs**: All virtual machines that belong to the sales business unit

Note: When I create a new object in vRealize Operations, I like to put an abbreviation of the type of object in the name. For example, for all custom groups, I add the abbreviation COG to the name. Similarly, for all custom group types, I add CGT. In addition, because this is a user-defined object, I also add the abbreviation USR. This makes filtering and searching for an object in vRealize Operations a lot easier. The other custom group types listed in this example are built into the product and can be used to categorize custom groups that you create. The list of custom group types appears in the Content area under group types (not shown in the screenshot).

Putting it all together

Before creating custom groups, group types must be defined. Group types are what will bind super metrics to custom groups and will help you organize categories of groups in vRealize Operations.

Because a group type is required when creating a custom group, it must be created in advance. Once the custom group is created, the group type can only be changed if the custom group is cloned.

For example, let's say we want to logically organize things into two group types: by organizational or business units and by application or server roles. In the **Organizational Business Units** group type, we want to have custom groups where we group objects by department or cloud tenant, such as All Development VMs, All Development DB VMs or All Cloud TenantA VMs.

In the **Application and Server Roles** object type, we want to have custom groups where we group objects by server or application role, such as All AppX VMs, All DB VMs, All SQL DB VMs or All Web VMs.

This is illustrated in the following diagram:

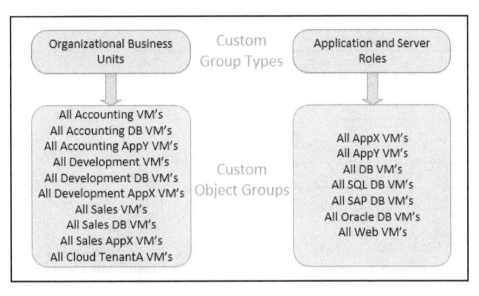

We create group types by navigating to the **Administration** tab, **Configuration**, and then **Group Types**. Click on the **Add Group Type** button and provide a descriptive name to create a group type.

In this example, I've created the following two group types:

- **Organizational Business Units** (CGT USR)
- **Applications and Server Roles** (CGT USR)

As we've mentioned, a custom group is a container that includes one or more objects. You can create static groups of objects. You can also create dynamic groups of objects with criteria that determines group membership as vRealize Operations discovers and collects data from new resources that are added to the environment.

We can create a new custom group by using the **New Group** icon on the **Environment Overview** page to create custom groups.

Let's create the All Development VMs custom group from our example, which will contain all the VMs belonging to the development business unit, as shown in the following screenshot:

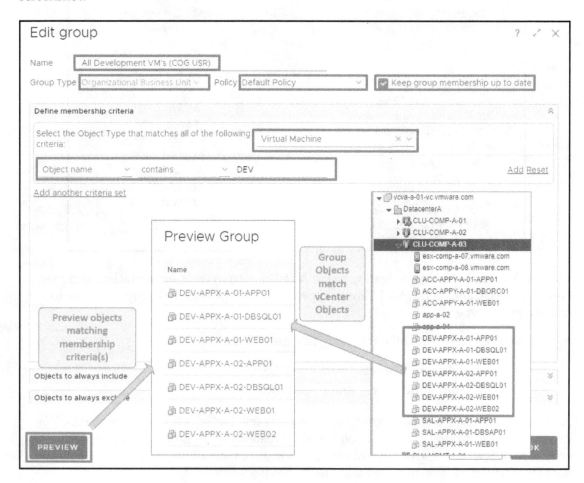

In this example, I've named the object group **All Development VMs (COG USR)**. I've given the custom group the **group type Organizational Business Units (CGT USR)**. I've assigned the **Default Policy** to the object group. A policy is a collection of thresholds, buffers, and settings that is used to map objects and applications to service-level agreements.

You can configure dynamic group membership by selecting the **Keep group membership up to date** check box. For dynamic groups, vRealize Operations discovers objects that match the criteria for the group membership according to the rules that you define. vRealize Operations updates the group members based on search results.

The object type indicates the type of objects to add to the object group. In this example, the objects are a virtual machines.

You can add one or more criteria. In this example, the criteria is based on the object's name. This means that members are selected based on their name matching a defined expression. Members must be from virtual machines and must contain in their object name the word **DEV**, which in our example notates a virtual machine belonging to the development department.

The **Objects to always include** panel is used to identify which objects are always part of the custom group, regardless of the membership criteria.

The **Objects to always exclude** panel is used to identify which objects are not a part of the custom group, regardless of the membership criteria.

Using the **Preview** button, you can validate that the criteria you defined matches the correct objects. As you can see, the defined matches correspond to the objects in vCenter that we want to group.

Let's now create the **All Development DB VMs** custom group from our example, which will contain all the database VM's belonging to the development business unit:

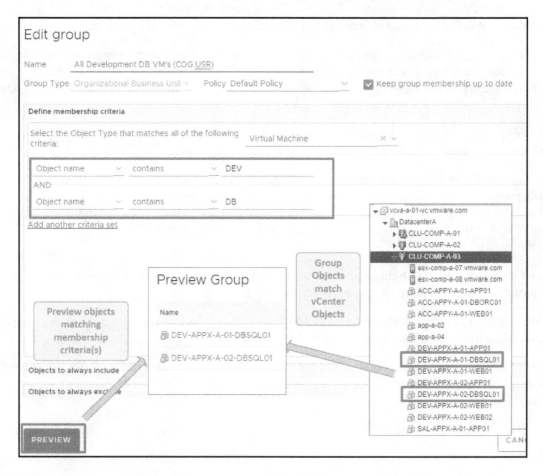

We are building on top of the previous example by adding an extra **AND** membership criteria rule that, in addition to filtering by **DEV** in the object name, will also filter by **DB**.

Next, let's create the **All AppX VMs** custom group from our example, which will contain all the **AppX VMs** across all business units:

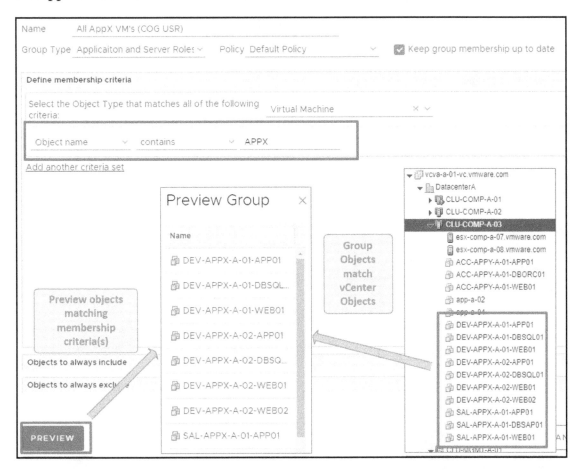

Again, similar to before, we can filter by **APPX** and get all the VMs across all the business units that build up **APPX**.

But what if we want to group not the individual VMs that build up an application, but rather all of the application instances? We can do this by using the application groups we created earlier.

Now let's create the **All AppX Instances** custom group from our example, which will contain all the AppX instances across all business units:

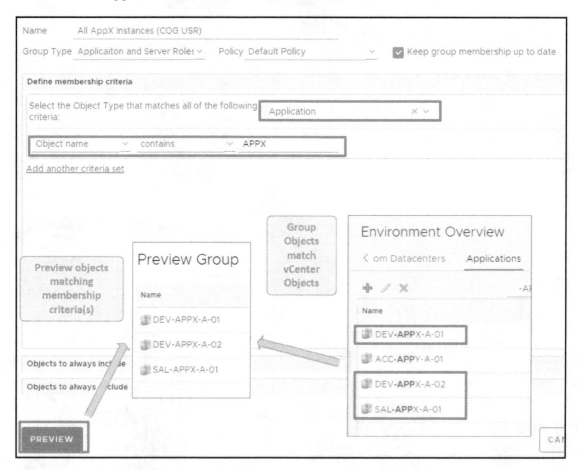

As you can see, we are now searching all of the application object types, not virtual machines. This will search within all the application groups we created earlier. The filtering criteria remain the same, as with the previous example.

Sometimes you may want to create a custom group of VMs based on the relationship to their vSphere cluster, as shown in the following screenshot:

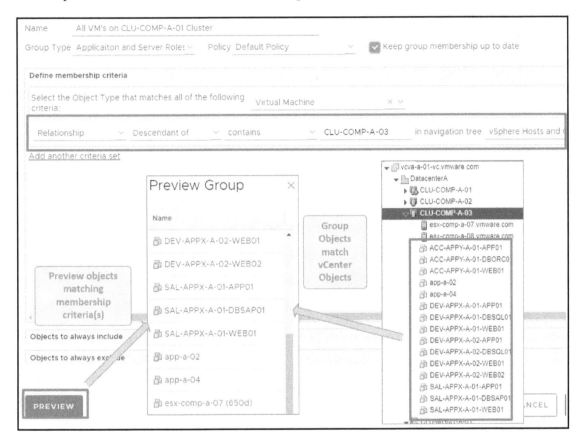

This time, instead of filtering by object name, we are going to filter by **Relationship**. We are going to filter for each VM that is a **Descendant** of a cluster (for example, CLU-COMP-A-03).

You can also group by vSphere folder, as shown in the following screenshot:

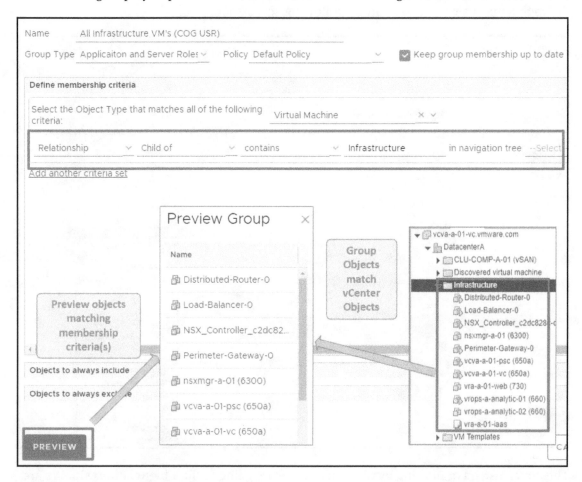

Another example of leveraging the **Relationship criteria** set involves the vCenter VM folder structure; this type we filter by **Child Of**.

Using vSphere tags to organize VMs in a vCenter provides another mechanism that can be used to create criteria sets based on VM vSphere tag properties. Cloud solutions, such as VMware's vRealize Automation and VMware's vRealize Orchestrator, may assign tags during VM provisioning to provide important metadata information.

Now let's create the **All Cloud TenantA VMs** custom group from our example, which will contain all the VMs that belong to cloud **TenantA**:

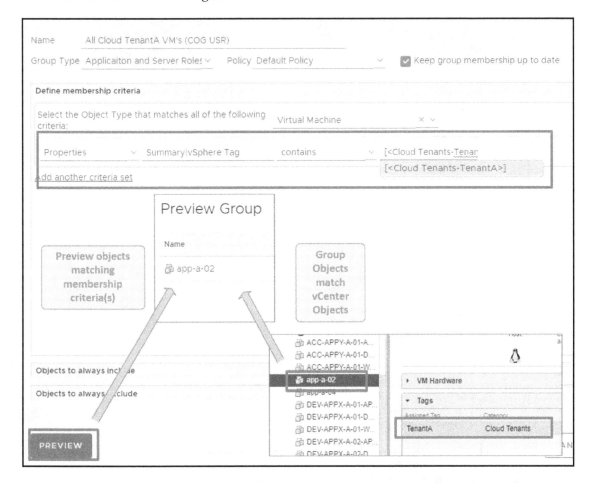

In this example, we are leveraging a **Properties** criteria set that involves the vCenter tagging feature. This type we filter by **Summary/vSphere Tag**.

Once you've created all the necessary **Custom Groups** and **Group Types**, you can view them by navigating to the **Environment** tab and then **Custom Groups**:

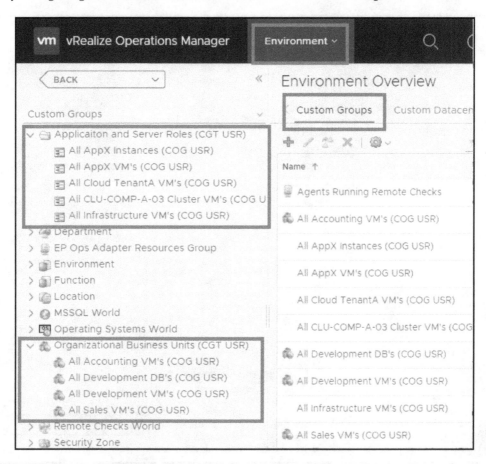

You can see all the custom groups we've created in the previous examples.

Once we've created all the **Custom Groups** we need, we can create super metrics using these groups. Typically, there are three categories that these fall into; these categories, which are all business-oriented, quantify performance, utilization, and the consumption of resources by related VMs in custom groups:

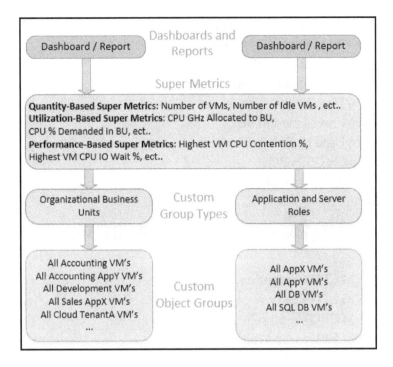

The following are some examples of **Quantity-based Super Metrics** that can be created for custom groups:

- Number of VMs
- Number of Powered ON VMs
- Number of Powered OFF VMs
- Number of Idle VMs
- Number of Oversized VMs
- Number of Stressed VMs

The following are examples of some **Utilization-based Super Metrics** that can be created for custom groups:

- CPU GHz Allocated to BU
- CPU GHz Demanded by BU
- CPU GHz Used by BU
- CPU % Demanded in BU
- CPU % Used in BU
- CPU Count in BU

- CPU Count Recommended to BU
- CPU Count Reclaimable from BU
- Memory GB Allocated to BU
- Memory GB Consumed by BU
- Memory % Used by BU
- Disk Space Provisioned to BU
- Disk Space Used by BU
- VM Snapshots GB in BU
- Disk Space % Used by BU
- Total BU IOPS

The following are examples of some **Performance-based Super Metrics** that can be created for custom groups:

- Highest VM CPU Contention %
- Highest VM CPU Ready % per Core
- Highest VM CPU Co-Stop %
- Highest VM CPU Swap Wait %
- Highest VM CPU IO Wait %
- Highest VM Mem Swap In Rate (KBps)
- Highest VM Mem Decompression Rate (KBps)
- Highest VM Mem Ballooned (KB)
- Highest VM Disk IOPS
- Highest VM Disk Latency (ms)
- Highest VM Network Packets Dropped
- Highest VM Network Usage Rate (KBps)

Once the super metrics are created, you will bind them to the appropriate custom groups and then use them to create dashboards and reports that provide visibility, utilization, consumption, and performance insights to key business and application stakeholders throughout the entire enterprise. We will not cover how to create super metrics or use them in dashboards, as this will be covered later on in this book.

Summary

In this chapter, we covered how to build reports around logical business structures, and how to provide stakeholders the business-oriented information they need. We accomplished this by using vRealize Operations tags, application groups, and custom groups. We also looked at how super metrics tie to custom groups, and how these can be used in dashboards and reports.

In the next chapter, we will cover super metrics in more detail.

9
Super Metrics Made Super Easy

As the name would suggest, super metrics are no ordinary metrics, and with great power comes great opportunity. In this chapter, we will discuss the following:

- Metric terminology and definitions
- Super metric types
- Building your own super metrics
- Applying super metrics to policies
- Using operators in super metric calculations
- Comparing super metrics to views

What are super metrics and when do I use them?

A super metric is an administrator-created custom metric based on a mathematical formula from existing metrics that can then be applied via policy. A super metric can be derived from either a single object or multiple objects across multiple environments.

A super metric is usually defined when an administrator notices a gap in the available metrics on a given object. For example, an administrator notices high CPU ready on a virtual machine and is curious as to whether it may be common across all VMs on the host, or even the vSphere cluster. The administrator would like to see what the average CPU ready value is for all VMs across the cluster to see if this has changed recently, or has progressively been getting worse.

Unfortunately, this metric is not available on a vSphere host or cluster (although other useful metrics may) and therefore the administrator is forced to look through several VMs individually to get this data. In this case, the administrator could create a super metric that rolls up the average CPU ready of all VMs to the cluster level, saving a lot of time having to view each object individually.

The easiest way is to imagine a super metric as a spreadsheet formula or cell. vRealize Operations offers a worksheet-like environment where you can combine existing metrics for an object in a formula to create a new one: a super metric. This metric can then be attached to an object and data collected like any other object. You can, of course, also visualize them in a dashboard, view, or report. Super metrics can be used to calculate averages, percentages, sums, min, and max, among others.

Let's take, for example, the following Microsoft Excel spreadsheet:

K4				f_x	=ROUND((AVERAGE(D4:J4)),2)						
	A	B	C	D	E	F	G	H	I	J	K
1			Metric				Super Metric				
2	Cluster	Virtual Machine	CPU Ready %				Avarage CPU Ready %				
3				Mo	Tu	We	Th	Fr	Sa	Su	Week
4		VM001	0.5	0.91	0.58	0.26	7	14.47	0.56	0.55	3.48
5		VM002	6.08	0.46	0.28	0.24	3.15	13.76	2.55	0.64	3.01
6	Payload Cluster 1	VM003	3	0.69	0.86	0.62	3.42	8.34	3.74	0.07	2.53
7		VM004	3.54	0.38	0.07	0.93	5.82	9.74	3.92	0.23	3.01
8		VM005	3	0.9	0.18	0.31	5.78	10.28	3.35	0.4	3.03
9		VM006	0.54	0.42	0.02	0	6.4	8.54	2.41	0.42	2.6
10		VM007	0.1	0.32	0.37	0.56	3.32	11.36	5.21	0.31	3.06
11		VM008	0.5	0.74	0.73	0.95	5.54	3.2	3.74	0.78	2.24

As you can see in the spreadsheet, we have our normal CPU Ready % showing the current CPU ready time for each VM in a payload cluster. If we want to calculate the Average CPU Ready % time for a VM for a given period (a day of the week or weeks average) we can use the AVERAGE Excel cell formula that can calculate that value for us. We can say that each of the cells representing that average value is super metric, like cells in Excel. In this particular example, what those super metric-like cell values tell us is that there was an increase of percent of time, from Thursday till Saturday, where there was work to be done for VM(s), but no physical CPU available to do it on a weeks average, though everything seems to be within the acceptable thresholds. If that spike in Average CPU Ready % is seen often, it may be good to investigate the cause.

> One rule of thumb is that below five percent CPU Ready per vCPU is normal; anything between five percent and ten percent, best keep an eye on the VM and the host. Over ten percent (for extended periods) you should be planning on taking some action.

Later in this chapter, we will cover how to create, in an analog way, super metrics in vRealize Operations. Although the previous use case is a valid example of when creating a super metric may be required, generally, the quality of the solution (known as Adapter) will determine how many super metrics are required.

Although there are different types of super metrics, a high-quality adapter will define most attribute types that an administrator should need. For example, this may include taking two opposite raw values, such as used capacity and free capacity, and dividing them to produce used capacity %. However, if this is not the case or an administrator is importing custom data via the API or HTTP Post adapter, super metrics can be very useful in providing a complete set of metrics to benefit from.

Using super metrics provides the following benefits:

- **Easier tracking**: You can watch a few metrics instead of many
- **Comprehensive views**: The super metric looks at one or more metrics, for one or more objects at a time
- **Investigation and forensics**: Super metrics are helpful in identifying recurring issues

Super metrics have the following limitations:

- Inability to address time bands (for example, last hour average), only time-slice metrics
- Dependent on consistent and manageable data collection

What's new with super metrics?

Although metrics in their essence have remained the same in the past few vRealize Operations releases, metric operators got a huge enhancement boost in vRealize Operations 6.3. It might seem like a somewhat trivial enhancement, but these operators are game changers for super metrics. With the introduction of vRealize Operations 6.3 and the new super metrics operators, it is now even easier to transform or create new metrics from the already collected metrics.

The new operators are as follows:

Operators	Function	Example
[]	Array	[A, B, C]
==	Equal	1==1
!=	Not equal	1!=2
<	Less than	1<2
<=	Less than or equal	1<=2
>	Greater than	2>1
>=	Greater than or equal	2=>1
||	Or	
&&	And	
? :	If then else	A ? B : C
!	Not	!(1>2)
Where	Where	1==1 where = "==1"

It may be difficult to grasp the value these operators bring at first, so let's jump straight to an example.

In vRealize Operations, you can get VM uptime. The inconvenience with uptime in vRealize Operations is that it is an ever-growing number until a reboot of the monitored object takes place. This means that for any given time period you will end up with some number that might be very high or very low, and as such it becomes very hard to make sense of it in terms of uptime statistics. Just look at the following graph:

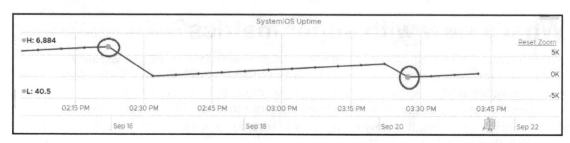

Every time there is a drop in the chart, the VM's OS has been restarted. vRealize Operations every 5 minutes (cycles or 300 seconds). It means that for every data point, 300 seconds is added to the previous value if the VMs OS has been up for the entire period. If not, the number will be lower, as the metric is reset on a reboot of the OS. Although not shown very clearly in the graph, the lowest number is 40.3 (around 03:30 PM) and the highest is 3.884 (around 2:20 PM).

 Note: you will see a lot higher values for a virtual machine that has been up for a longer period of time.

With the help of super metrics and the new operators, we turn these data points into something useful in the context of VM OS uptime statistics, which we can use for management or customer reports. As you can see, the VM OS has been up most of the time for that period:

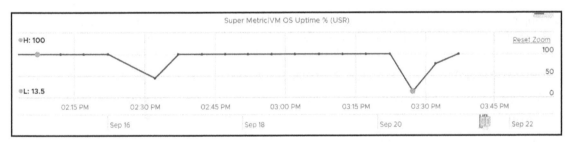

I will explain how to create the VM OS uptime % super metric shown with the help of the comparison operators later in this chapter.

Metric terminology and definitions

Now, granted this section heading may not sound like the most interesting subject, but before we get into building super metrics we need to understand the various definitions around metrics. Many administrators find super metrics too hard, not because they fail to have use cases or struggle with the math, but because they fail to understand the different terminology and how they should be built.

Objects

First up is understanding what an object is and what an object type is. An object is a single entity in vRealize Operations, such as a virtual machine, a Datastore, a switch, and so on. The individual object has a name and set of identifiers that make it unique inside vRealize Operations, even if there are multiple objects with the same name (for example, vCenter folders) they will all still be a unique object in the vRealize Operations inventory.

As mentioned in `Chapter 1`, *Going Ahead with vRealize Operations*, an object shares its GemFire shard key with its FSDB metric data and alarm data, this ensures that all elements that make up an object are persisted together on the same vRealize Operations node. In previous versions of vRealize Operations, an object was referred to as a resource, as such you may see the two terms used interchangeably.

Metrics

An object has metrics that are added to the FSDB and can be retrieved on request. Object metrics are the main concept that drives vRealize Operations, and includes examples such as VM CPU co-stop (ms), VM host disk usage rate (Kbps), and VDI desktop pool Avg PCoIP latency (ms).

Metrics are used in all areas of vRealize Operations including dashboards, views, widgets, and alarms. An individual metric always has a 1:1 mapping with its parent object.

An object type is a group of objects that share the same set of properties and metrics. This can also be seen as a category, and includes examples such as VM, Datastore, and a vSphere distributed switch. When creating and applying super metrics, object types are the most common selection, as it allows super metrics to be applied to all objects of the same object type with a single formula, rather than creating individual formulas for individual objects. Following the same name change as previously, object types were previously referred to as resource kinds, and an object can only have one object type.

Attribute types

Attribute types (previously known as attribute kinds) are the definition of what array of metrics an object type generally supports. Attribute types can be seen as the list of metrics you would expect an object to have, however, there is no guarantee that all objects in the given object type have data for every single attribute. For example, if an administrator selects a virtual machine and wishes to view the Snapshot space used (GB) metric and that VM has never had a snapshot, the **No Data** message will be displayed in the metrics graph window. Following the same use cases as object types, attribute types are commonly used in super metrics as they allow the formula to be applied to more than one object. One careful consideration when using attribute types in super metrics is that an object may have more than one instance of an attribute. For example, when a VM has more than one CPU or network adapter:

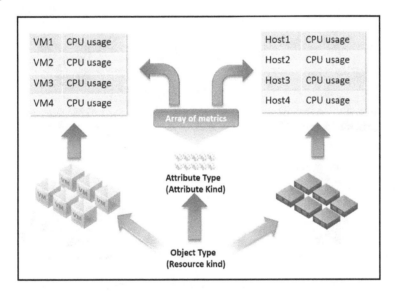

Super metric types

Now that we are ready to get into the details of super metrics, let's quickly discuss the three main types (or categories) of super metrics:

- Rollup
- Generic object
- Specific object (or pass-through)

Rollup

A rollup super metric is the most common example of a super metric. It uses transformation type functions such as sum, avg, min, and count. It then applies them through a looping function of all child objects matching the object and attribute type. The result of this calculation is then available as a super metric on the object where the super metric is applied.

Let's go through an example using Cluster Level Datastore free disk space. Now, before you email me and point out that this metric already exists by default in the vCenter adapter and there is no need to create a super metric, I will point out that you are correct, however, this example well illustrates the point of rollups. We will go through a unique example later:

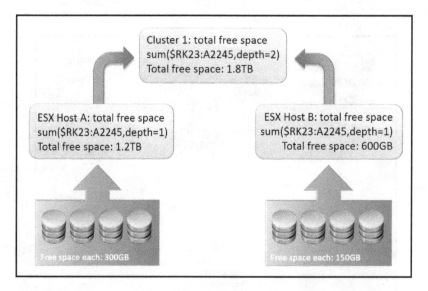

The preceding figure shows an example of two different super metrics of the rollup type applied at different levels. There are two different ESX hosts (**A** and **B**), both with only local storage. Each Datastore on **Host A** has **300 GB** free, and each Datastore on **Host B** has **150 GB** free. The administrator wishes to know at a cluster level how much free space is remaining. The administrator creates a super metric that uses the sum function to loop through all instances of free space GB for the Datastore object type. A depth value is also provided to indicate how many generations the super metric has to travel to loop through all of the objects. This super metric is then applied to the vSphere Cluster via policy and the result of 1.8 TB is given in the super metric.

Using the so-called **Multilayer Rollup** super metric, you can roll up or roll down data for multiple levels. In the previous example, the formula uses the depth value to calculate data at one or more layers in the inventory tree. You only need a single super metric to calculate values at all layers up to the desired depth.

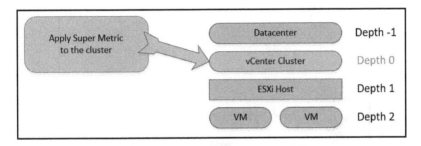

The depth indicates how far down, or up, in the inventory tree to go to get the metric value.

A negative depth value allows the formula to calculate values going up in the inventory tree.

A positive depth value allows the formula to calculate values going down in the inventory tree.

For example, if the super metric is applied at the cluster object, and you use a depth of one (Depth 1), the metric values are taken from host objects, but not from virtual machines. To get metric values from virtual machines, you must use a depth value of two (Depth 2), assuming that the super metric is assigned at the cluster object.

Generic resource

A generic resource super metric is when you combine existing metrics using mathematical operators and apply them back to the same object or another object with the same attributes. This essentially allows an administrator to create a completely new metric for an object type where a gap has been identified. What makes a generic resource super metric different from others is the use of the `This` option, which is substituted for the object type. The use of the `This` option allows the super metric to be placed on any object; however, it depends on all objects sharing an attitude with exactly the same name. On top of that, an administrator needs to ensure that the attribute has the same meaning or result if applied to different objects as sometimes the context of an attribute is important. As with views, it is recommended that administrators provide a meaningful name that indicates which object types can be associated with the super metric.

An example of a generic super metric is shown in the following diagram:

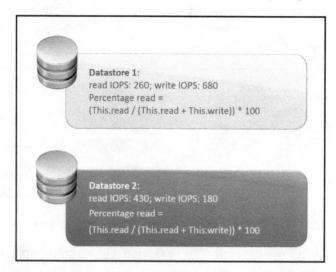

It is common when defining generic super metrics that an error is received: "Cannot convert the aggregated result to a number". This is due to the fact that an object may have multiple instances of an attribute, so the use of additional sum, avg, max, count, and so on is required to instruct the formula as to how to handle these occurrences. For example, `(avg($This.CPUusage)/(avg($This.CPULimit))`.

Specific resource/pass-through

A specific resource or pass-through is a super metric that targets a particular object rather than an object type. It is also referred to as pass-through because a particular object is being targeted and this super metric can be applied anywhere without the need to specify depth, as with Rollup super metrics. Unlike the other super metrics, this type generally also targets specific metrics rather than an attribute, as the super metric is already unique to an object.

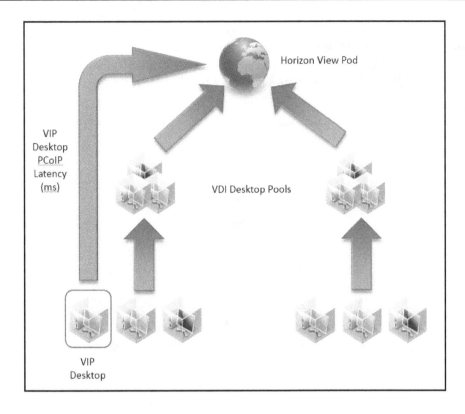

Building your own super metrics

Now it is time to start building your own super metrics, and we can walk through the process of doing so. The first step in designing and building a super metric is to have a clear use case or problem that you are trying to solve. In our example, an administrator is keen to know if CPU Ready % (or CPU contention) is increasing on all VMs in a cluster as the amount of provisioned VMs increases. Because the administrator wants to know the maximum value of a metric that is present on all virtual machines, a Rollup super metric is the most appropriate.

When creating Rollup super metrics, understanding parent/child relationships is critical as it helps determines the depth of the looping algorithm that is being defined. The parent/child relationships can be seen in some dashboards, the **Environment** tab of an object, and in the **Object Relationships** section under **Administration**. An example of these relationships is shown in the following screenshot:

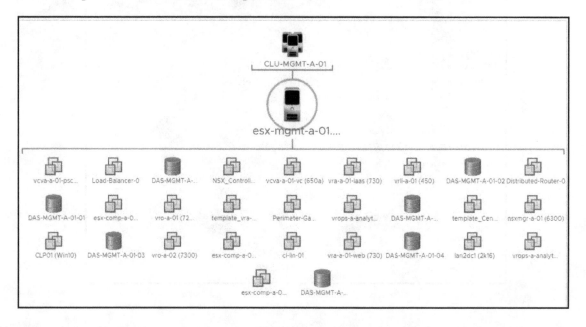

In our example, the **Administrator** has DRS set to **Fully Automatic**, so they are most interested in seeing if the maximum CPU ready across the VMs is increasing at the cluster level rather than the host level. For the super metric to apply correctly, the administrator needs to set the depth to a value of 2.

A VM with a single vCPU is assumed to be the norm if the CPU Ready time is below 5%. Usually, VM's with more vCPU's have higher CPU Ready. As a general guidance on a VM with four vCPUs, the CPU Ready should be below 10%, or 2.5 per vCPU.

Defining a new super metric

To define a new super metric, select **Administration** | **Configuration** | **Super Metrics** in the navigation bar and then select the plus symbol to open the wizard.

Now, let's step through the seven steps in creating the metric formula. These steps will be referring to the example in the following screenshot:

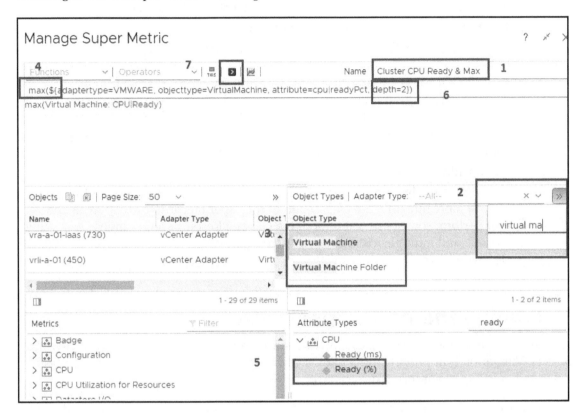

1. **Name the super metric**: Remembering from before that naming is critical in describing where a super metric should be applied and what its function is. Unlike Views, super metrics do not have a description field, so make good use of the name field.
2. **Filter on object types**: As there are a lot of object types out there, you can leverage the filter field to cut down the options.

3. **Select the virtual machine object type**: We know that we are after the maximum value of CPU ready across a cluster from each virtual machine. As our metrics are coming from virtual machines that are the object type we select.

4. **Enter the mathematical operand**: Before we select the attribute type we need to open the mathematical operand by typing `max()` or selecting it from the functions menu.

5. **Add the object type to the super metric**: With the `max()` operand in place, we can now scroll through the list and find the attribute type we are interested in `Ready (%)`. Double-clicking it will add it to the workspace.

6. **Change the depth**: By default, the depth is `1` and therefore this super metric could only be applied to the vSphere host level. Update the value to `2` to ensure we can add it at the Cluster level.

7. **Show formula description**: Selecting the show formula description button will allow a more human readable version of the super metric to be displayed and also perform some basic validation. If a Generic Resource super metric was being created, and multiple instances of an attribute were not taken into account, this step would error.

Validating the new super metric

Now that the super metric is created, it is time to validate it before applying it to real-world objects. Validation is important and it allows you to see the result of your formula and can help easily pick up major formulaic errors.

As mentioned earlier, super metrics do not start having a value until they are applied to an object through policy, therefore it is impossible to see the value of a super metric before it is created. There is one exception to this rule, however; the super metric validation allows you to model the value of a super metric from any time period. This is useful in ensuring that the result is what you expect before you apply the super metrics and find out the formula is incorrect, after waiting four weeks for Dynamic Thresholds to be calculated.

The following steps will be referring to the example given here:

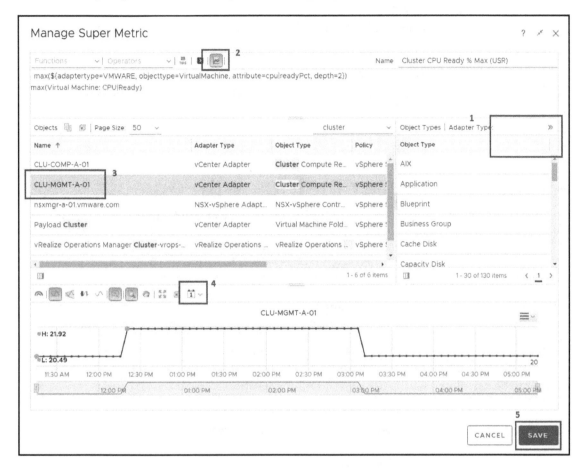

1. **Clear the object type filter**: Now that we are ready to visualize the super metric (validate it), we need to first clear the object type filter to allow us to select a cluster object.
2. **Open the super metric visualizer**: Sounds a bit Sci-Fi, but even so, select the button at the top of the wizard to replace the metrics and attribute types windows with the metric visualizer.
3. **Select a target object**: Find and select a target object that matches the object type of where the super metric will be applied. A preview of the super metric will now be shown.

4. **Set the time range (optional)**: Set the time range if you wish to preview data from a longer or different time period.

5. **Save the super metric**: If you're happy with the super metric, it is now time to save and close the wizard.

 It is important to preview your super metric and validate that it shows the data you expect. Super metrics can be misleading if proper care is not taken when defining the formula.

Associating super metrics with objects

Finally, we are up to the last stage of applying our recently created super metric into a policy and applying it to active objects.

When you associate your super metric to an object type, the super metric is calculated for the objects in that object type and appears as a metric for the object type.

After you have saved and closed your super metric, while focused on the metric, select the **Object Types** tab at the bottom of the screen and select the **Add Object Type** button.

Browse or search for the object type you wish to add to the super metric. This will allow us to specify that the super metric will only apply to certain object types and therefore not attempt to be calculated on the object that will not support it, such as Datastores, for example.

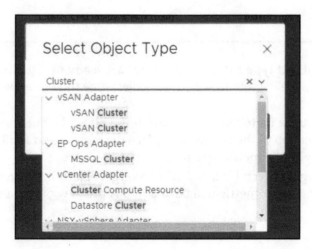

In this example, we want to monitor the entire vCenter Cluster (with a depth of 2), therefore we will select the **Cluster Compute Resource** object from the drop-down menu.

Now, we have to apply this metric to an appropriate policy from the policy library. To add the super metric to a policy, navigate to **Policies | Policy Library**. For the purpose of this example, we will be using the vSphere Solutions Default Policy. Select the policy and click **Edit Selected Policy**.

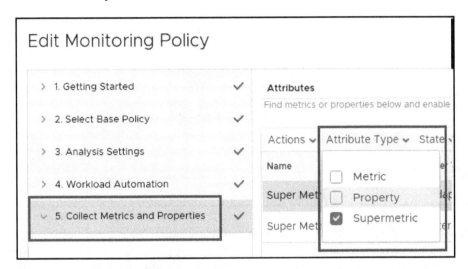

On the **Edit Monitoring Policy** window select **Collect Metrics and Properties**. Filter by **Attribute** type and leave only **Supermetric**.

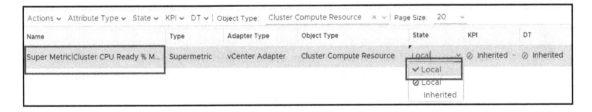

Finally, find your created super metric that matches your resource type and set the state to **Local** (enabled). **Save** and close the policy.

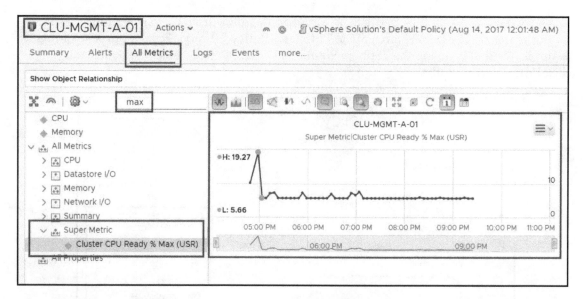

After a few collection cycles (5-10) your super metric should show some values on the selected object types within the inventory. As we have applied the metric to a computer cluster resource object type, we must navigate and select a vSphere Cluster from the inventory. We can find all metrics on the **All Metrics** tab. We can filter the available metrics to find what we are looking for more easily.

It is important to note that super metrics depend on accurate and consistent data collection from the metrics that are being transformed in a formula. For example, if an administrator is using a rollup super metric that is pulling data from multiple adapters and one goes offline the metric may skew heavy. As the saying goes, "garbage in, garbage out", so take care.

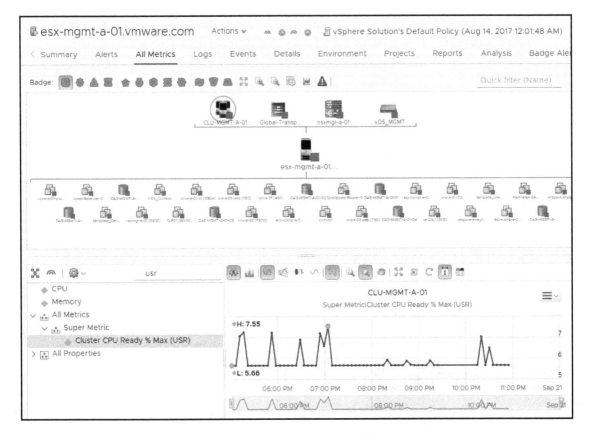

In certain scenarios, tracking a single super metric is easier than tracking the metrics on several separate objects. In this example, all the virtual machines on all hosts in the vSphere Cluster.

It is worth noting that you will find this metric for all objects in your environment. As we have associated this metric only with the Cluster computer resource object type, and enabled it only with that object type in the policy, the metric will only show data for that object type.

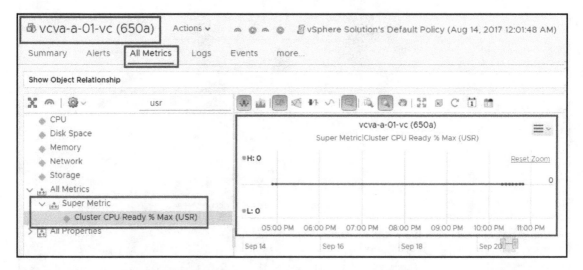

For example, if we look at the metrics at a virtual machine level and not vSphere Cluster level, we will still find our **Cluster CPU Ready % Max (USR)**, but it will not show any data.

Using operators in super metrics

Now that we've seen how to build our own super metrics, let's take a look at some of the operators we have available to supercharge our calculations.

Let's get back to the VM OS Uptime % example we have at the beginning of the chapter and recap it quickly. In vRealize Operations, you can get VM OS uptime via the OS Uptime metric. The metric shows an ever-growing number until a reboot of the monitored object takes place. This means that for any given time period you will end up with some number that might be very high or very low, and as such it becomes very hard to make sense of it in terms of uptime statistics.

We can use super metrics and the available comparison operators to turn these data points into something useful in the context of uptime statistics, which we can use for management or customer reports:

```
${this, metric=sys|osUptime_latest}<=300)?((((${this,
metric=sys|osUptime_latest}<300))*(${this,
metric=sys|osUptime_latest})))):(${this,
metric=sys|osUptime_latest}>=300)*300
```

This simple example will, for each data point, give you the OS uptime in seconds. It means that if every data point is 300, the VM OS Uptime is 100%.

So, how does it work? Let me break it down.

If

Let's start with the first part before the question mark, this is the `if` statement part of the super metric. If this is true, it will go to the `then` statement afterwards or else it will jump to the `else` statement. As we are doing the math, the true or false statement will come in the form of a Boolean value, a zero or a one. Zero means go to the `else` statement, and one means go to the `then` statement. Very basic stuff.

```
${this, metric=sys|osUptime_latest}<=300)
```

It will be true only if the metric `sys|osUptime_latest` is equal to or more than 300. The reason for this is that we know that if the value is 300 or more then the system has not been down, that is, rebooted. Then it is safe to jump to the conclusion that the update of the OS in the time period is 300 seconds or 100%.

Then

The `then` statement is anything between the question mark (?) and the colon (:). Again, this part of the super metric is only used if the first part (`if` statement), is zero as a Boolean value. This will mean that the OS has had downtime in the period. How much is what this part of the super metric statement is going to tell us:

```
((((${this, metric=sys|osUptime_latest}<300))*(${this,
metric=sys|osUptime_latest})))
```

The statement could have been shorter. I chose to have a way of validating the value of the statement. The first part, before the asterisk, looks at the time and validates that it is less than 300. If true it returns a value of one, which is multiplied by the OS uptime of the time period. This is what would be returned to vRealize Operations in OS Uptime for that time period.

Else

The `else` statement is the last part of the super metric. This is the all good scenario, and as such, the last part could just have been `300` as a value, because this is what it will always be. The only reason for having the validation in there is so you can see what is going on. Also, I used it a lot when I tried to figure out how this could be used:

```
(${this, metric=sys|osUptime_latest}>=300)*300
```

Simplified

How much can the super metric be shortened to you ask? This is how little! Once you know how it works, it is actually simpler to read it this way:

```
(${this, metric=sys|osUptime_latest}<=300)?(${this,
metric=sys|osUptime_latest}):300
```

Numbers to percentages

If you don't care for OS Uptime in seconds, you can always use the following example and get it as a percentage of the OS uptime over a given time period:

```
(${this, metric=sys|osUptime_latest}<=300)?((((${this,
metric=sys|osUptime_latest}<300))*(${this,
metric=sys|osUptime_latest})))/300*100:(${this,
metric=sys|osUptime_latest}>=300)*300/300*100
```

All I have done is divide the formula with `300`, which is the expected outcome, and then multiply it by `100` to get it into a percentage.

As every data point is now in a percentage, all you have to do to get the OS uptime for a given period is to get the average of the data point in the time period and you know the OS uptime for that VM.

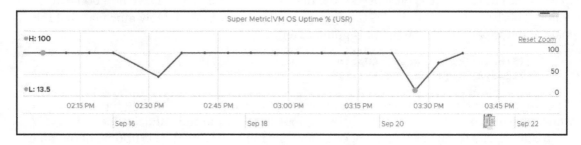

Consider the following graph from an OS uptime metric:

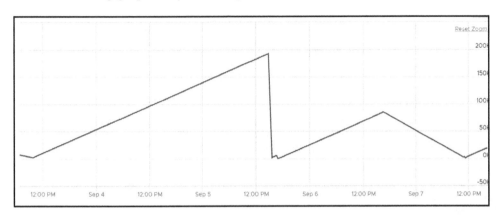

Same as before, every spike represents an OS reboot. As you can see, there are three distinct OS reboots:

- September 3rd around 11:00 AM
- September 5th around 5:00 PM
- September 7th around 12:00 PM

Here is the graph from a **VM OS Uptime %** super metric for the same period:

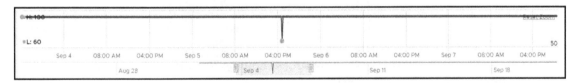

Notice that only one of the reboots (September 5th around 5:00 PM) is shown. The remaining OS reboots on September 3rd and September 7th are not detected.

The values for these are 2,209 and 377 respectively, which are above the vRealize Operations cycle of 300 seconds. This didn't show up as downtime on the graph as vRealize Operations was not running during that period and didn't capture the downtime. By the time vRealize Operations had started monitoring again, the VM OS was up for more than 300 seconds.

Let's look at another interesting use case. Consider the following graph:

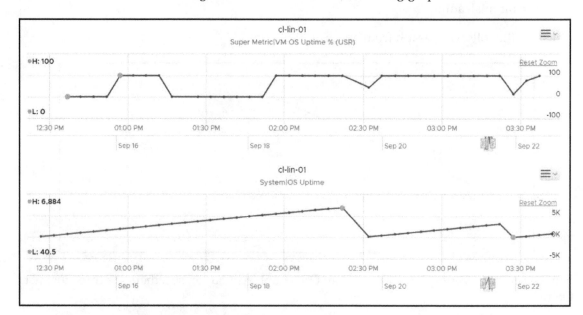

As you will notice, we are showing the **VM OS Uptime %** custom super metric we created earlier and the OS Uptime metric. Let's visually split the graph into two periods: before and after September 18th around 2:34 PM.

We can make the following observations for the before period based on the graph:

- The OS Uptime metric is constantly increasing and there are no spikes. As you must have learned by now, if you've paid attention, this means that there was on OS reboot.
- The **VM OS Uptime %** super metric is showing downtime for the same period of time as the OS Uptime metric.

In this case, the two observations contradict each other. One metric (graph) says there was downtime, the other one says there was none.

Why is that?

We will answer this in a moment, but first, let's take a look at the after period.

We can make the following observations for the after period based on the graph:

- The OS Uptime metric shows two spikes, which means two OS reboots took place
- The **VM OS Uptime %** super metric shows two downtime occurrences for the same period of time as the OS Uptime metric

In this case, both observations from both graphs for the after period match completely.

What has happened here is that between the two periods I have changed the formula in **VM OS Uptime %** super metric that calculates the uptime percentage. Once you change a formula for a metric it doesn't recalculate the data gathered from the past cycles (the before period). The new formula will be used to calculate data for all cycles onward (the after period).

As a rule of thumb, once a super metric has been created, applied to an Object type, and enabled for a policy, never change the formula of the super metric. In other words, once the metric has been used already in a cycle to gather data, do not change the metric. Instead, create a new metric and do the necessary corrections in the formula there.

As you can see, changing the metric formula can lead to inconsistent data. If you were to pull the OS uptime percentage statistics data as a report and present it to your stakeholders, it will be showing downtime when actually there was none. Sometimes the differences in data before and after a formula change may be unnoticeable, but sometimes they may be drastic, as in this case.

One more reason why you should create new metrics if you wish to change the formula is that if you change the formula of an existing metric this is not detectable anywhere and is unknown to anyone except you.

Comparing super metrics to views

Before ending our journey with super metrics, I think now would be a great time to explain how they are different from views. For example, a summary type view allows data from multiple objects to be transformed with operators such as sum, avg, max, and so on, in the same way that a rollup super metric does. Since you attach a super metric to an object, you can also specify if it is a key performance indicator or not. From there, you can decide if it is subject to normal vRealize Operations dynamic trending, or if you want a hard threshold.

The rule of thumb is if you need to create a view once with a metric, by all means, do. But if you need to repeatedly view a metric that is not available out of the box, you should consider a super metric. We will be talking more about views in the next chapter.

So, using a rollup super metric as an example, let's compare the two, with advantages and disadvantages of each.

Views

Views are quick and easy to create, especially compared to super metrics; when created they also have the ability to show past, present, and future data (trends). This is a big distinction from super metrics, which only have data from when they were created and attached to an object, as such you can't see the value of a super metric before it was applied.

Super metrics

A super metric is a metric in its own right, and, unlike views which are only dynamically generated when requested by a dashboard or report, a super metric once applied is always being calculated and stored in the FSDB as if it were a normal metric. Although the drawback of this, as mentioned previously, is that an administrator has no data for a super metric before it was applied, it does allow for a variety of benefits that views cannot provide.

First and foremost, a super metric is a real metric and both Dynamic Thresholds (once enough time has passed) and alerts can be applied to super metrics. This allows vRealize Operations to detect anomalies and alerts accordingly on a user-created super metric if the need arises. A super metric also has the granularity and regularity of any standard metric that makes it very easy to combine with other metric charts on all the metric windows.

Because of these pros and cons for both super metrics and views, it depends on the use case and situation as to which one might be the best fit. If you are in the situation where you need some basic data transformation on a group object, it might be a good idea to start with a view, and if the information is required on a regular basis, convert it into a super metric. However, if you need functionality such as advanced mathematical operands, or dynamic thresholds and alerts, skip straight to super metrics. Ensure that you put on a lab coat when defining them and do it on a whiteboard first, this will ensure that you gain the respect of your colleagues, who will see how smart you really are.

Summary

In this chapter, we explained what super metrics are and what they are used for. After that, we moved to building and applying our own super metrics. We also looked at some of the new calculation operators and how to use them. At the end, we compared super metrics to views.

In the next chapter, we will cover what vRealize Operations views and reports are. We will see how we can create custom views and custom reports to fit our needs.

10
Creating Custom Views

This chapter will cover what vRealize Operations views and reports are and how they assist in providing any piece of information about your environment at any time. You will discover the major improvements that these features bring to effectively managing your environment, as well as examples of how to create your own.

The following topics will be covered in this chapter:

- New additions to Views and Reports in vRealize Operations 6.6
- Views in vRealize Operations
- Reports in vRealize Operations

What's new in views and reports in vRealize Operations 6.6?

Views and reports haven't changed much since vRealize Operations 6.0, but one new feature worth mentioning is the ability to specify an Absolute Date Range for views.

To understand what Absolute Date Range is, let's consider the following use case. You have a customer that wants a monthly report, meaning no matter when the report was run in vRealize Operations, they wanted it to be for the last whole month or quarter.

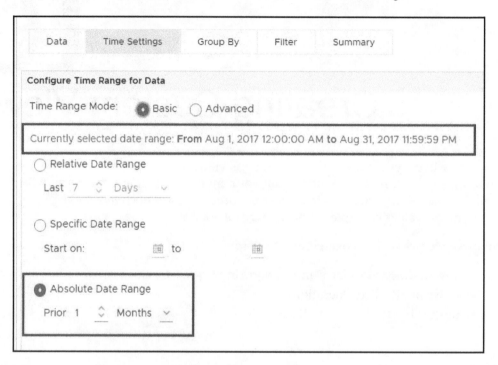

Now, there are two new things that can help you achieve that goal; the Absolute Date Range, which lets you specify the absolute time for this view, and the ability to understand the selections made. As can be seen, I have chosen one month back and I can verify my selection by looking at the "currently selected data range".

Views in vRealize Operations

A view presents collected information for an object in a certain way, depending on the view type. Each type of view helps you interpret properties, metrics, alerts, policies, and data from a different perspective.

Another way to interpret this is—a view is a window or a container that takes data from an object or group of objects and presents it in a way that provides useful information to the administrator. The first thing to take away from this statement is that a view is a container or object in its own right. It is the smallest component of a dashboard or report, but it can be linked to or used on its own.

It is also important to point out that views can be applied to any object type from any adapter. Different object types can be combined or compared in the same view if the objects have the same data types. These views can then be added to different parts of vRealize Operations to ensure they are available to administrators at the right time. We will discuss how to link views to other parts of the UI shortly.

vRealize Operations provides several types of views. Each view type helps you interpret metrics, and properties of various monitored objects, including alerts, symptoms, and so on from a different perspective.

Data in dashboards and reports can be displayed and transformed in several different ways using views.

Although many prebuilt views are available to choose from, any user with the correct privileges can create custom views. A view can be attached to an object of any type. Any data that is collected by any adapter can be used in a view or report.

Views are useful aids for the following tasks:

- Diagnosing and troubleshooting issues
- Gathering information about your environment

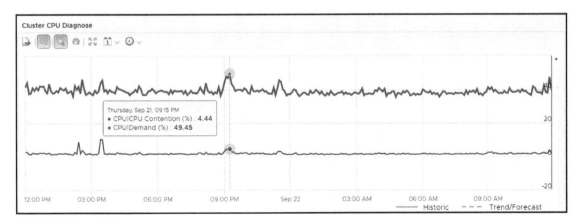

For example, the **Cluster CPU Diagnose** view provides trend information about CPU demand and contention in a cluster, which can be helpful for diagnosing system health issues.

 This view is available for data center or cluster objects.

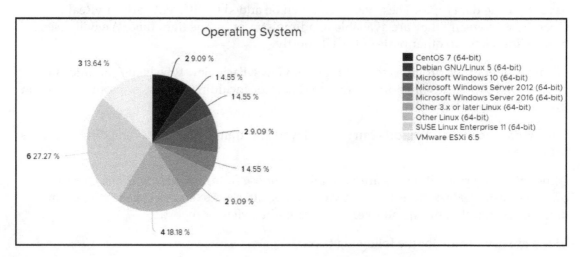

An example of an informational view can be the **Virtual Machine Guest OS Name** view, which categorizes virtual machines by the guest operating system that they are running on.

 Note: This view is available for data center, cluster, and Datastore objects.

Views are available from the following sources:

- Built into the product
- Installed management packs
- User-created (custom)

These are the only two view types available in vRealize Operations. The **Cluster CPU Diagnose** view is from type **Trend**, presenting information in a graph form. The **Virtual Machine Guest OS Name** view is from type **Distribution**, presenting information in a pie chart form. We will go through all available view types later in this chapter.

Views are accessible from a variety of places:

- From an object's **Details** tab
- From the Analysis section on the object **Analysis** tab
- From a custom dashboard
- From prebuilt or custom reports
- From the **Dashboards** tab under the **Views** section

Defining and building views

Before you start creating views, it is beneficial to have an understanding of the components that they are comprised of.

A view consists of the view type, subject, and data components:

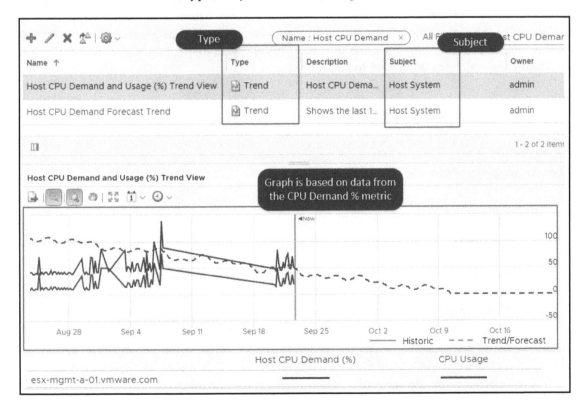

In this example, the view is a trend view, which gets its data from the **CPU Demand (%)** metric.

The subject is the object type, which a view is associated with.

A view presents the data of the subject. For example, if the selected object is a host and you select the view named **Host CPU Demand (%) Trend View**, the result is a trend of the host's CPU demand over a period of time.

Let's walk through what parts are needed to define and build our own custom views, and then apply them to real work situations.

Name and description

Although it might seem obvious, the first thing you need to define when creating a report is the name and description. Before you dismiss this requirement and simply enter `My View` or `Scott's Test`, the name and description fields are very useful in defining the scope and target of the view. This is because many views are not really designed to be run/applied on the subject, but rather on one of its parents. This is especially true for lists and distributions, which we will cover in just a moment.

View types (presentation)

The presentation is the format the view is created in and how the information is displayed.

The following types of views are available:

- **List**: A list view provides tabular data about specific objects in the environment that correspond to the selected view.
- **Summary**: A summary view presents tabular information about the current use of resources in the environment.
- **Trend**: A trend view uses historic data to generate trends and forecasts for resource use and availability in the environment.
- **Distribution**: A distribution view provides aggregated data about resource distribution in the monitored environment. Pie charts or bar charts are used to present the data.
- **Text**: A text view displays text that you provide when you create the view.
- **Image**: An image view allows you to insert a static image.

List

A list is one of the simplest presentation types to use and understand, and at the same time, is one of the most useful. A list provides a tabular layout of values for each data type, with the ability to provide an aggregation row such as sum or average at the end. Lists are the most useful presentation type for a large number of objects, and are able to provide information in the form of metrics and/or properties. Lists are also the most commonly used presentation when showing a collection of objects relative to its parent. An example of a list can be found in the following screenshot:

Datastore Inventory - Disk Space

Name	Time Remaining	Total	Usage (GB)	Provisioned (GB)	Overhead (GB)	Datastore capacity contention (%)
DAS-MGMT-A-01-02	> 1 Year	499.75 GB	127.92 GB	2,448.85 GB	53.99 GB	638.59 %
DAS-MGMT-A-01-04	50 Day(s)	499.75 GB	172.93 GB	998.63 GB	19.55 GB	253.32 %
DAS-MGMT-A-01-01	> 1 Year	492.5 GB	312.22 GB	319.96 GB	249.5 GB	133.63 %
DAS-MGMT-A-01-TI...	> 1 Year	499.75 GB	0.95 GB	0 GB	974 MB	0 %
DAS-MGMT-A-01-TI...	> 1 Year	499.75 GB	0.95 GB	0 GB	974 MB	0 %
DAS-MGMT-A-01-TI...	> 1 Year	499.75 GB	0.95 GB	0 GB	974 MB	0 %
DAS-MGMT-A-01-03	> 1 Year	499.75 GB	0.95 GB	0 GB	974 MB	0 %
Total	-	3,491 GB	616.87 GB	3,767.44 GB	326.84 GB	1,025.55 %

List summary

A summary is similar to a list, however the rows are the data types (rather than the objects) and the columns are aggregated values of all children of that subject type. Unlike a list, a summary field is compulsory, as the individual objects are not presented in the view. The summary view type is probably the least commonly used, but it is useful when you simply care about the end result and not the detail of how it was calculated.

The following example shows **Datastore Space Usage** from the cluster level; information such as the average used GB across each Datastore can be displayed without the need to show each Datastore present in a list:

Datastore Space Usage Breakdown

	Average Value	Peak Value	Standard Deviation
Disk Space|Capacity (GB)	498.71 GB	499.75 GB	2.54 GB
Disk Space|Provisioned Space	538.21 GB	2.39 TB	850.95 GB
Disk Space|Total used (GB)	88.12 GB	312.22 GB	113 GB
Disk Space|Virtual Machine used	46.3 GB	170.71 GB	60.84 GB
Disk Space|Virtual Disk Used (GB)	41.43 GB	153.37 GB	54.65 GB
Disk Space|Snapshot Space (GB)	0.0001 GB	0.001 GB	0.0003 GB
Disk Space|Swap File Space (GB)	4.71 GB	17 GB	7.46 GB
Disk Space|Overhead	46.69 GB	249.5 GB	84.76 GB

Although it will be discussed in more detail in the next chapter, the availability of creating simple summary views of child resources has partially removed the need for creating super metrics for simply rolling up data to parent objects.

Trend

A trend view is a line graph representation of metrics showing historical data that can be used to generate trends and forecasts. Unlike some of the other presentation types, a trend can only show data from that subject type. As such, trend views do not filter up to parent objects.

A trend view, in many ways, is similar to a standard metric chart widget with a set of combined preconfigured data types, with one major exception. The trend view has the ability to forecast data into the future for a specified period of time, as well as show the trend line for historical data for any object type.

This allows the trend view to provide detailed and useful capacity planning data for any object in the vRealize Operations inventory. When selecting the data types to use in the view, it is recommended that, if multiple data types are used, that they support the same unit of measurement. Although this is not a requirement, views that have different unit types on the same scale are relatively hard to compare. An example of a trend view is shown as follows:

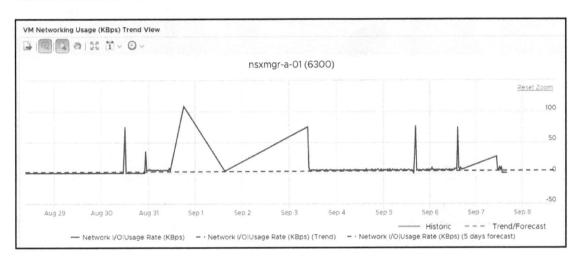

Distribution

A distribution view is a graphical representation of aggregated data which shows how resources fall within those aggregation groups. This essentially means that vRealize Operations finds a way of graphically representing a particular metric or property for a group of objects.

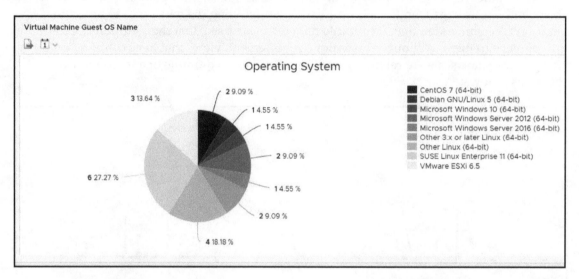

In this example, it is the distribution of VM OS types in a given vSphere cluster. A distribution like a summary is very useful in displaying a small amount of information about a large number of objects.

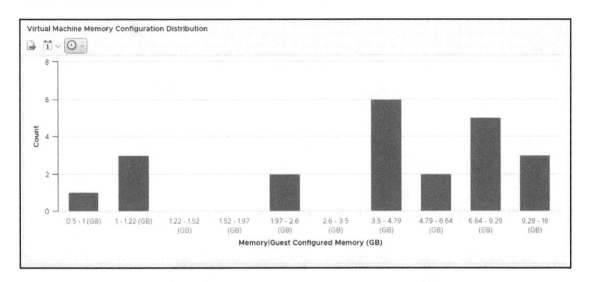

Distribution views can also be shown as bar charts. In this example, the distribution of **Virtual Machine Memory Configuration Distribution** is shown in a given vSphere cluster. This view can help spot virtual machines configured with a large amount of memory.

An important point when creating distribution views is that the subject must be a child of the preview or target object. This means that you can only see a view for the distribution on one of the subject's parent objects.

Both visualization methods essentially group the subjects into buckets, with the number of buckets and their values based on the distribution type. The three distribution types are as follows:

- **Dynamic distribution**: vRealize Operations automatically determines how many buckets to create based on an interval, a min/max value, or a logarithmic equation. When dealing with varying data values, this is generally the recommended display.
- **Manual distribution**: Allows the administrator to manually set the range of each bucket in the display.
- **Discrete distribution**: Used for displaying exact values of objects rather than ranges. A discrete distribution is recommended if most objects only have a few possible values, such as properties or other binary values.

Text and images

The text and image views are used to insert static text or image content for the purpose of reports and dashboards. They allow an administrator to add context to a report in combination with the dynamic views that are inserted when the reports are generated.

Subjects

Although the subjects are generally selected after the presentation, it makes sense to describe them first. The subject is the base object for which the view shows information. In other words, the subject is the object type that the data is coming from for the view. Any object type from any adapter can be selected. It is important to keep in mind that you may be designing a view for a parent object, however, the subject is actually the data of a child object. For example, if you wish to list all the **Datastore** free space in a vSphere Cluster itemized by Datastore, the subject will be a **Datastore**, not a **Cluster Compute Resource**. This is because although the list will always be viewed in the context of a cluster, the data listed is from **Datastore** objects themselves.

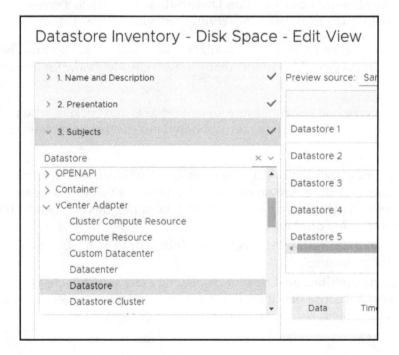

When selecting a subject, an option is provided to select multiple object types. If this is done, only data that is common to both types will be available.

Data

Data is the content that makes up the view based on the selected subject. The type of data that can be added and any additional options available depend on the select presentation type. An important feature with views is that they are able to display and filter based on properties, and not just standard metrics. This is particularly useful when filtering a list or distribution group. For example, the following screenshot shows badge information in a given vSphere Cluster, as long as they contain a vSphere tag of **BackupProtectedVM**. This allows a view to be filtered only to virtual machines that are deployed and managed by vRealize Automation:

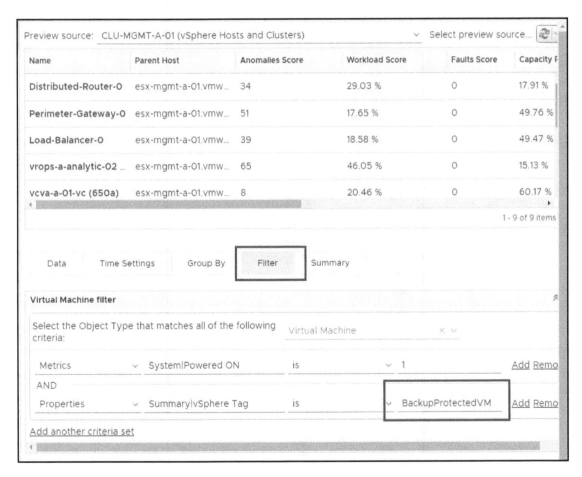

Visibility

One of the most useful features about views is that you have the ability to decide where they show up and where they can be linked from. The visibility layer defines where you can see a hyperlink to a view in vRealize Operations based on a series of checkboxes.

The visibility step is broken into three categories, which are **Availability**, **Further Analysis**, and **Blacklist**, as shown in the following screenshot:

Availability

Make the view available at:

- ☑ Dashboards through the View widget
- ☑ Report template creation and modification
- ☑ Details tab in the environment

Further Analysis

Make the view available at Further Analysis section for:

- ☐ Workload
- ☐ Anomalies
- ☐ Faults
- ☐ Time Remaining
- ☐ Capacity Remaining
- ☐ Stress
- ☐ Compliance
- ☐ Reclaimable Capacity
- ☐ Density

Blacklist

Hide the view for the selected Object Types:

Select an Object Type   ✕ ⌄

Add Object Type

Subsequently, you can also make the view available in a dashboard. To make this view available inside a dashboard, you can either edit an existing one or create a new dashboard by navigating to **Home**, **Actions**, then **Create Dashboard**. You can add the desired view within your dashboard configuration.

Availability

The availability checkboxes allow an administrator to devise how their view can be used and if there are cases where they wish to restrict its availability:

- **Dashboard through the view widget**: The view widget allows any created view to be displayed on a dashboard. This essentially allows an unlimited amount of data types to be displayed on the classic dashboards, with the flexibility of the different presentation types.
- **Report template creation and modification**: This setting allows views to be used in reports. If you are creating views explicitly to use in reports, ensure this box is checked.
- **Details tab in the environment**: The **Details** tab in the environment is the default location where administrators will use views. It is also the location where the **Further Analysis** links will take an administrator if selected. In most cases, it is recommended that this option be enabled, unless a view is not yet ready to be released to other users.

Further Analysis

The **Further Analysis** checkbox is a feature that allows an administrator to link views that they have created to the minor badges in the **Object Analysis** tab. Although this feature may seem comparatively small, it allows users to create relevant views for certain troubleshooting scenarios and link them directly to where administrators will be working. This allows administrators to leverage views more quickly for troubleshooting rather than simply jumping to the All Metrics tab and looking for dynamic threshold breaches.

Blacklist

The blacklist allows administrators to ensure that views cannot be used against certain object types. This is useful if you want to ensure that a view is only partially promoted up to a parent and not, for example, to a grandparent.

Deleting a view

Views show up in multiple places. When you're tempted to delete a view, ask yourself: Do I want to delete this entire view, or do I just want to no longer show it in one part of the UI?

Don't delete a view when you just want to hide it in one part of the UI. When you delete a view, areas in the UI that use the view are adjusted:

- **Report templates**: The view is removed from the report template
- **Dashboards**: The view widget displays the message **The view does not exist**
- **Further Analysis panel of badges on the Analysis tab: The link to the view is removed**
- **Details > Views tab for the selected object: The view is removed from the list**

vRealize Operations will display a message informing you that deleting the view will modify the report templates that are using the view.

Reports in vRealize Operations

vRealize Operations gives the ability to create custom reports for any object type. Out of the box, there are over 50 report templates to leverage straight away or use as examples for your own reports.

The creation of reports is very simple, since views are used as the delivery container for content in the reports. This includes the text and image presentation types, which can be used to add context and detail to manually or scheduled reports.

Like views, report templates can be imported and exported from other vRealize Operations systems, allowing administrators to share configuration across environments.

Creating reports

When you create reports, you have the option to add **Views and Dashboards** to the report. When you add a view to a report, the view is filled with sample data.

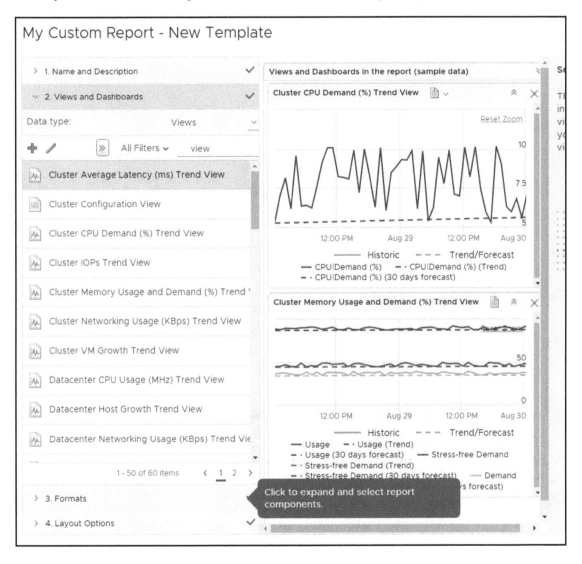

Previewing data in the view helps you verify that the information displayed meets your expectations. When you add a dashboard to a report, the dashboard fills with sample data.

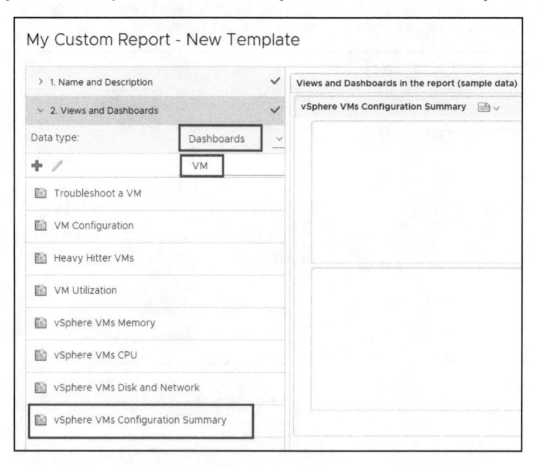

Select the dashboard from the list in the left pane and drag it to the main pane. Formats are the outputs in which you can generate a report. You can choose one or more of the following report formats:

- **PDF**: This output is best for sharing the report with users who need to print it
- **CSV**: This output is best for providing data to other data analysis applications

The report can contain the following layout options:

- Cover page
- Table of contents
- Footer

Scheduling reports

One common reason for creating reports for views is to allow them to be generated automatically on a schedule.

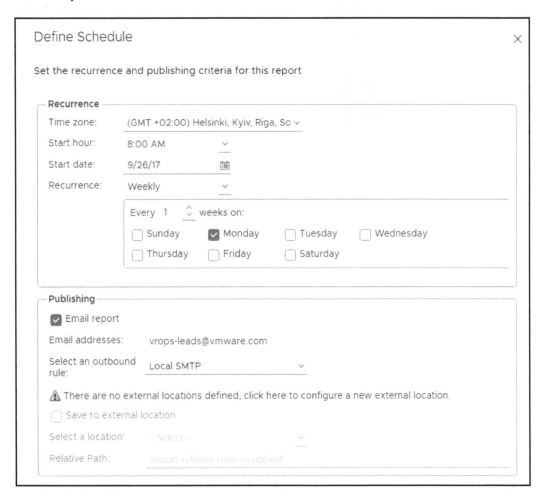

Scheduling reports can bring the following benefits to administrators:

- Allows views and data to be easily captured at a point in time and sent to interested stakeholders
- Allows for CSV copies of information to be sent to external systems that might also inject the data for their own requirements
- Allows different tailored reports to be sent to different teams, such as capacity management, on a regular basis without the need to log in to vRealize Operations

When setting up a scheduled report, the easiest way is to find the object in the environment and select the reports tab. From there, an administrator can select the relevant report template and under **Actions**, select schedule report.

Summary

In this chapter, we have covered the new powerful features that are in views and how they can be used in reports. We have covered the different view presentation types and their strengths and weaknesses for varying data types.

In the next chapter, we will discuss vRealize Operations Dashboards. We will look at some of the most commonly used widgets and how we can use them when creating custom dashboards.

11
Creating Custom Dashboards

In this chapter, we will discuss what a custom dashboard is and show how to create one. This will give you the foundation to create and build more that will suit any environment, application, or object being managed. This chapter will cover:

- What are dashboards?
- Types of widgets.
- Widget settings.
- Designing dashboards.
- Creating dashboards.
- Creating metric configuration files.

About dashboards

A dashboard provides a visual overview of an object. You can use different widgets and views to change the focus of information.

You can create various dashboards to meet your monitoring needs. You do not have to show every dashboard on the **Home** page. You can choose to show a subset of dashboards. You can select one dashboard as your default starting point.

To customize built-in dashboards, ensure that you clone the built-in dashboard before modifying the clone.

Designing dashboards

One of the greatest features of vRealize Operations is of course the ability to create custom dashboards. The power in custom dashboards is being able to display relevant information to the different areas of your organization.

Let's look at some of the reasons why we would want to create custom dashboards, and how they help to manage your environment more efficiently.

Dashboards are mainly used within different IT support teams. Generally, IT support is split up into different sections. This does vary from environment to environment with size and complexity. Typically, one would see the following infrastructure teams in an enterprise environment:

- Wintel server team
- Linux server team
- Storage team
- Database team
- Messaging team
- Applications middleware team
- Network team
- Monitoring team

Many of these teams will generally call on the VMware/Virtualization team or person when things are wrong, requesting metrics on disk, network, memory, and CPU to assist with troubleshooting issues, or blame the sole cause on it being a virtual machine; this is simply part of the philosophy that in IT operations generally the team lower down the stack is used as scapegoat.

What if a dashboard or two could be supplied with only the relevant information that each of those teams need? It will free up time, and hopefully make all the other teams more self-sufficient and less reliant on the VMware Admins. As such, creating dashboards for different teams or functions is a great way to provide self-service to performance management of a virtualized environment.

Different audiences have different needs. For example, executives usually want a high-level overview of the performance of the virtual infrastructure, and administrators want details and fast access to infrastructure data.

You need to identify relevant data sources. You might need to create additional data, such as super metrics. You might also want to add a management pack to monitor the correct metrics. For example, if you are monitoring VMware Horizon® View desktops, you must install the VMware vRealize® Operations for Horizon® solution to collect metrics and performance data from desktop agents. This management pack also provides its own set of dashboards.

We spoke about super metrics and management packs earlier in this book. You can use the following general guidelines to design a custom dashboard in vRealize Operations:

- Identify the audience or consumers of the dashboard
- Define how the dashboard must be used
- Define the functional aspects of the dashboard (operations, forensics, and support)
- Identify the data sources:
    - Create or add management packs, if necessary
    - Create or add super metrics, if necessary
- Identify the necessary widgets and interactions
- Build a prototype dashboard
- Share the dashboard with the intended audience

When designing the dashboard, you must consider the purpose for which the dashboard will be used. For example, the dashboard might be used to monitor line-of-business, which refers to the business-critical applications that are important to the enterprise.

You also may need to design dashboards to display the big picture, for example, of health or performance. Dashboards can be built to be clickable and focused on specific areas of your infrastructure or application. Some dashboards need interaction to display the expected information. For example, you might have to select a particular metric to see a graph of the metric values over a period of time.

You can create a dashboard that displays important information without user interaction and that automatically updates at a configured interval. These types of dashboards are often used for operations teams to display the big picture of the infrastructure or applications, or both.

You can create dashboards that monitor metrics that help you assess the health and performance of your environment. You can monitor the following:

- The overall operation of your clusters
- The capacity of your storage
- The capacity of your disaster recovery sites
- The performance and capacity of your Tier 1 applications

Here are a few use cases where you may want to create custom dashboards for specific metrics related to Cluster Operations:

- Display aggregate health, risk, and efficiency of each of these clusters and their trends
- Display unhealthy virtual machines for each cluster
- Display which hosts or clusters are stressed or underused
- Display which hosts in these clusters have high latencies to datastores

How much should I pay for storage: capacity consumed or provisioned?

Total virtual disk space used by all virtual machines (thin-provisioned) versus total provisioned disk space for all virtual machines in a line of business.

Do I have enough capacity in my failover data center?

- Display a side-by-side view of all clusters at site A
- Display the number of virtual machines deployed

How well am I using my Tier 1 clusters?

- Name each cluster by grade or generation of hardware
- List these clusters, their efficiency score, trend, and optimal consolidation ratio

How well am I using my Tier 1 storage?

- Display workload (and its trend), capacity remaining, time remaining, reclaimable capacity, and density

Widgets

Although dashboards are a powerful concept, a dashboard on its own is just a blank canvas. It is the ability for a dashboard to host widgets and their associated configuration that makes the difference. Widgets display the information we want to show in a large variety of different methods.

Most widgets display metric information in the form of scores, graphs, or lists. Widgets can also be linked by interactions, which means, when an object like a virtual machine is selected in one widget, the linked widget(s) will change its data based on the selected object. Some widgets require the use of an additional metric configuration XML file to show specific information that may be required.

Types of widgets

We will now have a look at all the available widgets and a quick explanation of each type. These widgets provide information about objects, metrics, alerts, and properties:

- **Alert List**: Displays alerts associated to the selected object(s).
- **Tag Picker**: Similar to object lists, but it lists all the tags such as object type, this cannot be modified.
- **Environment**: Displays the resources for which data is collected.
- **Environment Status**: Displays statistics for the overall environment: objects, metrics, applications, alerts, analytics, and users.
- **Metric Chart**: Ability to show multiple charts of any metric based on a selected time period. This widget is a common choice for an interactive troubleshooting type dashboard.
- **Metric Picker**: Displays all metrics for a selected object. This widget is commonly used in conjunction with the Metric Chart widget.
- **Object List**: As the name suggests, this widget lists objects, by default it will show every object available in vRealize Operations, but it can be limited to show specific objects by tags. This widget is designed to be used as an interactive widget allowing the user to see what is displayed in other widgets on the dashboard.
- **Sparkline Chart**: Displays a small chart over time that has just visual details with the metric name to the right of the small chart. This can display multiple metrics from multiple objects.
- **Top Alerts**: Shows the top alerts for the selected object or dependents of the selected object.

- **Property List**: Displays configuration metrics on the selected object.
- **Current Policy**: Displays information about the active policy that is assigned to an object or object group.
- **Data Collection Results:** Displays a list of all supported actions for an object.
- **DRS Cluster Settings:** Displays the workload of clusters and hosts.

These widgets can be used to provide useful visuals about the health of an object or application:

- **Container Details**: Shows all the child objects of the container object selected with summery of metrics, objects, and alarms for that container.
- **Health Chart**: Displays the historical health, risk, or efficiency badge data for a selected time period.
- **Container Overview**: Shows selected objects with health, risk, and efficiency badges with Sparklines.
- **Rolling View Chart**: Same as metric charts, but it only shows one chart at full size and allows manual selection of other charts, which can be cycled through automatically on a timer.
- **Mashup Chart**: Displays events that are overlaid on a health over time chart, alongside any anomalies over time for the object.
- **Anomaly Breakdown**: Shows the volume and anomaly score of the selected object.
- **Scoreboard Health**: Similar to Scoreboard, but it is displayed in circles. We can choose to display the score number of custom metrics.

These widgets can be used to provide information on health, object relationships, and metrics:

- **Object Relationship**: As the name suggests, it shows the parent and child relationships of the selected object along with the health, risk, and efficiency of all related objects.
- **Scoreboard**: This is a table of boxes that we can use to display any metric value with a custom label and a Sparkline if wanted. The box color values are also chosen or left to symptom state to determine.
- **Object Relationship (Advanced):** Identical to the normal Object Relationship, but it displays the information differently.
- **Environment Overview**: This was part of the earlier versions on vRealize Operations in what was the vSphere UI. It shows all the objects in a hierarchy, highlighting the object and all its relationships.

- **Topology Graph**: Shows a relationship mesh of all parent and child objects of the selected object.
- **Symptom Volume**: Displays the volume of symptoms over time for the selected object.
- **Top-N Analysis**: Allows the display of top *X* amount of objects by a specified metric or health score.
- **Recommended Actions:** Displays recommendations for problems found on vCenter Server instances.

These widgets can be used to analyze and visualize data:

- **View**: Displays views based on selected objects.
- **Heatmap**: This widget displays metrics represented as a color range grouped and sized by different object types. For example, colored by CPU usage, sized by VM, and grouped by host.
- **Forensics**: Shows the 75th, 90th, and 95th percentile overlaid with the objects metrics value to see how it compares.
- **Weather map**: This widget is similar to the heatmap widget, but it shows specific metric values over time, such as an animated GIF.
- **GEO**: Shows where your objects are located on a world map (if you use the GEO location object tag).
- **Text Display**: Shows text in the user interface.

These widgets can be used to provide badge information:

- **Health**: This widget can be seen on the default home screen of vRealize Operations , it shows the health badge for the object
- **Workload**: Displays the minor workload badge details for the selected object
- **Capacity Remaining**: Displays the capacity remaining details for the selected object
- **Stress**: Displays the minor badge with a heat map over 24/7
- **Anomalies**: Displays the anomaly minor badge with anomalies over time for the selected object
- **Faults**: Displays the faults minor badge with a list of all the faults for the selected object
- **Efficiency**: Displays the efficiency minor badge with a breakdown of what makes up the efficiency score via a pie chart
- **Reclaimable Capacity**: Displays the minor badge with a breakdown of what type of waste was reclaimable in a pie chart

- **Risk**: Displays the minor badge with a risk trend over time graph
- **Time Remaining**: Displays the time remaining minor badge with days remaining for resource types
- **Density**: Displays the minor badge with details on current density configurations
- **Capacity Utilization**: Displays objects that are underutilized, overutilized, and operating at optimum capacity levels

Widget configuration options

Each widget has a group of settings that will impact how the widget displays information and what information a widget will display. In this section, we will go through the common setting types and the layout of a widget.

Most widgets will have one or more of these common configuration options:

- **Title**: This is what is displayed as the title of the widget on the dashboard.
- **Refresh Content**: When enabled, the widget will refresh with the latest data automatically. This is recommended unless the widget is used in an interactive manner.
- **Refresh interval**: The interval when the widget will refresh data if enabled.
- **Self Provider**: When set to **on**, the widget becomes its own provider and will only show data on the objects and metrics selected within the widget itself and will not participate if linked to another widget.

Most widgets include options that must be configured individually to display information. The available configuration options vary depending on the widget type. The options listed in the slide are commonly used by most widgets.

If **Refresh Content** is **not enabled**, then the widget is updated only when the dashboard is opened or when you click **Refresh** on the widget in the dashboard.

If **Self Provider** is **Off**, then you configure other widgets to provide objects to the widget by using widget interactions or dashboard navigation.

It is recommended to set the refresh interval to the same as your collection interval, which is why 300 seconds is the default. If the widget is not displaying data that changes every data collection, such as capacity, it would be recommended not to enable refresh content.

Two more common settings that we will come across are as follows:

- **Res. Interaction Mode**: This setting is a drop-down menu of XML files that contains metrics we want to display for an object; this is only used when self-provider is set to off and linked to another widget through interactions.
- **Mode**: This has three settings:

  - **Self**: Displays information/metrics of the object, for example, Host A.
  - **Children**: The children of the selected object, if Host A, children would be, for example, Virtual Machines and datastores on Host A.
  - **Parent**: The parent of the object, if Host A then parent would be Cluster A. These settings are shown in the following screenshot.

Particular widgets will have specific settings related to only that widget, for example, generic scoreboard widget contains box size, text size, decimal places, or period length.

Widgets will generally have two or three sections: settings at the top, followed by object(s) or tags. If there is a third section it is generally additional settings such as box labels, measurement units, or to change the display order of metrics.

An example of the three sections is shown as follows:

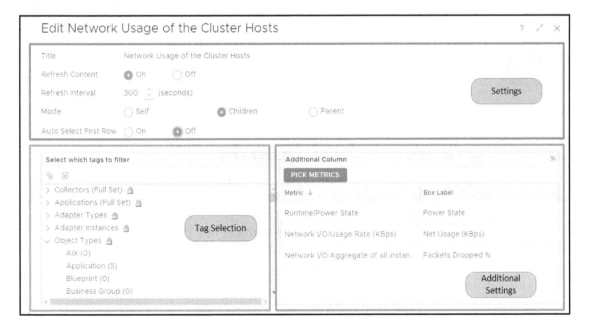

The following screenshot is an example of a widget with only two sections to it, which are settings and tag selection:

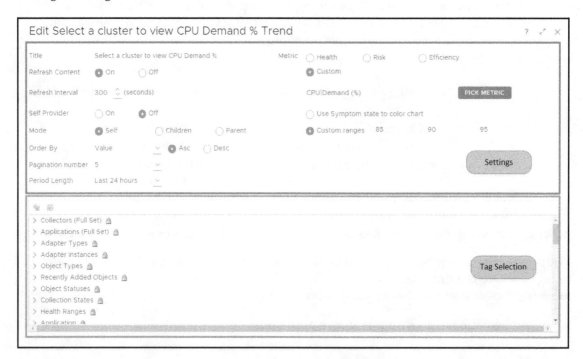

Widget settings will vary based on the widget, but most will share the previously mentioned configuration settings.

Creating custom dashboards

Creating a dashboard is a relatively simple exercise, creating a good dashboard will require tuning and some tweaking. The tricky part is displaying the information needed on a single screen, this is one of the biggest challenges when creating a dashboard; placing all the relevant information on a single pane of glass. The number one goal when creating a dashboard is to get all the information across in a glance.

Out of the 46 widgets vRealize Operations 6.6 has available, we will only use a handful of them regularly. The most commonly used widgets, from experience, are the scoreboard, metric selector, heat map, object list, and metric chart. The rest are generally only used for specific use cases.

There are basically two types of dashboards that we can create, an **interactive dashboard** or a **static dashboard**. An interactive dashboard is typically used for troubleshooting or similar activities where you are expecting the user to interact with widgets to get the information they are after. A static or display dashboard typically uses self-providing widgets such as scoreboards and heatmaps that are designed for display monitors, or other situations where an administrator is keeping an eye on environment changes.

Each of the widgets has the ability to be a self-provider that means we set the information we want to display directly in the widget. The other option is to set up interactions and have other widgets provide information based on object or metric selection in another widget.

Until the end of chapter, we will focus on the interactive dashboard; we will be looking at creating a dashboard that looks at vSphere cluster information, which at a glance will show us the overall health and general cluster information an administrator would need.

Working through this will give all the knowledge needed to be able to go away and create either type of dashboard. The dashboard we are about to create will show how to configure the more common widgets in a way that can be replicated on a greater scale.

When creating a dashboard, you will generally go through the following steps:

1. Start the **New Dashboard** wizard from the **Actions** menu.
2. Configure the general dashboard settings.
3. Add and configure individual widgets.
4. (Optional) Configure widget interactions.
5. (Optional) Configure dashboard navigation.

Creating an interactive dashboard

You can create a dashboard by using the **New Dashboard** wizard. Alternatively, you can clone an existing dashboard and modify the clone. Perform the following steps to create a new dashboard:

1. Navigate to the Dashboards page, click **Actions**, and then click **Create Dashboard**, as shown in the following screenshot:

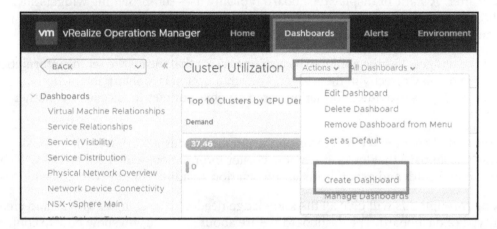

2. Under **Dashboard Configuration**, we need to give it a meaningful name and provide a description. If you click **Yes** for the **Is default** setting, the dashboard appears on the homepage when you log in.

   By default, the **Recommendations** dashboard is the dashboard that appears on the home page when a user logs in. You can change the default dashboard.

3. Next, we click on **Widget List** to bring up all the available widgets. Here we will click and drag the widgets we need from the left pane to the right. We will use the following:
   - Object List
   - Metric Picker
   - Metric Chart
   - Generic Scoreboard
   - Heat Map

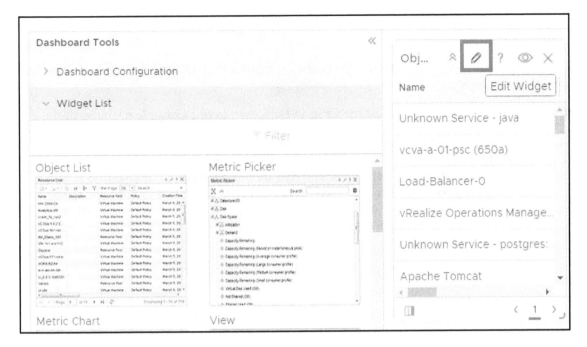

You can arrange widgets in the dashboard by dragging them to the desired column position. The left pane and the right pane are collapsed so that you have more room for your dashboard workspace, which is the center pane.

To edit the widgets, we click on the little pen icon sitting at the top of widget.

The Object List

The **Object List** widget configuration options, as shown in the following screenshot, include some of the more common options, such as **Title**, **Refresh Content**, and **Refresh Interval**.

Options also exist that are specific to this widget:

- **Mode:** You can select **Self**, **Children**, or **Parent** mode. This setting is used by widget interactions.
- **Auto Select First Row:** This enables you to select whether or not to start with the first row of data.
- **Select which tags to filter**: This enables you to select objects from an object tree to observe. For example, you can choose to observe information about objects managed by the vCenter Server instance named VCVA01.

You can add different metrics using the **Additional Column** option during widget configuration.

Using the **Additional Column** pane, you can add metrics that are specific for each object in the data grid columns.

Perform the following steps to edit the Object List widget in our example dashboard:

1. Click this on **Object List** and the **Edit Object List** window will appear. In here edit the **Title**, select **On** for **Auto Select First Row**, and select **Cluster Compute Resource** under **Object Types Tag**. We should have something similar to the following screenshot. Click **Save** to continue.

   With tag selection, multiple tags can be selected, if this is done then only objects that fall under both tag types will be shown in the widget.

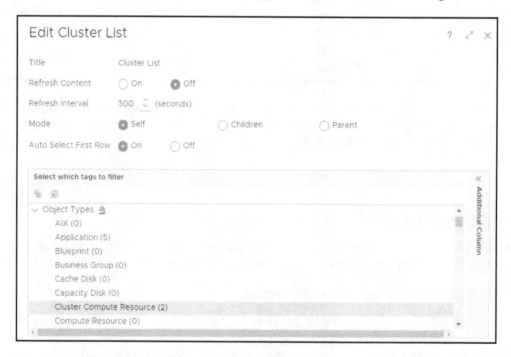

2. The next thing we want to do is click on **Widget Interactions** on the left pane; this is where we go to link the widgets, for example, we select a virtual machine from an object list widget and it would change any linked widgets to display the information of that object.

3. We will see a **Selected Object(s)** with a drop-down list followed by a green arrow pointing to our widgets. This is saying that what we select in the drop-down list will be linked to the associated widget.

4. Here our new **Cluster List** will feed **Metric Picker, Scoreboard,** and **Heatmap**, while **Metric Picker** will feed **Metric Chart**. Also we will notice that a widget like **Metric Chart** can be fed by more than one widget. Click **APPLY INTERACTIONS** and we should end up with something similar to the following screenshot:

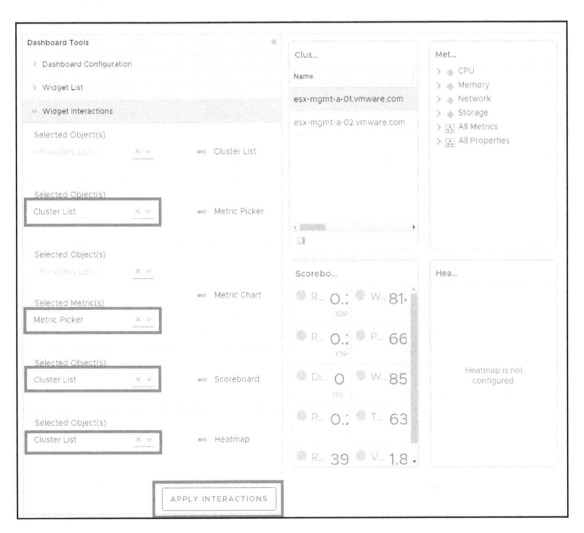

The Metric Picker

Now, if we select a metric under the **Metric Picker** widget it should show the metric in the **Metric Chart** widget, as displayed in the following screenshot:

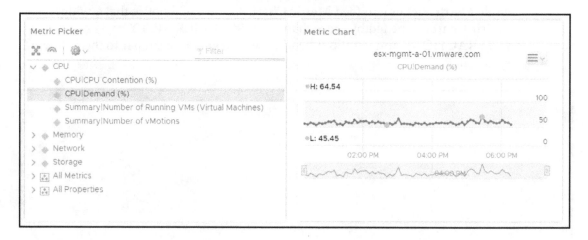

 Metric Picker will contain all the available metrics for the selected object, such as an ESXi host or a Virtual Machine.

The Heatmap

Next up, we will edit the **Heatmap** widget. For this example, we will use the Heatmap widget to display capacity remaining for the datastores attached to the vSphere cluster. This is the best way to see at a glance that none of the datastores are over 90% used or getting close. We need to make the following changes:

1. Give the widget a new name describing what we are trying to achieve.
2. Change Group By to Cluster Compute Resource - This is what we want the parent container to be.
3. Change mode to Instance - This mode type is best used when interacting with other widgets to get its objects.
4. Change Object Type to Datastore - This is the object that we want displayed.

5. Change Attribute Kind to Disk Space | Capacity Remaining (%) - The metric of the object that we want to use.

6. Change Colors around to 0 (Min), 20 (Max) - Because we really only want to know if a datastore is getting close to the threshold, minimizing the range will give us more granular colors. Change the colors around making it red on the left and green on the right. This is done by clicking on the little color square at each end and picking a new color. The reason this is done is because we have capacity remaining, so we need 0% remaining as red.

7. Click **Save** and we should now have something similar to the following screenshot, with each square representing a datastore:

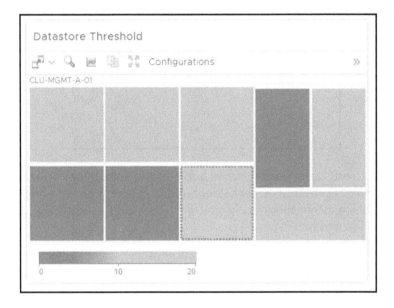

 Move the mouse over each box to reveal more detail of the object.

The Scoreboard

Time to modify the last widget. This one will be a little more complicated due to how we display what we want while being interactive. When we configured the widget interactions, we noticed that the scoreboard widget was populated automatically with a bunch of metrics, as shown in the following screenshot:

Now, let's go back to our dashboard creation and edit the Scoreboard widget. We will notice quite a lot of configuration options compared to others, most of which are how the boxes are laid out, such as number of columns, box size, and rounding out decimals. What we want to do for this widget is:

- Name the scoreboard something meaningful
- Round the decimals to 1 - this cuts down the amount of decimal places returned on the displayed value
- Under **Metric Configuration** choose the **Host-Util** file from the drop-down list

We should now see something similar to the following screenshot:

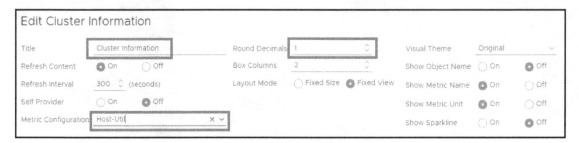

But what about the object selection you may have noticed in the lower half of the scoreboards widget? These are only used if we make the widget a self-provider, which we can see as an option to the top left of the edit window. We can choose objects and metrics, but they are ignored when **Self Provider** is set to **Off**.

If we now click **Save** we should see the new configuration of the scoreboard widget, as shown in the following screenshot:

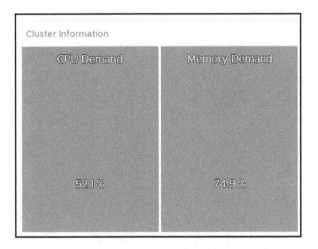

 I've also changed the **Visual Theme** to **Original** in the scoreboard widget configuration options to change the way the scoreboard visualizes the information.

The scoreboard widget may not always display the information we necessarily need. To get the widget to display the information we want while continuing to be interactive to our selections in the **Cluster List** widgets, we have to create a **metric configuration (XML) file**.

Metric Configuration Files (XML)

A lot of the widgets are edited through the GUI with the objects and metrics we want displayed, but some require a **metric configuration file** to define what metrics the widget should display.

Metric configuration files can create a custom set of metrics for the customization of supported widgets with meaningful data.

Metric configuration files store the metric attribute keys in **XML format.**

These widgets support customization using metric configuration files:

- Scoreboard
- Metric Chart
- Property List
- Rolling View Chart
- Sparkline Chart
- Topology Graph

To keep this simple, we will configure four metrics to be displayed, which are:

- CPU usage for the cluster in %
- CPU demand for the cluster
- Memory ballooning
- CPU usage for the cluster in MHz

Perform the following steps to create a metric configuration file:

1. Open a text editor, add the following code, and save it as an XML file; in this case we will call it `clusterexample.xml`:

```xml
<?xml version="1.0" encoding="UTF-8" standalone="yes"?>

<AdapterKinds>
   <AdapterKind adapterKindKey="VMWARE">
      <ResourceKind resourceKindKey="ClusterComputeResource">
        <Metric attrkey="cpu|capacity_usagepct_average" label="CPU"
unit="%" yellow="50" orange="75" red="90" />
        <Metric attrkey="cpu|demandPct" label="CPU Demand" unit="%"
yellow="50" orange="75" red="90" />
        <Metric attrkey="cpu|usagemhz_average" label="CPU Usage"
unit="GHz" yellow="8" orange="16" red="20" />
        <Metric attrkey="mem|vmmemctl_average" label="Balloon Mem"
unit="GB" yellow="100" orange="150" red="200" />
      </ResourceKind>
   </AdapterKind>
</AdapterKinds>
```

2. Using WinSCP or another similar product, upload this file to the following location on the vRealize Operations 6.0 virtual appliance:

```
/usr/lib/vmware-vcops/tomcat-web-app/webapps/vcops-web-ent/WEB-
INF/classes/resources/reskndmetrics
```

In this location, you will notice some built in sample XML files.

3. Alternatively, you can create the XML file from the vRealize Operations user interface. To do so, navigate to **Administration | Configuration**, and then **Metric Configuration**.

4. Now let's go back to our dashboard creation and edit the **Scoreboard** widget. Under **Metric Configuration** choose the `clusterexmaple.xml` file that we just created from the drop-down list. Click **Save** to save the configuration.

5. We have now completed the new dashboard; click **Save** on the bottom right to save the dashboard. We can go back and edit this dashboard whenever we need to. This new dashboard will now be available on the home page, this is shown in the following screenshot:

For the **Scoreboard** widget we have used an XML file so the widget will display the metrics we would like to see when an object is selected in another widget. How can we get the correct metric and adapter names to be used in this file?

Glad you asked. The simplest way to get the correct information we need for that XML file is to create a non-interactive dashboard with the widget we require with all the information we want to display for our interactive one.

For example, let's quickly create a temp dashboard with only one scoreboard widget and populate it with what we want by manually selecting the objects and metrics with self-provider set to yes:

1. Create another dashboard and drag and drop a single scoreboard widget. Edit the scoreboard widget and configure it with all the information we would like. Search for an object in the middle pane and select the widgets we want in the right pane.

2. Configure the box label and Measurement Unit. A thing to note here is that we have selected memory balloon metric as shown in the following screenshot, but we have given it a label of GB. This is because of a new feature in 6.0 it will automatically upscale the metrics when shown on a scoreboard, this also goes for datastore GB to TB, CPU MHz to GHz, and network throughput from KBps to MBps. Typically in 5.x we would create super metrics to make this happen.

   The downside to this is that the badge color still has to be set in the metrics base format.

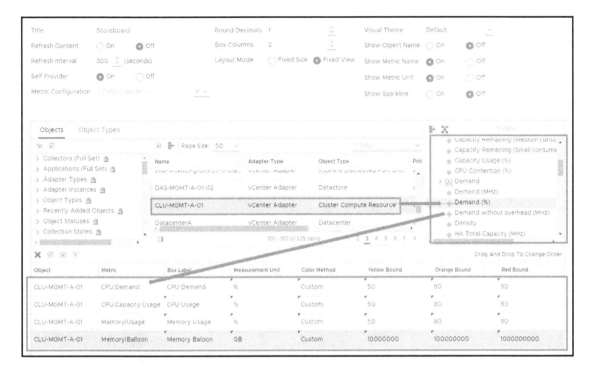

3. Save this dashboard once we have the metrics we want. Locate it under our dashboard list and select it, click on the little cog, and select **Export Dashboards** as shown in the following screenshot.

4. This will automatically download a file called `Dashboard<Date>.json`.

Open this file in a text editor and have a look through it and we will see all the information we require to write our XML interaction file.

First off is our `resourceKindKey` and `adapterKindKey`, as shown in the following screenshot. These are pretty self-explanatory, `resourceKind` being Cluster resource, and adapter is the adapter that's collecting the metrics, in this case the inbuilt vCenter one called VMWARE.

```
        }]
    }],
    "entries": {"resource": {
        "adapterKindKey": "VMWARE",
        "identifiers": [
            {
                "key": "VMEntityObjectID",
                "value": "domain-c26"
            },
            {
                "key": "VMEntityVCID",
                "value": "24c626fa-da61-4c79-8a0b-17740d485cca"
            }
        ],
        "internalId": "resource:id:0_::_",
        "name": "CLU-MGMT-A-01",
        "resourceKindKey": "ClusterComputeResource"
    }]},
    "uuid": "a2554b71-bfda-456f-9037-82b4faf2571a"
}
```

Next are our resources, as we can see from the following screenshot we have `metricKey`, which is the most important one as well as the color settings, unit, and the label:

```
    "resourceMetrics": [
        {
            "colorMethod": 0,
            "id": "extModel2608-1",
            "isStringMetric": false,
            "label": "CPU Demand",
            "metricKey": "cpu|demandPct",
            "metricName": "CPU|Demand",
            "metricUnitId": "percent",
            "orangeBound": 80,
            "redBound": 90,
            "resourceId": "resource:id:0_::_",
            "resourceKindId": "002006VMWAREClusterComputeResource",
            "resourceName": "CLU-MGMT-A-01",
            "unit": "%",
            "yellowBound": 50
        },
```

There it is, how we can get the information we require for XML files:

```xml
<?xml version="1.0" encoding="UTF-8" standalone="yes"?>
<AdapterKinds>
    <AdapterKind adapterKindKey="VMWARE">         <ResourceKind
resourceKindKey="ClusterComputeResource">          <Metric
attrkey="cpu|capacity_usagepct_average" label="CPU" unit="%" yellow="50"
orange="75" red="90" />    <Metric attrkey="cpu|demandPct" label="CPU
Demand" unit="%" yellow="50" orange="75" red="90" />     <Metric
attrkey="cpu|usagemhz_average" label="CPU Usage" unit="GHz" yellow="8"
orange="16" red="20" />    <Metric attrkey="mem|vmmemctl_average"
label="Balloon Mem" unit="GB" yellow="100" orange="150" red="200" />
      </ResourceKind>
    </AdapterKind>
</AdapterKinds>
```

Any widget with the setting Metric Configuration available can use the XML files you create. The XML format is as per the preceding code. An XML file can also have multiple Adapter kinds as there could be different adapter metrics that you require.

Summary

In this chapter, we've learned why you would want to create dashboards; mainly to get all the other support teams off our backs. We learned how each of the widgets function, then how we can link them together to make a dashboard that is interactive based on selections made within widgets. We also unraveled the mystery of the metric configuration XML file and how to get the information we require into it.

In the next chapter, we will cover how we can use vRealize Operations to monitor applications and services within our environment.

12
Using vRealize Operations to Monitor Applications

In this chapter, we will cover how you can use vRealize Operations to monitor operating systems and an application's compliance. We will also discuss what the Endpoint Operations Management Agent is.

This chapter will cover:

- What is Endpoint Operations Management?
- Endpoint Operations Management key components.
- Installing and reinstalling the Endpoint Operations Management Agent.
- Viewing and collecting metrics from the agent
- How to add more monitoring objects
- Using the remote checker and multiprocess Endpoint Operations Management functionalities

What is Endpoint Operations Management?

As we saw earlier in this book, the vSphere adapter, included out of the box with vRealize Operations, allows you to monitor your virtual infrastructure. Although it can gather an extensive amount of information, it cannot monitor everything in the virtual infrastructure. The vSphere adapter creates visibility for the vSphere hypervisor and management layers.

In the following example, the **Operations Overview** dashboard shows the status of a VMware vCenter Server system and the status of all running services. Monitoring the vCenter Server services ensures prompt action in the event of an anomaly before the anomaly escalates into a bigger issue:

The vSphere adapter collects information from those layers about networking, storage, and virtual machines, but only from hypervisors' point of view. It will let you know how virtual switches and virtual machines are behaving, but not how your VMware NSX Manager or network devices are behaving, or what is happening within the virtual machine guest operating system.

Here is where the Endpoint Operations Management Agent comes to help.

Endpoint Operations Management was previously called **Application Infrastructure Management** (**AIM**). I will occasionally refer to Endpoint Operations Management as EP-OPS and to the Endpoint Operations Management Agent as EP-OPS Agent. Neither EP-OPS nor EP-OPS Agent are official VMware names.

The Endpoint Operations Management Agent enables vRealize Operations to collect data directly from within a virtual machine guest or a physical system's operating system. This data includes the operating system, service, and application time series metrics. This provides holistic monitoring of the operating system and applications all the way down to services, processes, and the application layer.

For monitoring applications, you should install solutions specific to the applications. For example, the default endpoint operation solution will monitor the operating systems and remote services of a node. But, to monitor applications such as SQL databases and services, you will have to install the .pak file for the SQL Endpoint Operations solution.

The SQL Endpoint Operations Management solution will install the SQL plugin on vRealize Operations cluster nodes.

What is new in vRealize Operations 6.6?

Although not much, there are few new things related to the Endpoint Operations Management Agent in vRealize Operations 6.6 that are worth mentioning.

Agent support for IPv6 environments for Microsoft Windows Server 2016 is now available, which is something that has been asked for by customers for a while.

Now, the agent also collects the following metrics for NFS-mounted filesystems:

- **Resource availability**: Availability
- **Use percent (%)**: Utilization
- **Total bytes free (KB)**: Utilization

The vRealize Operations UI has also undergone a change related to the Endpoint Operations Management Agent.

The **Plugins** tab will show all the Endpoint Operations Management plugins which are installed. You can highlight a specific plugin and disable it from here. You can access the **Plugins** tab by navigating to **Administration** | **Configuration** | **Endpoint Operations**. When you disable a plugin, it is removed from all the agents on which it has existed, and the agent no longer collects the metrics and other data related to that plugin. The plugin is marked as disabled on the vRealize Operations server.

You cannot disable the default plugins that are installed during the vRealize Operations installation.

The **Operating Systems** plugin collects metrics for:

- Operating system object types such as Linux, AIX, Solaris, and Windows
- Windows services, script services, and multi process services

The **Remote Service Monitoring** plugin collects metrics for object types such HTTP check, TCP check, and ICMP check.

To monitor specific applications, you will have to install their respective solutions. For example, to monitor SQL databases and services, you have to install the .pak file for the Endpoint Operations Management solution. The solution will subsequently install the SQL plugin on vRealize Operations nodes.

Endpoint Operations Management key components

Let's take a look at some key components of the Endpoint Operations Management Agent, including how they looked before, in previous vRealize Operations versions, and how they look today:

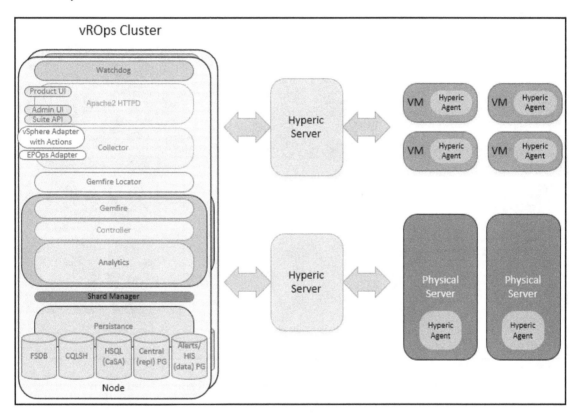

In previous versions of vRealize Operations, when you needed guest metrics for applications, middleware, and databases, you would have Hyperic agents installed on guests. You would also have a **Hyperic Server** to receive inventory and metrics from those agents:

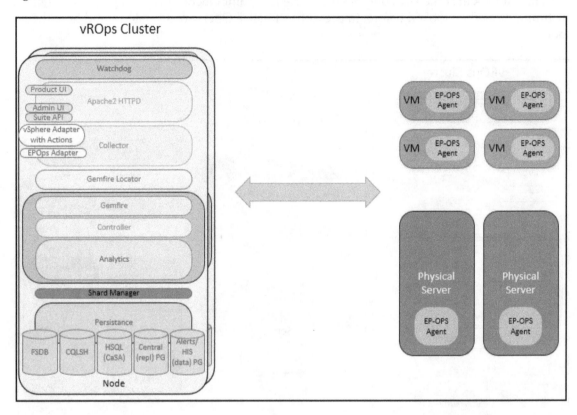

Since vRealize Operations 6.1, VMware merged some of the Hyperic solutions into vRealize Operations. This makes it a lot easier to get metrics from services, processes, and the application layer, without the need for a **Hyperic server**:

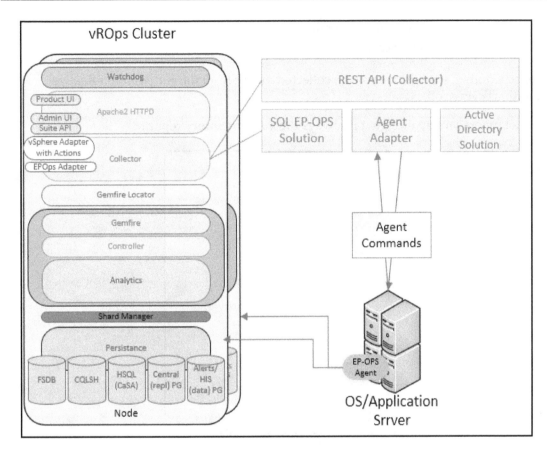

The Endpoint Operations Management solution is delivered with vRealize Operations and does not require the installation of a separate management pack. By default, Endpoint Operations Management adapters are installed on all data nodes.

The Endpoint Operations Management Agent is a piece of code installed on each endpoint. It talks to the OS layer to gather relevant information. Communication between the Endpoint Operations Management Agent and the vRealize Operations server is unidirectional. As we will see later in this chapter, the agent initiates a connection to vRealize Operations during installation.

Once the data is sent by the agent, the agent-adapter schedules the metric collection as per the collection cycle based on the metrics type:

- **Availability metrics**: One minute
- **Throughput metrics**: Five minutes

- **Performance metrics**: Five minutes
- **Utilization metrics**: Five minutes

After scheduling, the agent sends the collected metric from the endpoint to vRealize Operations every collection cycle.

The first report sent by the agent is always the **auto inventory** report:

About Me	
Agent Bundle Version:	agent-x86-64-linux-6.6.0
Description:	EP Ops Agent
Java Vendor:	Oracle Corporation
Java Version:	1.8.0_131
Name:	EP Ops Agent - cl-lin-01.vmware.com
Sigar Native Version:	1.6.6.0
Sigar Version:	1.6.6.0
User Home:	/home/epops
Agent Version:	6.6.0

The **About Me** section on the UI for the endpoint object is the auto inventory report, which contains all the properties of the object. Thereafter, the subsequent report sent by the agent is the metric report. Afterwards, the auto inventory runs every 15 mins on the endpoint.

Managing the Endpoint Operations Management Agent

You can install the Endpoint Operations Management Agent from a `tar.gz` or `.zip` archive, or from an operating system-specific installer for Windows or for Linux-like systems that support RPM.

The agent can come bundled with JRE or without JRE.

Installing the Agent

Before you start, you have to make sure you have vRealize Operations user credentials to ensure that you have enough permissions to deploy the agent.

Let's see how can we install the agent on both Linux and Windows machines.

Manually installing the Agent on a Linux Endpoint

Perform the following steps to install the Agent on a Linux machine:

1. Download the appropriate distributable package from `https://my.vmware.com` and copy it over to the machine. The Linux `.rpm` file should be installed with the `root` credentials. Log in to the machine and run the following command to install the agent:

       [root]# rpm -Uvh <DistributableFileName>

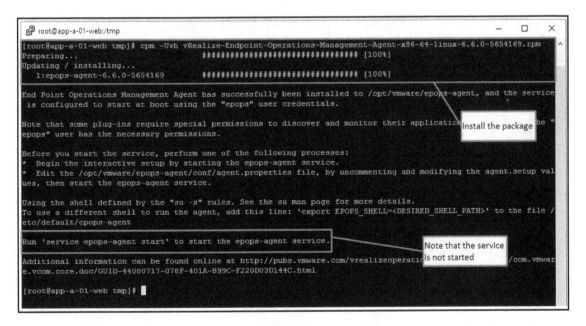

   In this example, we are installing on CentOS. Only when we start the service will it generate a token and ask for the server's details.

2. Start the Endpoint Operations Management Agent service by running:

```
service epops-agent start
```

The previous command will prompt you to enter the following information about the vRealize Operations instance:

- **vRealize Operations server hostname or IP:** If the server is on the same machine as the agent, you can enter the `localhost`. If a firewall is blocking traffic from the agent to the server, allow the traffic to that address through the firewall.
- **Default port:** Specify the SSL port on the vRealize Operations server to which the agent must connect. The default port is `443`.
- **Certificate to trust:** You can configure Endpoint Operations Management agents to trust the root or intermediate certificate to avoid having to reconfigure all agents if the certificate on the analytics nodes and remote collectors are modified.
- **vRealize Operations credentials:** Enter the name of a vRealize Operations user with agent manager permissions.

The agent token is generated by the Endpoint Operations Management Agent. It is only created the first time the endpoint is registered to the server. The name of the token is random and unique, and is based on the name and IP of the machine.

 If the agent is reinstalled on the Endpoint, the same token is used, unless it is deleted manually.

Provide the necessary information, as shown in the following screenshot:

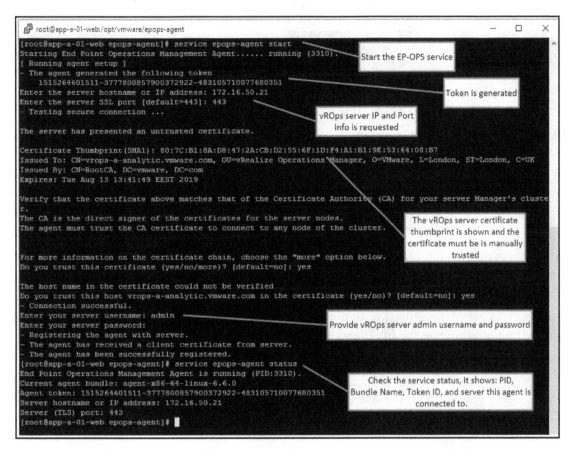

Go into the vRealize Operations UI and navigate to **Administration** | **Configuration** | **Endpoint Operations**, and select the **Agents** tab:

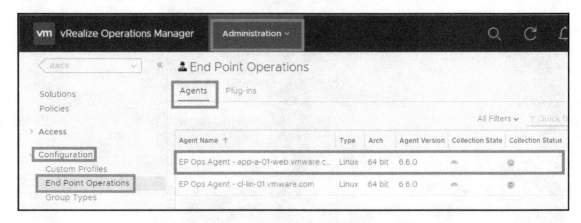

After it is deployed, the Endpoint Operations Management Agent starts sending monitoring data to vRealize Operations, where the data is collected by the Endpoint Operations Management adapter.

You can also verify the collection status of the Endpoint Operations Management Agent for your virtual machine on the **Inventory Explorer** page.

 If you encounter issues during the installation and configuration, you can check the `/opt/vmware/epops-agent/log/agent.log` log file for more information. We will examine this log file in more detail later in this book.

Manually installing the agent on a Windows Endpoint

On a Windows machine, the Endpoint Operations Management Agent is installed as a service.

The following steps outline how to install the Agent via the `.zip` archive bundle, but you can also install it via an executable file.

Perform the following steps to install the Agent on a Windows machine:

1. Download the agent .zip file. Make sure the file version matches your Microsoft Windows OS. Open Command Prompt and navigate to the bin folder within the extracted folder. Run the following command to install the agent:

   ```
   ep-agent.bat install
   ```

2. After the install, is complete, start the agent by executing:

   ```
   ep-agent.bat start
   ```

If this is the first time you are installing the agent, a setup process will be initiated. If you have specified configuration values in the agent properties file, those will be used.

Upon starting the service, it will prompt you for the same values as it did when we installed in on a Linux machine. Enter the following information about the vRealize Operations instance:

- vRealize Operations server hostname or IP
- Default port
- Certificate to trust
- vRealize Operations credentials

 If the agent is reinstalled on the endpoint, the same token is used, unless it is deleted manually.

After it is deployed, the Endpoint Operations Management Agent starts sending monitoring data to vRealize Operations, where the data is collected by the Endpoint Operations Management adapter. You can verify the collection status of the Endpoint Operations Management Agent for your virtual machine on the **Inventory Explorer** page:

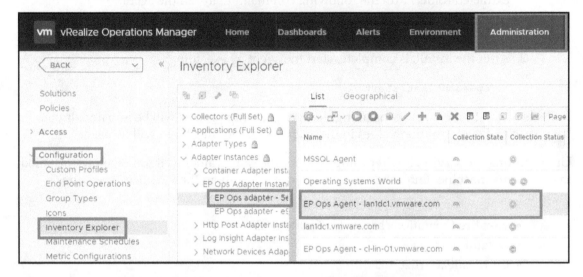

Because the agent is collecting data, the collection status of the agent is green.

Alternatively, you can also verify the collection status of the Endpoint Operations Management Agent by navigating to **Administration** | **Configuration** | **Endpoint Operations**, and selecting the **Agents** tab.

Automated agent installation using vRealize Automation

In a typical environment, the Endpoint Operations Management Agent will not be installed on many/all virtual machines or physical servers. Usually, only those servers holding critical applications or services will be monitored using the agent. Of those servers which are not, manually installing and updating the Endpoint Operations Management Agent can be done with reasonable administrative effort. If we have an environment where we need to install the agent on many VMs, and we are using some kind of provisioning and automation engine like Microsoft System Center Configuration Manager or VMware vRealize Automation, which has application-provisioning capabilities, it is not recommended to install the agent in the VM template that will be cloned.

If for whatever reason you have to do it, do not start the Endpoint Operations Management Agent, or remove the Endpoint Operations Management token and data before the cloning takes place. If the Agent is started before the cloning, a client token is created and all clones will be the same object in vRealize Operations.

In the following example, we will show how to install the Agent via vRealize Automation as part of the provisioning process. I will not go into too much detail on how to create blueprints in vRealize Automation, but I will give you the basic steps to create a software component that will install the agent and add it to a blueprint.

Perform the following steps to create a software component that will install the Endpoint Operations Management Agent and add it to a vRealize Automation Blueprint:

1. Open the vRealize Automation portal page and navigate to **Design**, the **Software Components** tab, and click **New** to create a new software component. On the **General** tab, fill in the information.

2. Click **Properties** and click **New** . Add the following six properties, as shown in the following table:

Name	Type	Value	Encrypted	Overridable	Required	Computed
RPMNAME	String	The name of the Agent RPM package	No	Yes	No	No
SERVERIP	String	The IP of the vRealize Operations server/cluster	No	Yes	No	No
SERVERLOGIN	String	Username with enough permission in vRealize Operations	No	Yes	No	No
SERVERPWORD	String	Password for the user	No	Yes	No	No

		The thumbprint of				
SRVCRTTHUMB	String	the vRealize Operations certificate	No	Yes	No	No
SSLPORT	String	The port on which to communicate with vRealize Operations	No	Yes	No	No

These values will be used to configure the Agent once it is installed. The following screenshot illustrates some example values:

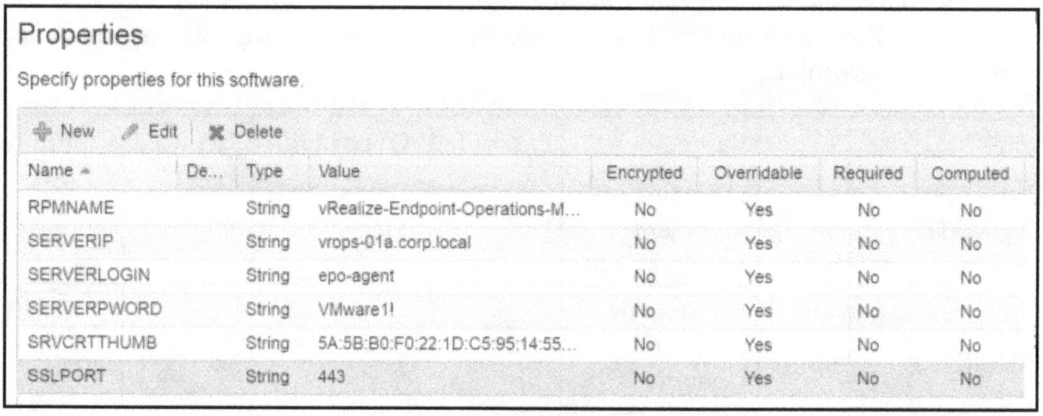

Properties

Specify properties for this software.

✛ New   ✎ Edit   ✖ Delete

Name ▲	De...	Type	Value	Encrypted	Overridable	Required	Computed
RPMNAME		String	vRealize-Endpoint-Operations-M...	No	Yes	No	No
SERVERIP		String	vrops-01a.corp.local	No	Yes	No	No
SERVERLOGIN		String	epo-agent	No	Yes	No	No
SERVERPWORD		String	VMware1!	No	Yes	No	No
SRVCRTTHUMB		String	5A:5B:B0:F0:22:1D:C5:95:14:55...	No	Yes	No	No
SSLPORT		String	443	No	Yes	No	No

3. Click **Actions** and configure the **Install**, **Configure**, and **Start** actions, as shown in the following table:

Life Cycle Stage	Script Type	Script	Reboot
Install	Bash	`rpm -i http://<FQDNOfThe ServerWhere theRPMFileIsLocated>/$RPMNAME`	No (unchecked)

Configure	Bash	`sed -i "s/#agent.setup.serverIP=localhost/agent.setup.serverIP=$SERVERIP/" /opt/vmware/epops-agent/conf/agent.properties`
		`sed -i "s/#agent.setup.serverSSLPort=443/agent.setup.serverSSLPort=$SSLPORT/" /opt/vmware/epops-agent/conf/agent.properties`
		`sed -i "s/#agent.setup.serverLogin=username/agent.setup.serverLogin=$SERVERLOGIN/" /opt/vmware/epops-agent/conf/agent.properties`
		`sed -i "s/#agent.setup.serverPword=password/agent.setup.serverPword=$SERVERPWORD/" /opt/vmware/epops-agent/conf/agent.properties`
		`sed -i "s/#agent.setup.serverCertificateThumbprint=/agent.setup.serverCertificateThumbprint=$SRVCRTTHUMB/" /opt/vmware/epops-agent/conf/agent.properties`
			No (unchecked)

Start	Bash	`/sbin/service epops-agent start` `/sbin/chkconfig epops-agent on`	No (unchecked)

The following screenshot illustrates some example values:

4. Click **Ready to Complete** and click **Finish**.

5. Edit the blueprint to where you want the agent to be installed. From **Categories**, select **Software Components**. Select the Endpoint Operations Management software component and drag and drop it over the machine type (virtual machine) where you want the object to be installed:

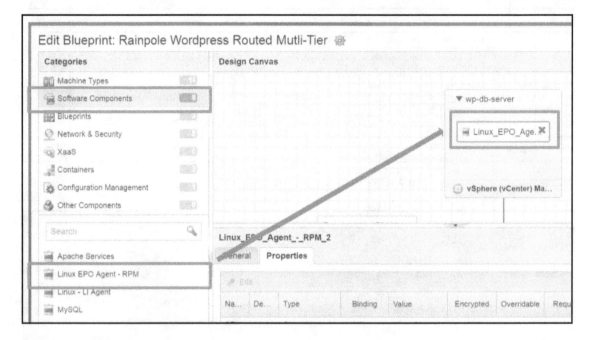

6. Click **Save** to save the blueprint.

This completes the necessary steps to automate the Endpoint Operations Management Agent installation as a software component in vRealize Automation. With every deployment of the blueprint, after cloning, the Agent will be installed and uniquely identified to vRealize Operations.

Reinstalling the agent

When reinstalling the agent, various elements are affected, like:

- Already-collected metrics
- Identification tokens that enable a reinstalled agent to report on the previously-discovered objects on the server

The following locations contain agent-related data which remains when the agent is uninstalled:

- The data folder containing the keystore
- The epops-token platform token file which is created before agent registration

Data continuity will not be affected when the data folder is deleted. This is not the case with the epops-token file. If you delete the token file, the agent will not be synchronized with the previously discovered objects upon a new installation.

Reinstalling the agent on a Linux Endpoint

Perform the following steps to reinstall the agent on a Linux machine:

1. If you are removing the agent completely and are not going to reinstall it, delete the data directory by running:

    ```
    $ rm -rf /opt/epops-agent/data
    ```

2. If you are completely removing the client and are not going to reinstall or upgrade it, delete the epops-token file:

    ```
    $ rm /etc/vmware/epops-token
    ```

3. Run the following command to uninstall the Agent:

    ```
    $ yum remove <AgentFullName>
    ```

4. If you are completely removing the client and are not going to reinstall it, make sure to delete the agent object from the Inventory Explorer in vRealize Operations.
5. You can now install the client again, the same way as we did earlier in this book.

Reinstalling the Agent on a Windows Endpoint

Perform the following steps to reinstall the Agent on a Windows machine:

1. From the CLI, change the directory to the agent `bin` directory:

   ```
   cd C:\epops-agent\bin
   ```

2. Stop the agent by running:

   ```
   C:\epops-agent\bin> ep-agent.bat stop
   ```

3. Remove the agent service by running:

   ```
   C:\epops-agent\bin> ep-agent.bat remove
   ```

4. If you are completely removing the client and are not going to reinstall it, delete the data directory by running:

   ```
   C:\epops-agent> rd /s data
   ```

5. If you are completely removing the client and are not going to reinstall it, delete the epops-token file using the CLI or Windows Explorer:

   ```
   C:\epops-agent> del "C:\ProgramData\VMware\EP Ops agent\epops-token"
   ```

6. Uninstall the agent from the **Control Panel**.
7. If you are completely removing the client and are not going to reinstall it, make sure to delete the agent object from the Inventory Explorer in vRealize Operations.
8. You can now install the client again, the same way as we did earlier in this book.

Viewing and collecting metrics

As we said previously, Endpoint Operations Management gathers operating system metrics through agent-based collections:

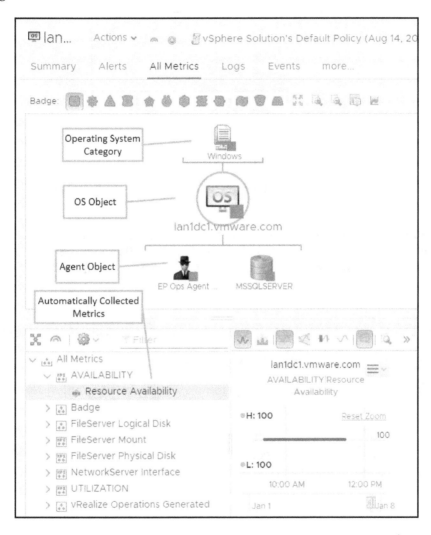

In the example, the agent has supplied the discovery information about the objects related to the operating system. The relationship tree in the center pane shows the operating system category (Windows, in this case), `lan1dc1.vmware.com` (the operating system object), and the agent.

Not all vRealize Operations metrics are enabled by default. To collect additional operating system metrics, create a policy and apply it to the operating system object type.

In the following example, the **System Uptime** metric is added by applying the policy:

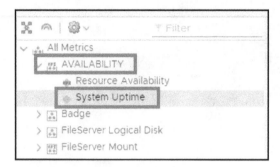

If you take a look at the **All Metrics** tab of the object again, you will notice that we can now see the **System Uptime** metric.

In addition to the features available after the initial configuration of Endpoint Operations Management, you can enable remote monitoring, enable or disable plugins for additional monitoring, and customize Endpoint Operations Management logging.

Other Endpoint Operations Management monitoring functionalities

Let's take a look at some other Endpoint Operations Management monitoring functionalities:

- How to add additional monitoring objects, or how to monitor services
- How to monitor remote objects
- How to monitor multi processes

Adding monitoring objects

The Endpoint Operations Management Agent auto discovers some of the operating system objects to monitor.

You can add objects (such as files, scripts, and processes) for the endpoint agent to monitor.

Let's add a service to monitor as an example. Let's add a Windows service object in vRealize Operations that will monitor a DNS service running on the Windows Server.

Perform the following steps to add DNS as a monitored service in vRealize Operations:

1. In vRealize Operations, navigate to the object (server) where the service is running:

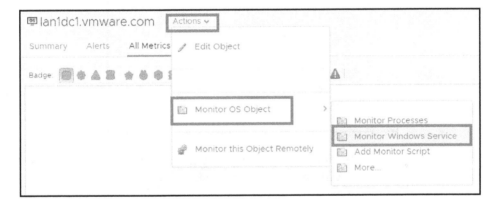

2. Click **Actions** | **Monitor OS Object**, and select **Monitor Windows Service**.

3. Enter a display name for the monitored service, and for `service_name` enter DNS. Make sure to spell out the name correctly. On a Windows machine, you can list the services and find the name by running the `Get-Services` PowerShell cmdlet:

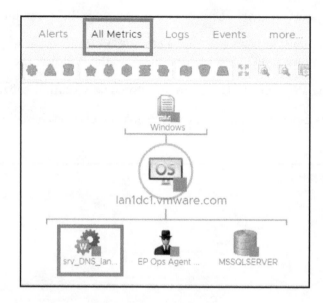

If you take a look at the **All Metrics** tab of the object again, you will notice that now, the object relationship shows the monitored service as well.

Using remote check

Endpoint Operations Management allows the user to monitor a particular application resource or a service from various geographies.

You can configure remote monitoring using the following methods:

- HTTP
- ICMP
- TCP

When you configure a remote HTTP, ICMP or TCP check, it is created as a child object of the tested object that you are monitoring and of the monitoring agent.

A remote check can be configured on the Operating System and the Endpoint Operations Management Agent object type.

Here are a few examples where the remote checker can be used:

- Let's say there is an application server that runs in Buffalo. The same Tomcat server also provides services to Cork and Munich. This is a perfect use case for remote check. You can configure a remote check of the application service that resides in Buffalo from Cork and Munich.
- Let's say you configured the ICMP test. Now, if the communication between the sites is broken, the remote check should fail and the same would be visible in vRealize Operations in the form of alerts and symptoms.
- Remote check is an option to monitor an object without having an agent installed on it.

Let's configure an example check.

Perform the following steps to configure an ICMP check:

1. In vRealize Operations, navigate to the object (server) you want to monitor.
2. Click **Actions** and select **Monitor this Object Remotely**.
3. Fill in the following information for the ICMP check:
    - **Display Name**: Enter a display name for the check
    - **Monitored From**: Select the system from which the check will be displayed
    - **Check Method**: Select **ICMP check**
    - **Hostname**: Type the FQDN or IP of the object which the check will be performed against

In this example, the server I selected in Monitored From and the server I entered in Hostname are in two different geographical locations:

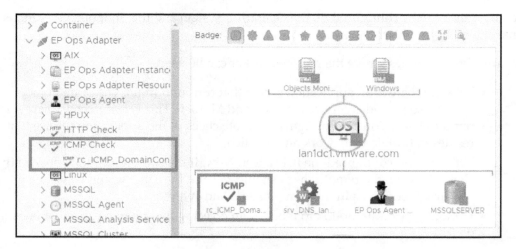

If you take a look at the **All Metrics** tab of the object again, you will notice that now, the object relationship shows the remote checker as well.

Using multiprocess

Multiprocess can only be configured on the object type operating system. This is a feature by which you can monitor the processes and services of an operating system. Once configured, it will be listed in the objects list as sub-object of the **MultiProcess**.

In this example, we will show you how to configure multiprocess to monitor the VMware Tools service:

1. In vRealize Operations, navigate to the object (server) you want to monitor. Click **Actions** | **Monitor OS Object** and select **Monitor Processes**:

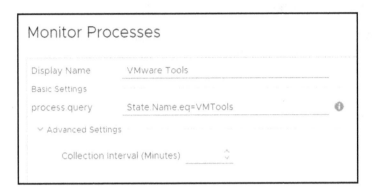

2. Enter a **Display Name** and the process name to monitor:

You should see the process in the Inventory Explorer under the **MultiProcess** group.

Summary

In this chapter, we've become familiar with the Endpoint Operations Management Agent and what it can do. We discussed how to install and reinstall it on both Linux and Windows operating systems. We also covered how to use some of its additional functionalities, like remote checker and multi process.

In the next chapter, we will cover how we can use vRealize Operations to optimize vSphere and vRealize Automation workload placement.

13
Leveraging vRealize Operations for vSphere and vRealize Automation Workload Placement

In this chapter, we will take a look at an exciting new feature in vRealize Operations called Intelligent Workload Placement, and how it can help us deal with underutilized and overutilized clusters in our environment. We will also see how it can integrate with vRealize Automation to provide the same effect for workloads provisioned through the portal.

In this chapter, we will cover the following topics:

- What is Intelligent Workload Placement
- How to use the Workload Balance dashboard
- How to rebalance workloads with vRealize Operations and DRS
- How to automate rebalancing
- How to optimize vRealize Automation Workload Placement with vRealize Operations

What is Intelligent Workload Placement?

Workloads are often placed suboptimally, resulting in the inefficient use of clusters and chronic resource contentions. Resolving contention by balancing resources is a difficult, time-consuming, and nonstrategic activity.

Using vRealize Operations Intelligent Workload Placement, you can visualize how your workloads are distributed and used across the environment, and you can see trends. When the workload in your environment becomes imbalanced, Intelligent Workload Placement recommends rebalance actions to resolve resource contention and improve performance of applications and infrastructure:

I will occasionally refer to vRealize Operations Intelligent Workload Placement as WLP. WLP is not an official VMware acronym.

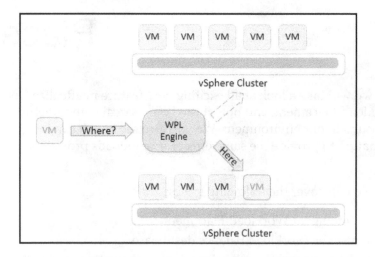

Intelligent Workload Placement determines the best destination to run your workload by rebalancing existing workloads inside a container. The container for the rebalance action can be a data center or a **Custom Data Center** (**CDC**). Intelligent Workload Placement provides you with a prioritized list of recommended places to put or move the workload.

A custom data center can be used to perform capacity management and planning across disparate groupings of capacity providers. You can associate all the Analysis Badge data for these groupings. Using custom data centers, you can group various capacity provider objects such as hosts, clusters, virtual data centers, and VMware vCenter Server® instances. These objects might span multiple vCenter Server instances.

VMware vSphere's **Distributed Resource Scheduler** (**DRS**) plays several, very important roles within VMware vSphere.

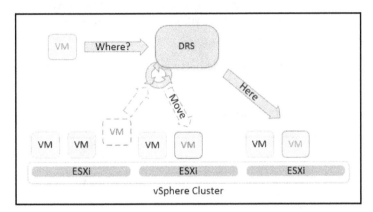

It can decide where to deploy a **new VM**, or move an **existing VM**, within a cluster to ensure virtual machines are always running on a host with adequate resources to support it. It can also help migrate VMs off a host when we place it in maintenance mode:

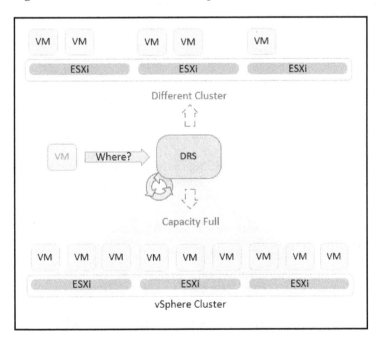

However, there are some limitations to what DRS can do on its own. For example, because **DRS can only move VMs between hosts within a cluster**, there's very little that it can do when that cluster runs out of resources. Once a cluster has been completely utilized, vSphere DRS cannot move the workloads to other underutilized clusters in the data center or Custom Data Center.

Question: Can we allow DRS to move VMs between clusters or to move VMs before resource contention even occurs?

The answer is, yes! vRealize Operations allows us to do this:

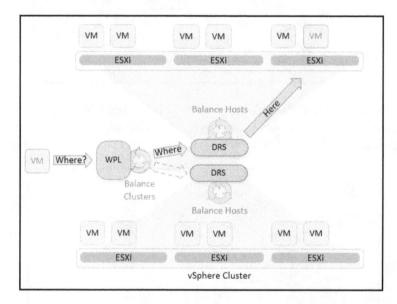

vRealize Operations enhances vSphere DRS further by providing the **Rebalance Container feature**, which moves virtual machines between clusters, thus ensuring that the clusters are balanced in the environment.

The vRealize Operations rebalance feature works with vSphere DRS to help virtual machines get the required resources:

- vRealize Operations determines how to best balance clusters within the CDC or the data center:
  - Creates a rebalance plan recommending the migration of virtual machines from overutilized clusters to underutilized clusters
  - Moves virtual machines to the underutilized clusters

- Hands over the virtual machine to vSphere DRS
- vSphere DRS can then optimally balance virtual machines within a cluster by determining the best host in the cluster to place the virtual machine

The Workload Balance dashboard

The **Workload Balance** dashboard in vRealize Operations is a great place to see how your workloads are distributed:

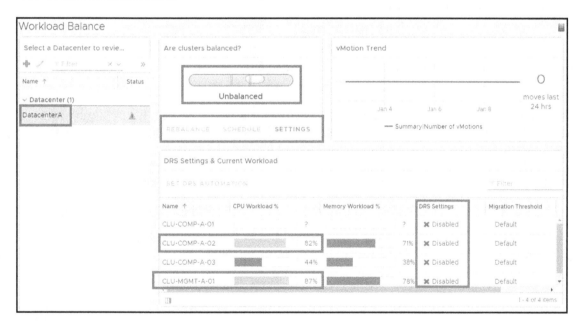

You start by selecting a data center or custom data center. At the top, you will see a spirit level that looks very similiar to the DRS level in the center, but **instead of measuring the balance of a single cluster, we're now measuring the balance of an entire data center**.

In the Datacenter Workload Status widget, you can also find links for direct access to the rebalance, schedule, and settings dialog. You may notice that the **Rebalance** and **Schedule** buttons are grayed out. vRealize Operations will **not allow the rebalance action or to set rebalance plans** for the following reasons:

- vSphere DRS is not running in automatic mode on all the clusters
- The host is in maintenance mode, powered off in standby mode, or on a disconnected datastore
- Virtual machines have active affinity, or anti-affinity rules
- Virtual machines need to be migrated to separate datastores
- Virtual machines need to be migrated to a separate data center or vCenter Server system

If we scroll down, we can see that two of our clusters are running a bit hot. We can also see that **DRS is disabled** on all of our clusters, which in this example is one of the reasons we cannot currently rebalance the datacenter. A cool feature of the dashboard is that you can activate DRS for a cluster from within the dashboard by selecting the cluster and clicking the **Set DRS Automation** button, as we will demonstrate later in this chapter.

 One of the clusters isn't showing any Workload data. This is because the cluster is offline at the moment, and it is not being taken into account for workload balancing.

If you scroll further down, you will see the **Capacity Utilization of Datacenter Resources** widget:

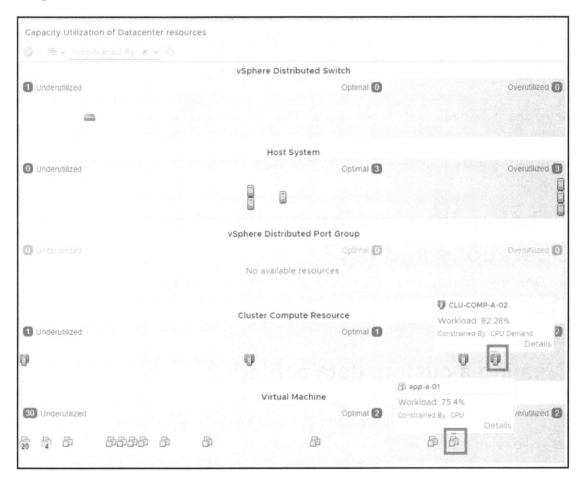

You can use this widget to view a visual summary of the capacity and workload distribution of resources used by the objects in your environment.

The widget shows the workload distribution of the objects in the data center or the CDC. Its zones are based on workload levels:

- **Underutilized** zone: Workload score 0-33
- **Optimal** zone: Workload score 34-66
- **Overutilized** zone: Workload score 67-100

You can use the **Capacity Utilization** widget to infer whether a rebalance action is required in your environment.

In the example, some clusters in your data center are overutilized, while other clusters are underutilized. As you can see, the **CLU-COMP-A-02** cluster has a **Workload badge** score of **82.28%**, and it's **Constrained By: CPU Demand**. As expected, the **app-a-01 VM**, which is running on the cluster, has a **Workload** badge score of **75.4%**, and it is also **Constrained By: CPU**.

At the end of the dashboard, we will find the **What is the workload trend?** (a Metric Chart) widget.

The widget shows the historical workload balance over time.

Rebalancing workloads with vRealize Operations and DRS

The Datacenter Workload Status may show the **Rebalance** and **Schedule** buttons as grayed out if you are not meeting all the requirements for Intelligent Workload Placement, which will not allow you to rebalance workload distribution in your data center or CDC.

Creating a custom data center

As we already mentioned in this book, a Custom Data Center (CDC) can be used to perform capacity management and planning across disparate groupings of capacity providers.

Let's take a look at all the workloads in our datacenter:

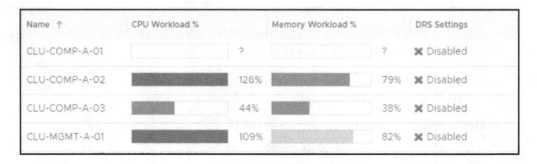

Name ↑	CPU Workload %		Memory Workload %		DRS Settings
CLU-COMP-A-01		?		?	✖ Disabled
CLU-COMP-A-02		126%		79%	✖ Disabled
CLU-COMP-A-03		44%		38%	✖ Disabled
CLU-MGMT-A-01		109%		82%	✖ Disabled

In this example, as we mentioned already, we can have the following clusters:

- **CLU-COMP-A-01:** A compute cluster, which is powered off and in this lab used as a cold standby
- **CLU-COMP-A-02**: A compute cluster being utilized
- **CLU-COMP-A-03**: A compute cluster being utilized
- **CLU-MGMT-A-02**: A management cluster being utilized

Again, for the purpose of this example, let's say I do not want to use Intelligent Workload Placement and balance between all the clusters in my datacenter. I only want to balance between the currently-running computer clusters: **CLU-COMP-A-02** and **CLU-COMP-A-03**.

Let's create a CDC to group these together.

1. On the left-hand side of the dashboard, in the **Select a Datacenter to review** widget, click the plus sign to create a new CDC.
2. In the **New Custom Datacenter** window, enter the appropriate **Name** and **Description** for the CDC.

   Select the clusters you want to group.

   Although a CDC can span across multiple clusters, datacenters and vCenter Server environments, make sure to select the cluster object with all its host objects. If you do not select a cluster object, but rather only select a subset of hosts within a cluster, the cluster and the hosts you've selected will not be taken into account for Intelligent Workload Placement. This is also true for single hosts that are not part of a cluster. If you have single hosts in your selection that are not part of a cluster, these will be taken into consideration when doing workload balancing.

3. On the left hand side of the dashboard, in the **Select a Datacenter to review worked** widget, under **Custom Datacenters**, select the custom datacenter you just created.

Again, take a look at the workloads in our datacenter:

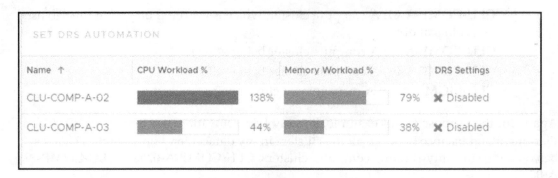

Now, you can see that we only have a subset of all clusters in the data center.

Unfortunately, we still cannot rebalance the CDC because the hosts still don't meet all Intelligent Workload Placement prerequisites, therefore the **Rebalanced Clusters** button in the **Are Clusters balanced?** widget is still grayed out.

In the previous screenshot, notice that DRS is set to Disabled for both clusters. Next, we are going to activate it.

Setting DRS automation

How cool it is that you can now activate DRS for a cluster from within the vRealize Operations interface, without the need to go to vCenter?

First, let's activate DRS for only one of the clusters:

1. In the **DRS Settings & Current Workload** widget, select the cluster you want to activate DRS on, and click the **Set DRS Automation** button.
2. In the **Set DRS Automation** window, under **Automation Level**, select the drop-down menu and select **Fully Automated**, then click **Begin Action**:

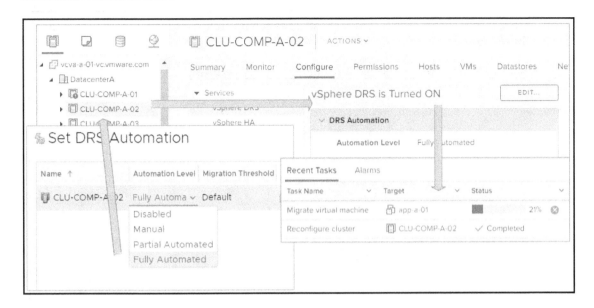

If you take a look in vCenter using the vSphere Web Client, you will see that the cluster is now configured for DRS, which in turn triggers workload balancing within the cluster. We can see a VM being migrated to a different cluster node.

Let's take a look at the workloads in our custom datacenter:

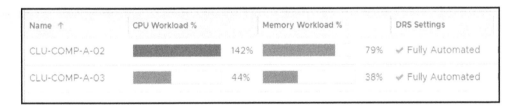

As you can see, although DRS kicked in and rebalanced the **CLU-COMP-A-02** cluster, the situation is still the same. The load on the cluster is still very high. Although the second cluster, **CLU-COMP-A-03**, is underutilized and has resources to handle more load, DRS cannot span between different clusters.

This is where Integrated Workload Balancing kicks in and resolves the problem.

Before actually rebalancing the datacenter, let's see what other configuration settings we have in the dashboard.

First, let's take a look at the workload automation policy settings:

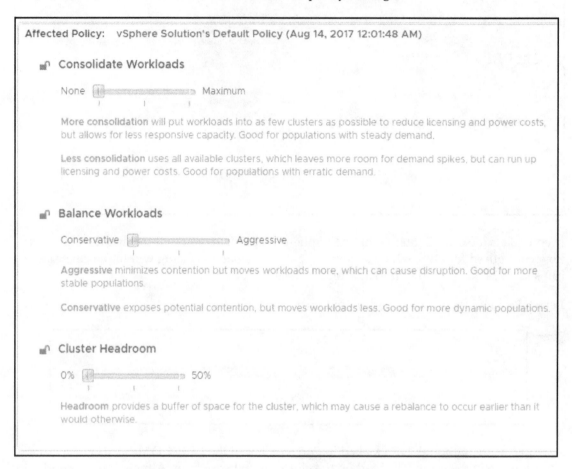

You can access these settings by navigating to the **Datacenter Workload Status** widget and clicking the **Settings** button.

You can customize workload automation by using the Workload Automation options on the left-hand side of the **Add** or **Edit Monitoring** policy workspace:

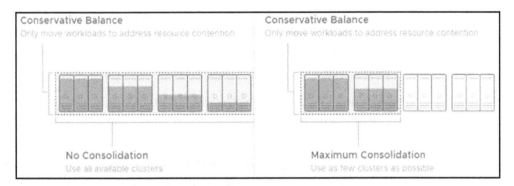

The **Consolidate Workload** setting determines how well all of your virtual machines are combined, that is, if they should all live within a few clusters or across many.

Select **Aggressive** balancing when you have stable populations. It minimizes contention but moves workloads more often, which can cause disruption.

Select **Conservative** balancing when you have dynamic populations. It exposes potential contention, but moves workloads less often:

 This setting only applies to **new** virtual machines deployed through vRealize Automation.

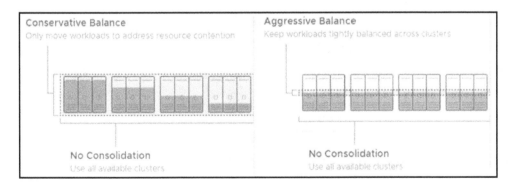

The **Balanced Workload** setting is effectively the same as the migration threshold in DRS. This determines how aggressively or conservatively you want to move workloads around.

Conservative Balance (default): Provides recommendations if one of the clusters is at over 100 percent workload:

- vRealize Operations moves virtual machines to other clusters to alleviate contention.
- Balancing for improving performance does not occur. For example, clusters with between 20% and 90% workload do not cause a rebalance.

Moderate Balance and **Aggressive Balance**: vRealize Operations moves virtual machines to other available clusters if one of the clusters is over 100% workload or if one of the following scenarios is true:

- Moderate: Provides recommendations if imbalance ratio between clusters is 70%
- Aggressive: Provides recommendations if imbalance ratio between clusters is 80%

The **Cluster Headroom** setting is an additional buffer which provides your clusters with a little extra headroom. This can help reduce the risk of your clusters running out of resources.

The following example illustrates how workloads will be consolidated by setting the **Consolidate Workloads** and **Balanced Workloads** settings to **Moderate**:

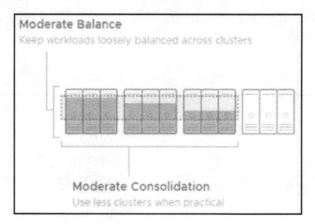

For this example, we will not be changing the policy settings.

Rebalancing clusters

After we saw that DRS cannot resolve our cluster overutilization issues, let's combine it with vRealize Operations Integrated Workload Balancing and see the result.

Perform the following steps to balance the datacenter:

1. On the left-hand side of the dashboard, in the **Select a Datacenter to review worked** widget, select a datacenter or a CDC that you want to balance:

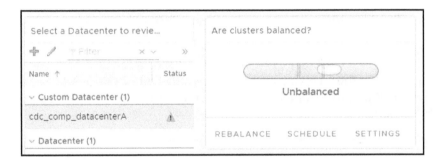

As you will notice, the Rebalance Cluster is not grayed out anymore. In this particular example, from all the prerequisites for Integrated Workload Balancing, we didn't have DRS enabled. If the button is still grayed out in your case, go back in this chapter and make sure your environment meets all of the prerequisites.

Alternatively, you can trigger rebalance by navigating to the custom datacenter or datacenter object and clicking **Actions** and then **Rebalance Container.**

In the first case, if the custom datacenter or datacenter you want to rebalance does not meet the prerequisites for rebalancing, the option is grayed out.

In the second case, the option is not listed at all under the Actions menu.

Make sure **all clusters have DRS enabled**, although the Rebalance Cluster button will appear if you have DRS enabled only on some of the hosts in the datacenter. This will not have optimal results on the workload placement. Activating DRS on all clusters ensures that.

OK, let's rebalance:

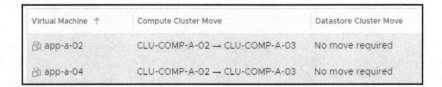

The **Compare Cluster Balance** window shows us our current state and the state after the move.

For example, here, our **CLU-COMP-A-02** cluster **CPU Workload** is at **163%**, and after the move it'll be at **80%**. On the receiving end, of course, the **CLU-COMP-A-03** cluster will see an increase in **CPU Workload** from **22%** to **63%**, which is similar for the **Memory Workload**, % for both clusters:

Virtual Machine ↑	Compute Cluster Move	Datastore Cluster Move
app-a-02	CLU-COMP-A-02 → CLU-COMP-A-03	No move required
app-a-04	CLU-COMP-A-02 → CLU-COMP-A-03	No move required

Next, on the **Review Rebalance Moves** page, we can view the rebalance moves, As you can see, virtual machine **app-a-02** will be moving from cluster **CLU-COMP-A-02** to **CLU-COMP-A-03**. We will not be changing storage, but if the storage was overutilized or we were moving to a different datastore cluster, VMware vSphere **Storage DRS** and **Storage vMotion** can kick in and help us move between datastore clusters as well. The same goes for **app-a-04**.

After you have reviewed the moves, click **Begin Action** to rebalance the datacenter:

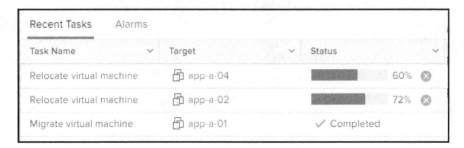

Jump back over to the vCenter, where you can see the reallocations taking place:

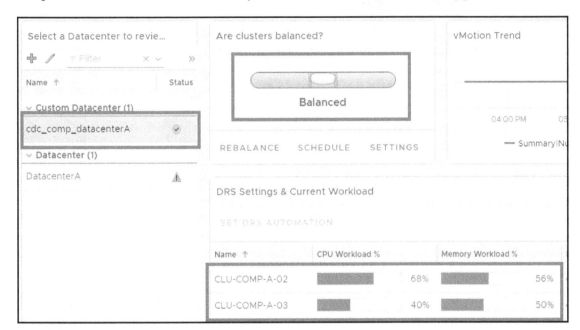

After the migrations are complete, vRealize Operations shows that cluster workloads our custom datacenter uses are now balanced.

 In this example, I'm using a nested environment, and because small deviations in CPU and Memory Workload were seen during the move, the percentages vRealize Operations predicted deviate a bit from the actual percentages after the rebalance action.

Automated rebalancing

Since the Rebalance Cluster Action runs so well, we may want to implement some kind of repeatable or automatic rebalancing action to balance our datacenter.

We will take a look at various ways to achieve this. All of the options we are going to discuss can be mixed together to achieve the desired result.

Scheduling a rebalance action

The first option we are going to discuss is to schedule a rebalance action.

We can do this from the **Are Clusters balanced?** widget, by clicking on the **Schedule** rebalance action button:

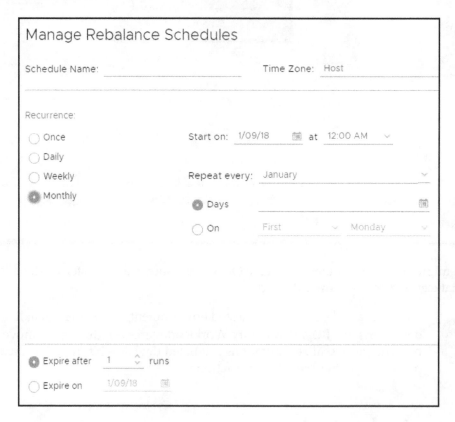

We can then schedule rebalances to run once daily, weekly, or monthly.

The drawback here is that the rebalance will take place on a fixed schedule. What if contention occurs outside of the defined schedule and we want vRealize Operations to react quickly and rebalance the datacenter and not wait till the scheduled date comes?

Let's see what other options we have.

Using rebalance alerts

The next option to achieve automatic rebalancing is to configure vRealize Operations to automatically rebalance your clusters when a rebalance alert is raised.

We can achieve this for datacenters and custom data centers by enabling the following Alert Definitions:

- Custom datacenter may require rebalancing to relieve heavy resource utilization in one or more clusters
- Datacenter may require rebalancing to relieve heavy resource utilization in one or more clusters

Are you satisfied with what vRealize Operations can do?

Well, I'm not. Let's see what else vRealize Operations has to offer.

Predictive DRS with vRealize Operations

What about preventing contention in the first place?

With vSphere Predictive DRS (pDRS), this is not an issue.

Predictive DRS is a new feature in vSphere 6.5 that leverages the predictive analytics of vRealize Operations with the powerful resource scheduler algorithm of vSphere DRS. It identifies workload patterns of the virtual machines in order to predict future resource needs. If a host doesn't have enough resources to keep up with future demands, predictive DRS will move workloads to other hosts in the cluster before contention can even occur.

Enabling pDRS is easy. Perform the following steps to enable pDRS:

1. Log in to the vSphere Web Client and select the cluster where you want to enable pDRS. Navigate to the **Configure** tab, **Services**, and select **vSphere DRS**. Click on the **Edit** button:

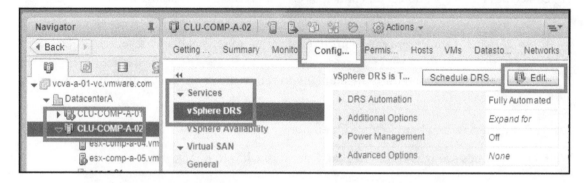

2. Expand **DRS Automation** and select **Enable Predictive DRS**.
3. Click **OK** to apply the change.
4. Navigate to the **Administration** tab and then **Solutions**, and find the **VMware vSphere** solution. Click on the gear icon to configure it. Expand **Advanced Settings**, and in the **Provide data to vSphere Predictive DRS** drop-down menu, select **True**. Click **Save Settings** and you are done:

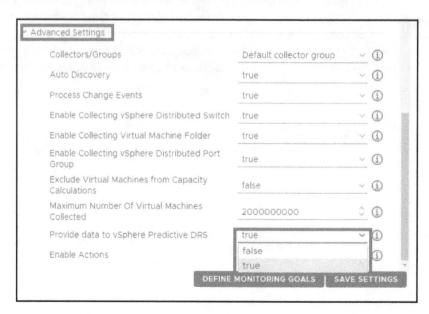

vRealize Automation Workload Placement with vRealize Operations

Now that you have a good understanding of how vRealize Operations Intelligent Workload Placement, vSphere DRS, and vSphere Storage DRS work together, let's see how we can leverage this in vRealize Automation.

Beginning with vRealize Automation 7.3 and vRealize Operations 6.6, you can leverage the capabilities of both products to optimize your workload placement.

vRealize Automation is playing the role of a governance engine. When a blueprint request for a new virtual machine comes to vRealize Automation, it determines which business group the requestor is a member of and the eligible reservations the business group has access to. A reservation policy is configured with a vSphere cluster and one or more Datastores or datastore clusters. A business group may be assigned multiple reservations, some or all of which may reside on different vSphere clusters.

So, how does vRealize Automation determine the best placement option?

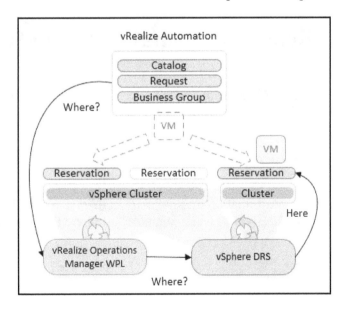

The following is the process used by vRealize Automation and vRealize Operations to determine the best (most optimized) reservation upon request for a blueprint from the catalog:

1. A request for a VM comes to vRealize Automation.
2. vRealize Automation determines the eligible reservations, following the process mentioned above. In this example, there are only two eligible reservations for the request. vRealize Automation has no insight into the utilization of different clusters, or hosts within a cluster. It cannot determine, from a utilization point of view, which is the best reservation to be used.
3. vRealize Automation passes all eligible reservations, or the clusters those reservations are configured for, to vRealize Operations for optimization recommendation.
4. vRealize Operations uses a combination of Intelligent Workload Placement and vSphere DRS to determine the most optimized workload placement.
5. vRealize Operations returns a recommendation from the options presented by vRealize Automation.

Integrating vRealize Automation with vRealize Operations

Now that we have seen how vRealize Automation works in conjunction with vRealize Operations to optimize placement of vRealize Automation managed workloads, let's see what needs to be configured to enable this integration.

Perform the following steps to configure integration between vRealize Automation and vRealize Operations:

- Log in to vRealize Automation and navigate to **Infrastructure** | **Endpoints**, and then **Endpoints**. Click **New** | **Management**, and then **vRealize Operations**:

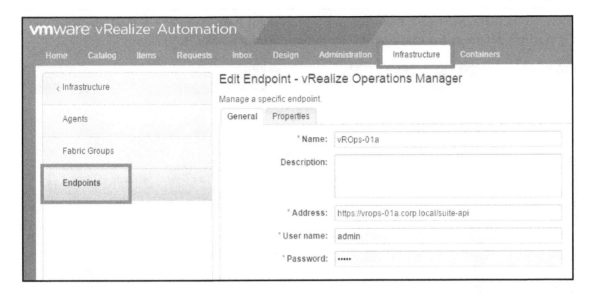

Enter the following information:

- **Name**: Friendly name for the vRealize Operations instance
- **Address**: `https://FQDN_Of_vROPS/suite-api`
- **Username**: vRealize Operations Administrator username
- **Password**: Password for the administrator user

If asked, accept the certificate and verify that the connection is set up correctly by clicking the **Test Connection** button. Click **OK** to save and exit.

Navigate to **Infrastructure** | **Reservations** | **Placement Policy** and check the **Use vRealize Operations Manager for Placement Recommendations**. Click **OK** to save:

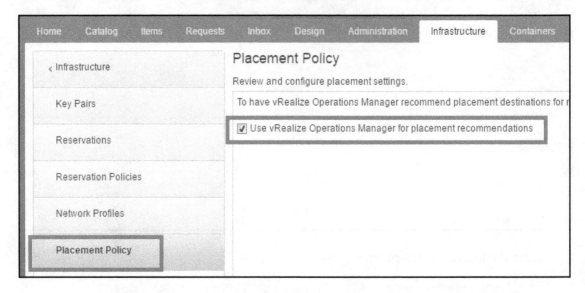

- Log in to vRealize Operations. Navigate to the **Administration** tab and then **Solutions**, and find the **VMware vRealize Automation** solution. Click on the gear icon to configure it.

Under instance name, add the following information:

- **Display Name**
- **vRealize Automation URL**

Click on the plus sign under credentials and fill in the SysAdmin and SuperUser information. Click **OK** to save once finished. Accept the certificates and verify the connection is successful:

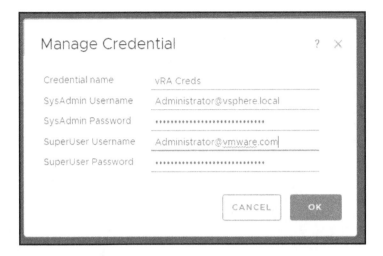

The SysAdmin user is typically the Administrator user in the default vsphere.local vRealize Automation tenant. In this example, SuperUser is a user that has Tenant and Infrastructure Admin permissions in all vRealize Automation tenants.

> Note: If the user you configure here does not have those permissions in all tenants, you will not see results for the respective tenants.

Previously in this chapter, we discussed the **Workload Policy Settings**. We said that the **Consolidate Workload** setting determines how well all of your virtual machines are combined. This policy affects new virtual machines deployed through vRealize Automation. Make sure to review the policy and make adjustments if necessary to meet your business needs.

Summary

In this chapter, we become familiar with vRealize Operations Intelligent Workload Placement and how it can work together with vSphere DRS and vSphere Storage DRS to bring us the most optimized placement of workloads within our datacenter. We then explored some advanced options and configurations available.

In the next chapter, we will discuss how we can use vRealize Operations for infrastructure compliance.

14
Using vRealize Operations for Infrastructure Compliance

In this chapter, we will discuss how we can use vRealize Operations to monitor configuration compliance, as well as how we can configure vRealize Operations to meet industry standard compliance standards such as PCI and HIPAA.

This chapter will cover the following topics:

- How vRealize Operations monitors compliance
- The Compliance badge
- Compliance alerts
- Compliance dashboards
- How to enable vSphere Hardening compliance
- How to enable PCI and HIPAA Compliance

Integrated compliance

Compliance is all about ensuring objects in your environment meet industrial, governmental, regulatory, or internal standards. For example, you can check compliance against the vSphere 5.5 or 6.0 Security Hardening Guide.

Compliance in vRealize Operations can be achieved with the following mechanisms:

- **Alerts**: Use alert-based compliance to ensure that objects in your environment are meeting the required standards
- **VMware vRealize Configuration Manager (VCM)**: Use the results of the compliance templates to ensure that objects are in compliance

In vRealize Operations, you can use the alert-based compliance that is provided, or if you also use VMware vRealize® Configuration™ in your environment, you can add the adapter that provides configuration compliance information in place of the alert-based compliance.

In vRealize Operations 6.6, VMware now offers compliance packs for two of the industry's most widely used standards of today:

- **Payment Card Industry Data Security Standard** (**PCI DSS**) compliance for vSphere
- **Health Insurance Portability and Accountability Act** (**HIPAA**) compliance for vSphere

Both compliance packs provide alerts, policies, and reports to validate the VMware vSphere resources against the PCI (v3.2) and HIPAA hardening guides.

The following resources are being validated using the compliance pack:

- vCenter
- ESXi Host
- Virtual machines (three risk profiles available, with risk profile 1 being the most restrictive)
- Distributed port group
- Distributed virtual switch

The compliance badge

The compliance badge value is a score based on one or more compliance policies that you run in vRealize Operations against the data collected from vRealize Operations. Compliance policies are a set of rules which your environment must comply with to meet corporate or industry standards.

The compliance score is based on the number of violations against those policies. The compliance percentage is a calculation, as follows:

```
100 - ((triggered symptom count(TR)/total symptom count(TS)) * 100)
```

The compliance badge displays one of the following values:

- 100 if there are no triggered standards. The badge color is green.
- 75 if the most critical triggered standard is a warning. The badge color is yellow.
- 25 if the most critical triggered standard is immediate. The badge color is orange.
- 0 if the most critical triggered standard is critical. The badge color is red.

If you are using VMware vRealize Configuration Manager to achieve compliance in vRealize Operations, the compliance badge value is a score based on one or more compliance templates that you run in vRealize Configuration Manager against the data collected from vSphere objects that are managed by vRealize Operations and by vRealize Configuration Manager.

The following compliance profiles are available:

- **Risk Profile 1**: This is the default profile, which enforces the highest security. It enables all compliance rules.
- **Risk Profile 2**: This is a medium-security level profile, which enforces only a subset of the symptoms that are available.
- **Risk Profile 3**: This is a low-security level profile, which enforces even less symptoms than Risk Profile 2.

Risk Profile 1 is the strictest, while Risk Profile 3 is the most relaxed compliance profile. It is recommended that by default, at the very least, Risk Profile 3 should be implemented in every environment.

vRealize Operations 6.3 introduced the term Risk Profile. Risk Profiles are created as vRealize Operations policies, which you can enable the same way as you would any other policy. The Risk Profiles in vRealize Operations now match the risk profiles in the VMware Security Hardening Guides and makes it easy for the monitoring administrator to activate the necessary vRealize Operations policies to adhere to a particular hardening guide risk profile.

The Security Hardening Guide provides prescriptive guidance on how to deploy and operate VMware products in a secure manner. Guidance for vSphere is provided in a spreadsheet format. You can find the hardening guide at `http://www.vmware.com/security/hardening-guides`.

If you have different environments with different requirements for compliance, you just have to set up the correct policy for that part of the environment and you are good to go.

vSphere Hardening compliance

If hosts of VMs in your environment are not configured in compliance with the vSphere Hardening Guide, you will receive an alert notification. Alerts are triggered when settings or properties are not in compliance. Alert-based compliance is not activated by default. You have to override and enable at least one of two policy settings. One is for alerts related to hosts, and one is for VMs.

It is worth noticing that since vSphere 6.5, it is no longer called a Security Hardening Guide, but a Security Configuration Guide. Unfortunately, at the time of writing this book, there is no vRealize Operations management pack available for download at VMware Marketplace's site to enable vRealize Operations 6.6 to monitor vSphere 6.5 for security configuration compliance.

Enabling vSphere hardening compliance

Now, let's see how we can enable those policies.

Perform the following steps to enable security hardening, or as it's now called, configuration compliance, in vRealize Operations:

1. Before we enable the policies in our environment, let's first check what the compliance level is for all environment objects in the vSpehre World custom group. To do so, navigate to **Environment, Custom Groups**, and select the **vSphere World custom group**.

2. Click on the **Analysis** tab and then click on **Compliance**. You will see something similar to the following image. As you will notice, although we have not yet enabled vSphere configuration compliance, there are already some compliance issues found and therefore we have a compliance badge score of 98%. Again, the percentage may differ in your environment:

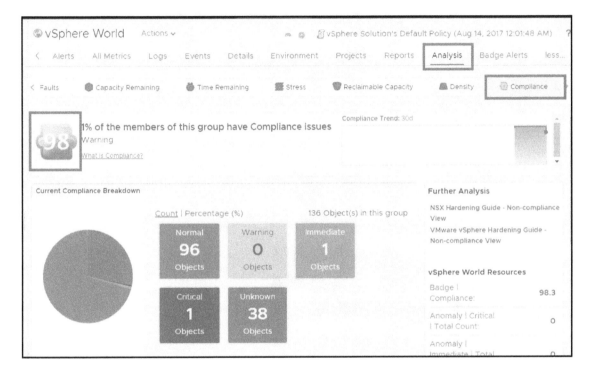

3. If we scroll down, we will see that the compliance violations come from a couple of NSX objects. By default, the VMware Management Pack for NSX-vSphere monitors its objects for compliance. Once we created an NSX-vSphere adapter and connected it to our NSX Manager, it started monitoring, and has already found some compliance violations:

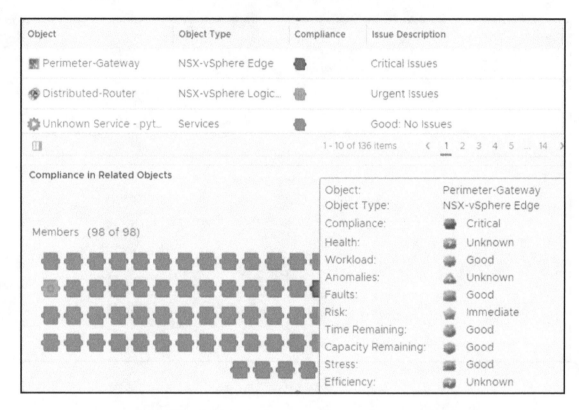

4. Now, to enable the vSphere security compliance policies, navigate to **Administration**, **Policies**, and then **Policy Library**. Select the current active policy. In our case, this is the **vSphere Solutions Default Policy**. Click on the pencil icon to edit the policy. The **Edit Monitoring Policy** window opens.

5. In the **Edit Monitoring Policy** window, navigate to **Alert /Symptom Definitions**. In the **Alert Definitions** area in the `filter criteria` file, type **hardening**, and sort by the state column until you see the five policies, which are shown as follows. Note the state column value for all is **Local = disabled**:

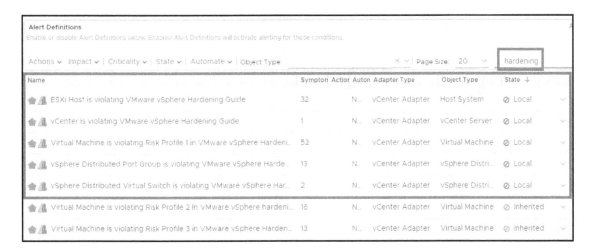

6. For each of the five compliance alerts, click the **State** drop-down menu and click **Local = enabled**. Click **Save**.

Once you've saved the changes, the corresponding configured symptom definitions become active for your vCenter Server instance(s), host(s), virtual machine(s), distributed port group(s), and distributed switch(es). vRealize Operations will not start to generate the configuration compliance alerts.

Monitoring compliance

Let's take a deeper look into how to view compliance alerts and what dashboards there are that can help us monitor our environment.

Compliance Alerts

Now that we have enabled vSphere configuration compliance, let's check how compliant our vSphere environment is:

    1. Select the **vSphere World** custom group as you did in the previous example. Navigate to the **Analysis** tab and select **Compliance.** As you will notice from the following image, the compliance badge score has dropped to 83% after we activated all the configuration compliance policies:

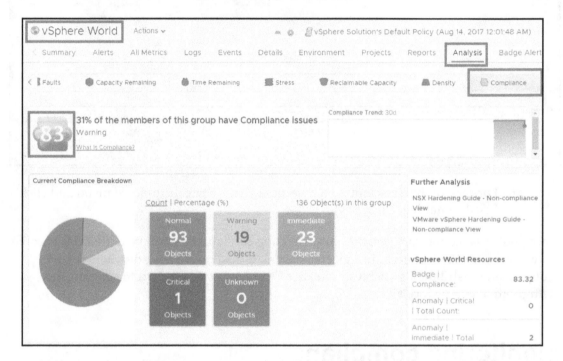

    It may take a few minutes until the Compliance badge score changes, reflecting the newly activated compliance alerts.

2. If you scroll down, you will see all the objects that violate the Compliance policies. Let's go and select one of the objects that violates compliance and examine what exactly is causing the violation. In this example, I will be selecting one of the ESXi **Host Systems**:

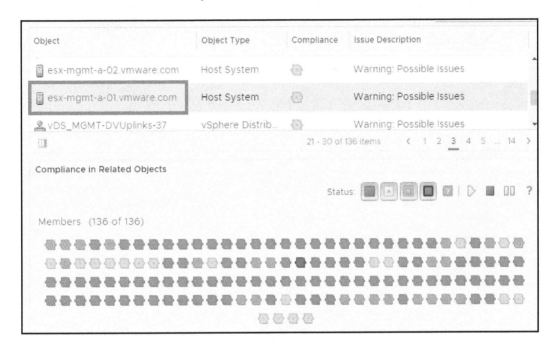

3. In the **Compliance Breakdow**n area, you can select to either show all the violated standards or all standards. Upon selecting **Violated Standards**, you are presented with a list of the standards/policies that this object violates. As you can see in this example, the host system violates the ESXi Host, which is violating the VMware vSphere Hardening Guide policy. Upon selecting the violated policy, you will be presented further down with a list of all **Violated Rules** (or **Symptom Definitions**):

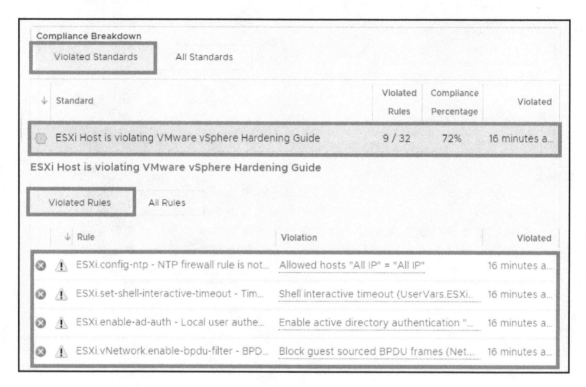

In this example, the named ESXi host system is violating the vSphere Hardening Guide. The following are some of the rules that the host system is violating according to the triggered symptoms:

- `ESXi.config-ntp`: NTP firewall rule is not configured
- `ESXi.set-shell-interactive-timeout`: Timeout is not configured for idle ESXi Shell and SSH sessions
- `ESXi.enable-ad-auth`: Local user authentication is not configured with `Ldap`
- `ESXi.vNetwork.enable-bpdu-filter`: BPDU filter on the ESXi host to prevent being locked out of physical switch ports with Portfast, and BPDU Guard not enabled

If you navigate to the **Alerts** tab and review the recent alerts, you will notice that a compliance alert is being raised. A compliance alert is triggered because a standard is violated. Click on generated compliance alert:

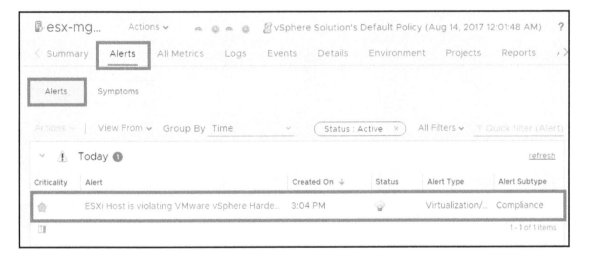

The symptoms that triggered this alert appear as rules violating a particular configuration:

⬠ ESXi Host is violating VMware vSphere Hardening Guide

Symptoms

> ⚠ esx-mgmt-a-01.vmware.com (Self) has symptom vNetwork.reject-forged-transmit -
Forged Transmits policy is not set to reject (5.5/6.0 Hardening Guide)

  Aggregated Forged Transmits "true" = "true"

> ⚠ esx-mgmt-a-01.vmware.com (Self) has symptom ESXi.config-ntp - NTP firewall rule is not
configured (5.5/6.0 Hardening Guide)

  Allowed hosts "All IP" = "All IP"

> ⚠ esx-mgmt-a-01.vmware.com (Self) has symptom ESXi.set-shell-interactive-timeout -
Timeout is not configured for idle ESXi Shell and SSH sessions (5.5/6.0 Hardening Guide)

  Shell interactive timeout (UserVars.ESXiShellInteractiveTimeOut) 0.0 = Threshold 0.0

> ⚠ esx-mgmt-a-01.vmware.com (Self) has symptom ESXi.set-shell-timeout - Timeout is not
set to limit the duration of ESXi Shell and SSH services session (5.5/6.0 Hardening Guide)

  Shell timeout (UserVars.ESXiShellTimeOut) 0.0 = Threshold 0.0

> ⚠ esx-mgmt-a-01.vmware.com (Self) has symptom ESXi.enable-ad-auth - Local user
authentication is not configured with Ldap (5.5/6.0 Hardening Guide)

  Enable active directory authentication "false" != "true"

If a symptom is triggered for any of the compliance alerts, the standard is violated and affects the badge score on the **Compliance** tab.

The Getting Started dashboard

The **Getting Started** dashboard is a guide to answering the most frequently asked questions from your IT staff.

This dashboard groups tasks into the following five broad categories:

- **Operations**
- **Capacity and Utilization**
- **Performance Troubleshooting**
- **Workload Balance**
- **Configuration and Compliance**

Use each of the categories featured on the **Getting Started** dashboard to focus on a particular problem or challenge you are trying to tackle. Each category is associated with one or more related dashboards which you can access straight away.

Because the **Getting Started** dashboard is not available by default, you might need to enable it by clicking **Dashboards** | **Actions** | **Manage Dashboards**, and then selecting the **Getting Started** checkbox. Once enabled, you can access it from the navigation pane on the **Dashboards** page.

Once you've opened the **Getting Started** dashboard, you will be presented with all the dashboard groups. vRealize Operations 6.6. also offers the **vSphere Hardening Compliance** dashboard. The dashboard is located under the **Configuration and Compliance** group:

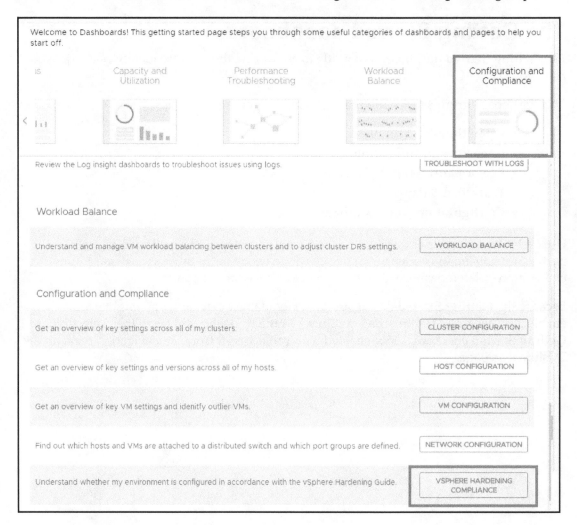

The dashboard measures your environment against the vSphere Hardening Guide and shows you the results, along with affected objects, which are shown as follows:

As you may have noticed, the Compliance badge score of `83%` is the same as we saw earlier for the vSphere World custom group.

The dashboard shows the `High Risk`, `Medium Risk`, and **Low Risk** violations trend as well as the **Hardening Compliance** score. You can drill down into the headmaps and further examine Compliance for related objects.

The remaining dashboards under the **Configuration and Complianc**e dashboard group also provide important information to help you monitor configuration compliance in your environment. Make sure to explore them and examine the information they provide.

PCI and HIPAA compliance

Both PCI and HIPAA compliance policies do not come out of the box with vRealize Operations. Both of them come in the form of management packs. The installation and configuration for both packs is the same. In this example, we will be installing and configuring the vRealize Operations Compliance Pack for HIPAA.

The pack will provide alerts, policies, and reports to validate the vSphere environment against the HIPAA hardening guide.

Enabling the HIPAA compliance pack

Perform the following steps to install the vRealize Operations Compliance Pack for HIPAA:

1. Navigate to the VMware Marketplace at `https://marketplace.vmware.com` and download the HIPAA management pack. In vRealize Operations, navigate to **Administration, Solutions**, and click the plus (+) sign.

2. Select the management pack, click **Upload**, and after the upload has completed, click **Next**. Read and accept the EULA. Wait until the solution has been installed on all vRealize Operations nodes.

3. Now, we have to edit a policy and activate the HIPAA policies the same way we did when we enabled vSphere hardening compliance previously. Navigate to **Administration, Policies**, and then **Policy Library**. Select and edit the **vSphere Solution's Default Policy**.

4. In the **Edit Monitoring Policy** window, navigate to **Alert /Symptom Definitions** in the **Alert Definitions** area in the filter criteria file type `HIPAA`. For each of the HIPAA compliance alerts, click the **State** drop-down menu and click **Local = enabled**. Click **Save**.

Now, let's check the compliance for an object. For this example, I will select the same host system I did earlier when configuring vSphere hardening compliance, and examine the **Compliance Breakdown** area. As you will notice, in addition to the VMware vSphere Hardening Guide, we now see the HIPAA Hardening Guide being applied. Selecting the violated HIPAA standard will give us a list of violated rules:

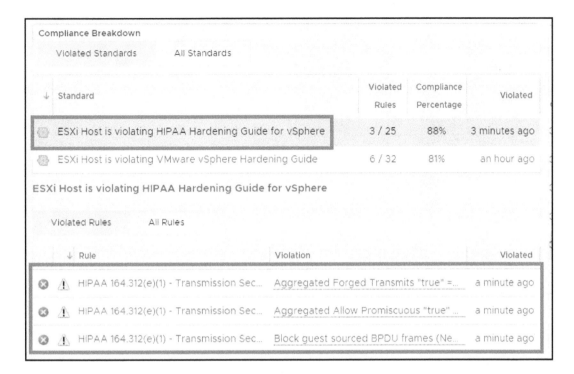

Compliance Breakdown

Violated Standards   All Standards

↓ Standard	Violated Rules	Compliance Percentage	Violated
ESXi Host is violating HIPAA Hardening Guide for vSphere	3 / 25	88%	3 minutes ago
ESXi Host is violating VMware vSphere Hardening Guide	6 / 32	81%	an hour ago

ESXi Host is violating HIPAA Hardening Guide for vSphere

Violated Rules   All Rules

↓ Rule	Violation	Violated
HIPAA 164.312(e)(1) - Transmission Sec...	Aggregated Forged Transmits "true" =...	a minute ago
HIPAA 164.312(e)(1) - Transmission Sec...	Aggregated Allow Promiscuous "true" ...	a minute ago
HIPAA 164.312(e)(1) - Transmission Sec...	Block guest sourced BPDU frames (Ne...	a minute ago

 It may take few minutes until the Compliance badge score changes, reflecting the newly activated compliance alerts.

In the same manner, you can install and configure the vRealize Operations Compliance Pack for PCI DSS.

Summary

In this chapter, we've become familiar with enhanced compliance capabilities in vRealize Operations and how to leverage hardening guides for PCI or HIPAA. We discussed the benefits of using vRealize Operations for Infrastructure Compliance and how to configure it.

In the next chapter, We are going to learn more how we can use vRealize Operations for troubleshooting purposes.

15
Troubleshooting vRealize Operations

In this chapter, we will take a look at some of the built-in tools vRealize Operations offers for troubleshooting its components and services. We will also discuss what the best practices are when adding, removing, extending, or rebooting a cluster or a cluster node. Finally, we will also cover how to troubleshoot issues during the upgrade process.

This chapter will cover:

- Self-monitoring dashboards
- Managing nodes best practices
- Troubleshooting vRealize Operations components
- Troubleshooting vRealize Operations upgrade process

Self-monitoring dashboards

vRealize Operations offers out-of-the-box dashboards that can help you monitor the overall status of a cluster and its nodes, including main services and key components.

These dashboards are fed with information by the built-in adapter for node and cluster status self-monitoring. They give a holistic picture of what vRealize Operations is doing, and makes it easier for users to check alerts or symptoms on the self-monitoring objects and troubleshoot vRealize Operations. It is worth mentioning that these dashboards were created keeping technical support engineers in mind, not vRealize Operations end users.

By default, the dashboards are not listed:

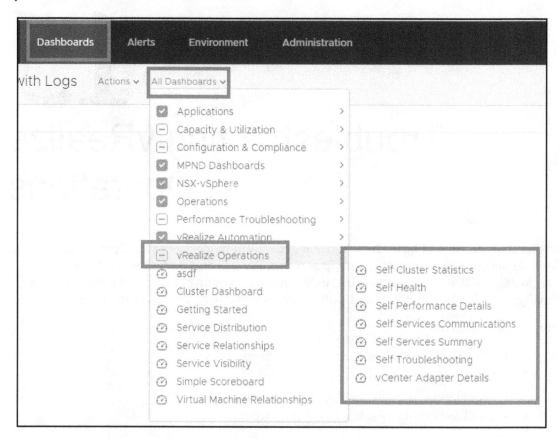

You can access them by navigating to the **Dashboards** tab, **All Dashboards**, and then **vRealize Operations**. Let's take a deeper look at some of those self-monitoring dashboards and how they can be useful for us when troubleshooting vRealize Operations.

The first part of the **Self Cluster Statistics** dashboard is the **Top Processing Info** widget:

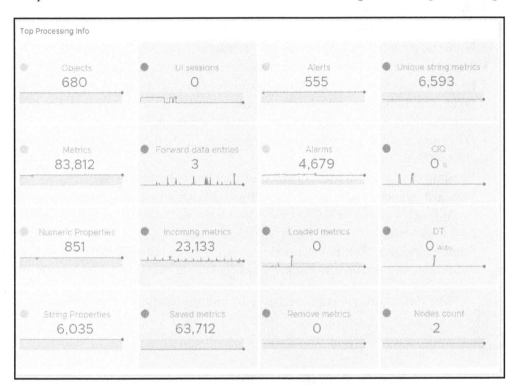

The widget shows the following information:

- **Objects**: Number of objects data collected in the vRealize Operations Cluster.
- **UI sessions**: Number of users accessing the vRealize Operations Product UI.
- **Alerts**: Depends on management packs, but something close to 1M may result in performance problems.
- **Unique string metrics**: Depends on management packs, but something close to 1M may be result in performance problems.
- **Metrics**: Number of metrics data collected.
- **Forward data entries**: Each vRealize Operations node has a maximum capacity of storing 19,999 entries. If it continuously stays at this value, it indicates that analytics may be busy.
- **Alarms**: Depends on management packs, but something close to 1M may result in performance problems.

- **CIQ**: There should not be frequent invocations. It should start at night and finish after several hours.
- **Node count**: Number of nodes available in the cluster.
- **Numeric properties**: Total number of numeric properties in the cluster.
- **String properties**: Total number of numeric properties in the cluster.
- **Load metrics**: Metrics loaded into the analytics cache during the last collection cycle. Should be close to 0. Some amount of spikes may be expected, but this should not be very frequent in case of stable environments.
- **DT**: There should not be frequent invocations. It should start at night and finish after several hours.
- **Incoming metrics**: Metrics collected during last collection cycle.
- **Forward data entries**: Summation of forward data queue size on all nodes (usually, greater than 20,000 means that some of the nodes may have an issue in data processing).
- **Remove metrics**: Should be close to 0. Some amount of spikes may be expected, but this should not be very frequent spikes in case of stable environments.

 The dashboard gets updated every 5 minutes (default collection cycle).

Scrolling down, we can see the **CPU/Memory/Disk** widget:

The metrics useful for troubleshooting here are mainly:

- **Free Mem**: Shows free memory available in the cluster
- **Swap**: Shows whether any swap is happening in the cluster
- **Used space**: Shows used space in the cluster

Next, let's take a look at the **Self Services Summary** dashboard:

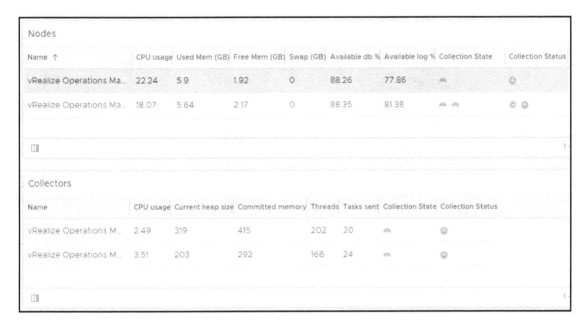

The **Available db%** value in the **Nodes** widget should be mostly equal for all nodes if they have all been deployed together since the very beginning. If the **Threads** value in the **Collectors** widget is something close to 30,000 threads, this may result in problems. You may need to check which management packs are running on those collectors.

Next, let's take a look at the **Self Performance Details** dashboard:

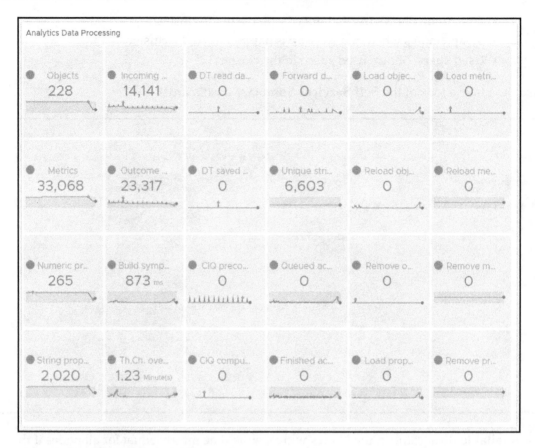

On the **Analytics Data Processing** widget, we can find the following metrics:

- **DT read data points**: The amount of data points read from FSDB during DT calculation on the selected node.
- **Load object**: The amount of object cache load operations on the selected node (vRealize Operations loads the cache for an object when we start monitoring it, for example, the new object gets autodiscovered). On the stable environments, when there are no variations happening in the objects count, this metric should remain as 0. The operation has some overhead on performance so you must watch out for this. If it is having high non-zero values in each cycle, then it may be an indication of an issue.

- **Load metrics**: The amount of metric cache load operations on the selected node (the amount of metrics that vRealize Operations has loaded for newly loaded objects).
- **Outcome metrics**: The amount of metrics that were returned after threshold checking was completed (incoming metrics + metrics generated by vRealize Operations).
- **Reload object**: The amount of object cache reload operations (happens when an object is updated, the policy updates, or the object changes its effective policy). Spikes can be expected, but in general should remain close to 0.
- **Reload metrics**: The amount of metric cache reload operations.
- **Build symptom time**: The summation of the build symptom phase during threshold checking of the threshold checking threads.
- **Th.ch. overall time**: The summation of threshold checking duration the threshold checking threads.
- **Load property**: The amount of property cache load operations. Should be close to 0. Some amount of spikes may be expected, but these should not be very frequent in case of stable environments.
- **Remove property**: The amount of property cache reload operations.
- **Forward data entries**: Should be close to 0. If it is close to 20,000, then data is being dropped.
- **CIQ Precomputations**: Should be spikes every 1 hour 40 minutes. If it doesn't happen at this interval, it indicates that precomputation is taking a long time.
- **CIQ Computations**: There should not be frequent invocations. It should start at night and finish after several hours.

Some of the metrics worth mentioning on the **FSDB Data Processing** widget are:

- **Store operations count**: How many story operations are performed on the FSDB of the selected node.
- **Work items**: The value should be close to 0. Some amount of spikes may be expected, but there shouldn't be frequent spikes. If you see values close to 400, then it may degrade the threshold checking performance and may result in data being dropped. In this case, it usually means the underlying storage performance is not sufficient. Make sure vRealize Operations VMs are not running on snapshots for a long time.
- **FSDB state**: Numerical representation of FSDB state (**Initial, Synchronizing, Running, Balancing,** and more).
- **Store time**: Summation of store operations and time spent by all storage threads.

Next is the **Self Service Communications** dashboard:

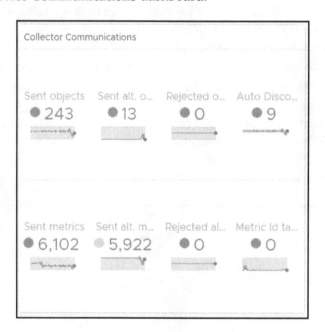

On the **Collector Communications** widget, the **Rejected Objects** value should be 0, otherwise, it means data was dropped because the forward data region was full—analytics was not able to process the incoming data in time.

Finally, let's take a look at the **vCenter Adapter Details** dashboard:

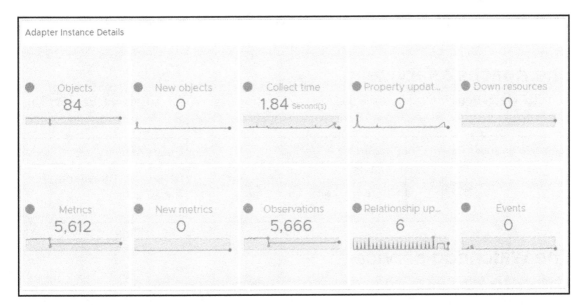

Our interest falls to the **Adapter Instance Details** widget. The metrics of interest here are:

- **New objects**: In environments where there is not much object churn, this should be close to 0.
- **Collect time**: Data collection should be complete within the monitoring interval (by default, 5 minutes).
- **Down resources**: Depends on management packs, but something close to 1M for property updates, relationship updates, and events may result in performance problems. Check these metrics for all management packs, not just vSphere.

We didn't cover all available self-monitoring dashboards. Make sure to familiarize yourself with all the dashboards and the information they provide as it may turn out to be very valuable for troubleshooting vROps issues.

Troubleshooting vRealize Operations components

Let's see what we can do to monitor and troubleshoot some of the key vRealize Operations components and services.

Services

Let's first take a look into some of the most important vRealize Operations services.

The Apache2 service

vRealize Operations internally uses the Apache2 web server to host Admin UI, Product UI, and Suite API. Here are some useful service log locations:

Log file name	Location	Purpose
`access_log` & `error_log`	`storage/log/var/log/apache2`	Stores log information for the Apache service

The Watchdog service

Watchdog is a vRealize Operations service that maintains the necessary daemons/services and attempts to restart them as necessary should there be a failure. The `vcops-watchdog` is a Python script that runs every 5 minutes by means of the `vcops-watchdog-daemon` with the purpose of monitoring the various vRealize Operations services, including CaSA.

The Watchdog service performs the following checks:

- PID file of the service
- Service status

Here are some useful service log locations:

Log file name	Location	Purpose
`vcops-watchdog.log`	`/usr/lib/vmware-vcops/user/log/vcops-watchdog/`	Stores log information for the WatchDog service

The Collector service

The Collector service sends a heartbeat to the controller every 30 seconds. By default, the Collector will wait for 30 minutes for adapters to synchronize.

 The collector properties, including enabling or disabling **Self Protection**, can be configured from the `collector.properties` properties file located in `/usr/lib/vmware-vcops/user/conf/collector`.

Here are some useful service log locations:

Log file name	Location	Purpose
`collector.log`	`/storage/log/vcops/log/`	Stores log information for the Collector service

The Controller service

The Controller service is part of the analytics engine. The controller does the decision making on where new objects should reside. The controller manages the storage and retrieval of the inventory of the objects within the system.

The Controller service has the following uses:

- It will monitor the collector status every minute
- How long a deleted resource is available in the inventory
- How long a non-existing resource is stored in the database

Here are some useful service file locations:

Log file name	Location	Purpose
`controller.properties`	`/usr/lib/vmware-vcops/user/conf/controller/`	Stores properties information for the Controller service

Databases

As we learned in previous chapters, vRealize Operations contains quite a few databases, all of which are of great importance for the function of the product. Let's take a deeper look into those databases.

Cassandra DB

Currently, Cassandra DB stores the following information:

- User Preferences and Config
- Alerts definition
- Customizations
- Dashboards, Policies, and View
- Reports and Licensing
- Shard Maps
- Activities

Cassandra stores all the information which we see under the `content` folder; basically, any settings which are applied globally.

You are able to log into the Cassandra database from any Analytic Node. The information is the same across nodes.

There are two ways to connect to the Cassandra database:

1. `cqlshrc` is a command-line tool used to get the data within Cassandra, in a SQL-like fashion (inbuilt).

To connect to the DB, run the following from the command line (SSH):

```
$VMWARE_PYTHON_BIN $ALIVE_BASE/cassandra/apache-cassandra-2.1.8/bin/cqlsh --ssl --cqlshrc $ALIVE_BASE/user/conf/cassandra/cqlshrc
```

Once you are connected to the DB, we need to navigate to the `globalpersistence` key space using the following command:

```
vcops_user@cqlsh&gt; use globalpersistence ;
```

2. The `nodetool` command-line tool

Once you are logged on to the Cassandra DB, we can run the following commands to see information:

Command syntax	Purpose
Describe tables	To list all the `relation` (tables) in the current database instance
Describe <table_name>	To list the content of that particular table
Exit	To exit the Cassandra command line
select command	To select any `Column` data from a table
delete command	To delete any `Column` data from a table

Some of the important tables in Cassandra are:

Table name	Purpose
`activity_2_tbl`	Stores all the activities
`tbl_2a8b303a3ed03a4ebae2700cbfae90bf`	Stores the Shard mapping information of an object (table name may be differ in each environment)
`supermetric`	Stores the defined super metrics
`policy`	Stores all the defined policies
`Auth`	Stores all the user details in the cluster
`global_settings`	All the configured global settings are stored here
`namespace_to_classtype`	Informs what type of data is stored in what table under Cassandra
`symptomproblemdefinition`	All the defined symptoms
`certificates`	Stores all the adapter and data source certificates

The Cassandra database has the following configuration files:

File type	Location
Cassandra.yaml	/usr/lib/vmware-vcops/user/conf/cassandra/
vcops_cassandra.properties	/usr/lib/vmware-vcops/user/conf/cassandra/
Cassandra conf scripts	/usr/lib/vmware_vcopssuite/utilities/vmware/vcops/cassandra/

The `Cassandra.yaml` file stores certain information such as the default location to save data (`/storage/db/vcops/cassandra/data`). The file contains information about all the nodes. When a new node joins the cluster, it refers to this file to make sure it contacts the right node (master node). It also has all the SSL certificate information.

 Cassandra is started and stopped via the CaSA service, but just because CaSA is running does not mean that the Cassandra service is necessarily running.

The service command to check the status of the Cassandra DB service from the command line (SSH) is:

```
service vmware-vcops status cassandra
```

The Cassandra `cassandraservice.Sh` is located in:

```
$VCOPS_BASE/cassandra/bin/
```

Here are some useful Cassandra DB log locations:

Log File Name	Location	Purpose
System.log	/usr/lib/vmware-vcops/user/log/cassandra	Stores all the Cassandra-related activities
watchdog_monitor.log	/usr/lib/vmware-vcops/user/log/cassandra	Stores Cassandra Watchdog logs
wrapper.log	/usr/lib/vmware-vcops/user/log/cassandra	Stores Cassandra start and stop-related logs
configure.log	/usr/lib/vmware-vcops/user/log/cassandra	Stores logs related to Python scripts of vRops

initial_cluster_setup.log	/usr/lib/vmware-vcops/user/log/cassandra	Stores logs related to Python scripts of vRops
validate_cluster.log	/usr/lib/vmware-vcops/user/log/cassandra	Stores logs related to Python scripts of vRops

To enable debug logging for the Cassandra database, edit the `logback.xml` XML file located in:

/usr/lib/vmware-vcops/user/conf/cassandra/

Change `&lt;root level="INFO"&gt;` to `&lt;root level="DEBUG"&gt;`.

The `System.log` will not show the debug logs for Cassandra.

If you experience any of the following issues, this may be an indicator that the database has performance issues, and so you may need to take the appropriate steps to resolve them:

- Relationship changes are not be reflected immediately
- Deleted objects still show up in the tree
- View and Reports takes slow in processing and take a long time to open.
- Logging on to the Product UI takes a long time for any user
- Alert was supposed to trigger but it never happened

 Cassandra can tolerate 5 ms of latency at any given point of time.

You can validate the cluster by running the following command from the command line (SSH). First, navigate to the following folder:

/usr/lib/vmware-vcopssuite/utilities/

Run the following command to validate the cluster:

```
$VMWARE_PYTHON_BIN –m vmware.vcops.cassandra.validate_cluster
&lt;IP_ADDRESS_1  IP_ADDRESS_2&gt;
```

You can also use the `nodetool` to perform a health check, and possibly resolve database load issues.

The command to check the load status of the activity tables in vRealize Operations version 6.3 and older is as follows:

```
$VCOPS_BASE/cassandra/apache-cassandra-2.1.8/bin/nodetool --port 9008
status
```

For the 6.5 release and newer, VMware added the requirement of using a 'maintenanceAdmin' user along with a password file. The new command is as follows:

```
$VCOPS_BASE/cassandra/apache-cassandra-2.1.8/bin/nodetool -p 9008 --ssl -u
maintenanceAdmin --password-file /usr/lib/vmware-
vcops/user/conf/jmxremote.password status
```

Regardless of which method you choose to perform the health check, if any of the nodes have over 600 MB of load, you should consult with VMware Global Support Services on the next steps to take, and how to elevate the load issues.

Central (Repl DB)

The Postgres database was introduced in 6.1. It has two instances in version 6.6. The Central Postgres DB, also called `repl`, and the Alerts/HIS Postgres DB, also called `data`, are two separate database instances under the database called `vcopsdb`.

The central DB exists only on the master and the master replica nodes when HA is enabled. It is accessible via port `5433` and it is located in `/storage/db/vcops/vpostgres/repl`.

Currently, the database stores the Resources inventory.

You can connect to the central DB from the command line (SSH). Log in on the analytic node you wish to connect to and run:

```
su - postgres
```

The command should not prompt for a password if ran as `root`.

Once logged in, connect to the database instance by running:

```
/opt/vmware/vpostgres/current/bin/psql -d vcopsdb -p 5433
```

The service command to start the central DB from the command line (SSH) is:

```
service vpostgres-repl start
```

Here are some useful log locations:

Log file name	Location	Purpose
postgresql-<xx>.log	/storage/db/vcops/vpostgres/data/pg_log	Provides information on Postgres database cleanup and other disk-related information

Alerts/HIS (Data) DB

The Alerts DB is called data on all the data nodes including the master and master replica node.

It was again introduced in 6.1. Starting from 6.2, the Historical Inventory Service xDB was merged with the Alerts DB. It is accessible via port 5432 and it is located in /storage/db/vcops/vpostgres/data.

Currently, the database stores:

- Alerts and alarm history
- History of resource property data
- History of resource relationship

You can connect to the Alerts DB from the command line (SSH). Log in on the analytic node you wish to connect to and run:

```
su - postgres
```

The command should not prompt for a password if ran as root.

Once logged in, connect to the database instance by running:

```
/opt/vmware/vpostgres/current/bin/psql -d vcopsdb -p 5432
```

The service command to start the Alerts DB from the command line (SSH) is:

```
service vpostgres start
```

FSDB

The **File System Database** (**FSDB**) contains all raw time series metrics and super metrics data for the discovered resources.

What is FSDB in vRealize Operations Manager?:

- FSDB is a GemFire server and runs inside analytics JVM.
- FSDB in vRealize Operations uses the Sharding Manager to distribute data between nodes (new objects). (We will discuss what vRealize Operations cluster nodes are later in this chapter.)
- The File System Database is available in all the nodes of a vRops Cluster deployment.
- It has its own properties file.
- FSDB stores data (time series data) collected by adapters and data which is generated/calculated (system, super, badge, CIQ metrics, and so on) based on analysis of that data.

If you are troubleshooting FSDB performance issues, you should start from the **Self Performance Details** dashboard, more precisely, the **FSDB Data Processing** widget. We covered both of these earlier in this chapter.

You can also take a look at the metrics provided by the **FSDB Metric Picker**:

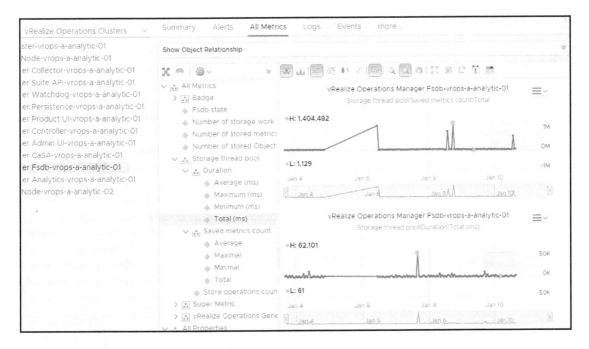

You can access it by navigating to the **Environment** tab, **vRealize Operations Clusters**, selecting a node, and selecting vRealize Operations Manager FSDB. Then, select the **All Metrics** tab.

You can check the synchronization state of the FSDB to determine the overall health of the cluster by running the following command from the command line (SSH):

```
$VMWARE_PYTHON_BIN /usr/lib/vmware-vcops/tools/vrops-platform-cli/vrops-
platform-cli.py getShardStateMappingInfo
```

By restarting the FSDB, you can trigger synchronization of all the data by getting missing data from other FSDBs. Synchronization takes place only when you have vRealize Operations HA configured.

Here are some useful log locations for FSDB:

Log file name	Locaiton	Purpose
Analytics-<UUID>.log	/usr/lib/vmware-vcops/user/log	Used to check the Sharding Module functionality Can trace which objects have synced
ShardingManager_<UUID>.log	/usr/lib/vmware-vcops/user/log	Can be used to get the total time the sync took
fsdb-accessor-<UUID>.log	/usr/lib/vmware-vcops/user/log	Provides information on FSDB database cleanup and other disk-related information

Platform-cli

Platform-cli is a tool by which we can get information from various databases, including the GemFire cache, Cassandra, and the Alerts/HIS persistence databases.

In order to run this Python script, you need to run the following command:

```
$VMWARE_PYTHON_BIN /usr/lib/vmware-vcops/tools/vrops-platform-cli/vrops-
platform-cli.py
```

The following example of using this command will list all the resources in ascending order and also show you which shard it is stored on:

```
$VMWARE_PYTHON_BIN /usr/lib/vmware-vcops/tools/vrops-platform-cli/vrops-
platform-cli.py getResourceToShardMapping
```

Summary

In this final chapter, we discussed how to use the self-monitoring dashboards in vRealize Operations to monitor the product itself and all its components. We also covered how to troubleshoot some of the most important components like services and databases. Finally, we also covered how to troubleshoot failures in the upgrade process.

Other Books You May Enjoy

If you enjoyed this book, you may be interested in these other books by Packt:

Learning VMware NSX - Second Edition
Ranjit Singh Thakurratan

ISBN: 978-1-78839-898-5

- Understand software-defined networks
- Deploy and configure VXLAN-enabled logical switches
- Secure your environment using Distributed Firewall and Data Security
- Configure third-party services in NSX
- Manage, configure, and deploy edge gateway services
- Perform various Edge operations including configuring CA certificates
- Explore the different monitoring options to check their traffic flow

Mastering VMware vSphere 6.5
Andrea Mauro, Paolo Valsecchi, Karel Novak

ISBN: 978-1-78728-601-6

- Get a deep understanding of vSphere 6.5 functionalities
- Design and plan a virtualization environment based on vSphere 6.5
- Manage and administer a vSphere 6.5 environment and resources
- Get tips for the VCP6-DCV and VCIX6-DCV exams (along with use of the vSphere 6 documentation)
- Implement different migration techniques to move your workload across different environments
- Save your configuration, data and workload from your virtual infrastructure

Leave a review - let other readers know what you think

Please share your thoughts on this book with others by leaving a review on the site that you bought it from. If you purchased the book from Amazon, please leave us an honest review on this book's Amazon page. This is vital so that other potential readers can see and use your unbiased opinion to make purchasing decisions, we can understand what our customers think about our products, and our authors can see your feedback on the title that they have worked with Packt to create. It will only take a few minutes of your time, but is valuable to other potential customers, our authors, and Packt. Thank you!

Index

C

capacity management policies
  buffers 190, 191
  defining 176
  defining, scenarios 178, 179
  High Availability (HA) 190, 191
  overcommitment, setting 186
  peak consideration 188, 189, 190
  resource containers, selecting 177
capacity management
  demand, versus allocation 183
  for vRealize Operations policies 176
  monitoring 175
capacity planning
  benefits 169
  preparing 174
Capacity Reclaimable dashboard 132
Capacity Remaining badge 122, 123, 124, 175
Cassandra DB
  about 28, 386
  commands 387
  configuration files 388
  log locations 388
  service command 388
  tables 387
Central (Repl DB)
  about 28, 390
  service command 391
Certificate Authority (CA) 61
Cluster and Slice Administrator (CaSA) 21
Cluster Headroom 344
cluster
  rebalancing 345, 346, 347
Collector 23, 24
Collector Communications widget 382
collector group, benefits
  adapter resiliency 46
  load balancing 46
Collector service 385
committed projects
  versus planned projects 195, 196
Common Information Model (CIM) 98
Compliance badge 128, 129, 175, 358, 359, 360
compliance

monitoring 363
monitoring, with alerts 364, 365, 366, 367, 368, 369
monitoring, with Getting Started dashboard 369, 371
Conservative Balance 344
Consolidate Workloads 344, 355
Controller 25
Controller service 385
CPU allocation
  about 184
  recommendation 184
CPU demand
  about 184
  recommendation 184
CPU/Memory/Disk widget
  metrics 378
criticality 139
custom dashboards
  creating 286, 287
Custom Data Center (CDC)
  about 196, 332
  creating 196, 197, 338, 339, 340
custom groups
  about 204
  using 211, 212, 213
custom profiles
  creating 199
custom types
  using 211, 212, 213
Customer Experience Improvement Program (CEIP) 67

D

dashboards
  about 277
  designing 278, 279, 280
  interactive dashboard 287
  static dashboard 287
data duplication
  working 40, 41, 42
data node 32
data storage solutions
  FSDB 26
  Postgres 26

CPSIA information can be obtained
at www.ICGtesting.com
Printed in the USA
BVHW081252130123
656213BV00012B/247